Pastoral Diagnosis

PASTORAL DIAGNOSIS

❧

A Resource for Ministries of Care and Counseling

Nancy J. Ramsay

FORTRESS PRESS   Minneapolis

Permission to use material has been kindly granted by:
The Journal on Supervision and Training in Ministry (portions of chapter 2); *The Quarterly Review: A Journal of Theological Resources for Ministry* (portions of chapter 4); Trinity Press International, *Theology and the Interhuman: Essays in Honor of Edward Farley*, edited by Robert R. Williams, 1995 (an earlier version of chapter 6). John Wiley & Sons, Inc. and Wm. C. Brown Publishers for material from *Counseling the Culturally Different: Theory and Practice.*

PASTORAL DIAGNOSIS
A Resource for Ministries of Care and Counseling

Cover design: Joseph Bonyata
Book design: Peregrine Graphics Services

Library of Congress Cataloging in Publication Data

Ramsay, Nancy J. (Nancy Jean), 1949–
    Pastoral diagnosis : a resource for ministries of care and counseling /
  Nancy J. Ramsay.
      p. cm.
    Includes bibliographical references (p.   ).
    ISBN 0-8006-2629-X (alk. paper)
    1. Pastoral psychology.   I. Title.
  BV4012.R35   1998
  253.5'2—dc21   98-43074
                                           CIP

Manufactured in the U.S.A.   AF 1-2629
02   01   00   99   98   1   2   3   4   5   6   7   8   9   10

For
Josephine Campbell Ramsay, 1895–1933
Martha Crouse Ramsay, 1911–1987
Edna Ingham Douglas, 1898–1996
With love.

CONTENTS

ACKNOWLEDGMENTS

I want to express my gratitude to the Board of Directors of Louisville Presbyterian Theological Seminary for granting me sabbatical leaves to complete this book. I am especially appreciative for the support of Dean W. Eugene March. Many students, colleagues in professional meetings, and continuing education participants have helped me refine these ideas with their perceptive questions and insights. Clients have also informed my reflection.

Friends and colleagues have generously shared their time and energy to reflect with me about the issues addressed here. This is particularly so of friends in the Society for Pastoral Theology. Members of its anthropology study group gave me valuable assistance. Andy Lester, Joretta Marshall, and Ted Smith have read large portions of the manuscript and offered very helpful advice with unfailing good humor and encouragement. I am forever in their debt. Cliff Guthrie kindly lent his expertise on issues of authority and ritual practice in reviewing a related chapter. I am also grateful to Carroll Saussy for the constancy of her encouragement. Here at Louisville Presbyterian Seminary many colleagues have reviewed portions of my work and contributed bibliographic ideas. Particular thanks go to Charles Brockwell, Joe Coalter, Chris Elwood, David Hester, Kathryn Johnson, John McClure, and Amy Plantinga Pauw.

Timothy Staveteig, formerly with Fortress Press, encouraged me to proceed with this project. I am also grateful to Marshall Johnson and Hank French for their subsequent invaluable editorial advice and patient encouragement. Fortunately I work with a most remarkable faculty secretary, Melissa Nebelsick. She has met every challenge in the production of this book with her usual aplomb and competence. She has exorcised countless word-processing demons and offered me her urgent patience when my energy languished.

During the years I was working on this project, I developed a special relationship with my maternal grandmother, Edna Ingham Douglas, who died recently a few months shy of her ninety-ninth birthday. Through her I have become more aware of the particular legacy my grandmothers have given to me. Grandmother Douglas showed this middle-aged granddaughter that one can approach the limits of advanced age with courage, dignity, humor, a continuing interest in learning new ideas, and abiding faith. In this way she has been a blessing to me in her life and in her death. Josephine Campbell Ramsay, my father's mother, died when my father was a boy. But through my father, aunts, and uncle I am aware of the legacy of her keen interest in teaching and learning; her faith; love expressed through gentle encouragement and quiet provision; and her sense of humor. Martha Crouse Ramsay, my father's stepmother, was a daily part of my childhood. She was a woman of deep faith. She had an infectious vitality and sense of humor. She taught me to dance before I could walk and to find joy in music. With profound gratitude I dedicate this book to these three grandmothers in faith and life.

TABLES

INTRODUCTION

At first blush, diagnosis may seem an obscure topic best understood as simply a technical therapeutic strategy. This is especially so in North America. Here practitioners of pastoral care and counseling face the challenges of an increasingly pluralistic culture in which the usefulness and truthfulness of Christian faith is an open question for many who find therapeutic resources more familiar if not more compelling.

Pastoral diagnosis offers important resources for such a time as this. Diagnosis is an evaluative process of discerning the nature of another's difficulty in order to provide an appropriate and restorative response. Diagnosis is never neutral. It always reiterates the anthropological and philosophical assumptions of the practitioner. It is an inherently hermeneutical process. It also has constructive possibilities, especially when practiced collaboratively with those whose operative worldview is inadequate for their predicament. Pastoral diagnosis is such a resource with those whose theological worldview is not sufficiently developed to sustain them at a time of crisis or needs revision in order to be adequate.

Pastoral diagnosis differs from diagnosis defined by various therapeutic paradigms because of the explicit theological contexts in which the anthropological and philosophical assumptions of practitioners are rooted. For this reason it is a constructive resource not only for those who seek care but also for us who intend to respond with theological integrity. Diagnosis is the practice of strategic knowledge in the sense that how a situation is named has everything to do with the interventions one develops in order to respond.

Pastoral diagnosis has at least two possible focii. On the one hand, it is pursued as attending to the significance of religious experience. Forerunners such as Wayne Oates and Edgar Draper have made significant contributions in assessing the significance of religious ideation in mental illness.[1] More recently Steven Ivy, David Stancil, and George Fitchett, among others, have adapted faith development theory in behalf of attending to the rich significance of religious language and experience for healing and spiritual growth.[2]

In this book, on the other hand, pastoral diagnosis is understood as attending to the religious significance of experience. My focus is with the breadth of human experience, which includes religious experience. With this broader focus the truthfulness and usefulness of Christian faith for comprehending human experience is even more apparent.

In *The Minister as Diagnostician*, published in 1976, Paul Pruyser, a psychologist on the staff of the Menninger Institute, challenged pastors and pastoral care specialists to articulate their theological perspectives in multidisciplinary diagnostic conversations.[3] Pruyser rightly complained that pastors were reluctant to value the richness of the biblical and theological resources in which they were trained.

In the past twenty years practitioners of pastoral care and counseling have reasserted the priority of theological and biblical resources for this ministry. But neither of these resources is adequate to replace the valuable insights of contemporary psychological and developmental theory, nor were they intended to do so. Yet, therapeutic paradigms are themselves rooted in anthropological and philosophical assumptions. The practice of pastoral diagnosis requires careful reflection in order to adapt such therapeutic resources critically. This involves skill in discerning the assumptions informing various therapeutic paradigms as well as the ability to articulate those theological assumptions that shape one's practice of ministry.

All diagnosis rests on three dynamically interdependent criteria: anthropological assumptions, communally shared guiding values, and mutually understood dynamics of authority in the helping relationship.[4] These three criteria can be defined quite differently, even competitively, depending on the practitioner's paradigm. This is so, of course, among therapeutic paradigms as well as theological ones and between the two. I will use these three criteria to organize comparative analyses of several therapeutic paradigms regularly used by pastors and pastoral care specialists. I will also use them to disclose the assumptions informing an ecclesial paradigm. Such analyses are illustrative of the critical reflection pastoral diagnosis requires.

Because pastoral diagnosis is a hermeneutical process the person of the practitioner is particularly important as the lens through which the process of diagnosis takes place. For this reason a heightened self-consciousness of one's pastoral identity as it is shaped by a theological tradition and one's place within that tradition is very important. Similarly, the influence of one's social location and embodiment also needs to be acknowledged.

My theological commitments are shaped particularly by my heritage within the Reformed tradition and the Presbyterian Church (U.S.A.). Within that tradition I find myself drawn particularly to feminist and womanist voices who sound liberative themes of love, justice, and empowerment. I find themes of freedom, power, and accountability pervasively relevant for the practice of pastoral diagnosis. The systemic insights of process theological approaches also inform my reflections here. Certainly, I acknowledge the influence of my social location as a Caucasian, middle-class, educated, North American woman. I hope the reader will recognize my efforts to correct the limitations of this location where possible and to appreciate its distinctive contributions.

Pastoral diagnosis is an exercise in practical theological reflection with a praxis orientation. It begins with experience and draws on theological and other disciplines in order to mediate more effectively the transformative, redemptive love of God so as to empower for discipleship. This practical theological method is used in each of the following chapters. The case material around which the chapters evolve represents either disguised or conflated pastoral experiences of others or myself. I have located these pastoral experiences in several different theological traditions to illustrate how diagnosis regularly requires critical reflection on one's own tradition in order to respond effectively to the experience at hand.

Part One
I have developed this book in two parts. The first several chapters are concerned with helping to describe how pastoral diagnosis is useful in our current theological and cultural context and what its practice

entails. These three chapters share a common case to lend continuity to the analyses involved. The second part of this book contains four chapters that describe critical concerns for enhancing the practice of contemporary pastoral diagnosis. Here the case material differs from chapter to chapter.

In the first chapter, I define diagnosis as a hermeneutical process invariably reflecting the values and assumptions of the perspectives of the practitioner. I demonstrate its critical role in care and healing because it projects the interventions a practitioner will adopt and the goals he or she envisions for the one seeking help. Diagnosis depends on three dynamically interdependent criteria: anthropological assumptions, guiding values shared by the practitioner and the one seeking care, and shared assumptions about the nature of authority in the helping relationship. Using these three criteria, I illustrate the anthropological and philosophical assumptions they disclose in medical or psychiatric, humanistic or growth, and family systems therapeutic paradigms. These are paradigms pastors and pastoral care specialists regularly use in the practice of care and counseling.

It is important for practitioners of pastoral diagnosis to be aware of the assumptions and ethical values on which their therapeutic approaches rest. Because diagnosis inevitably projects the assumptions and values of the paradigm from which it arises, pastoral practitioners of care need to be skillful in engaging these philosophical foundations in critical conversation so as to disclose areas of continuity and discontinuity with their theological assumptions. Of course, genuine conversation includes openness to the possibility of revising one's own ideas in light of new insights.

The mutually critical conversation pastoral diagnosis requires presumes that pastors are able to articulate the theological assumptions grounding their worldview. Using the same categories developed in the first chapter, I suggest how the assumptions of a particular ecclesial paradigm inform the experience that focuses the first three chapters. In this way I am able to identify points of continuity and discontinuity relevant for pastoral practice that depends on one of the three therapeutic paradigms described earlier. Of course, the comparative analyses offered here are intended to illustrate the process that diagnosis requires regardless of the particular therapeutic and theological paradigms of the practitioner.

The knowledge that diagnosis requires is not some objective data that can be abstracted from the person and experience of the practitioner. Rather, it presumes a unity of being and doing. In fact, it involves a highly dynamic, collaborative, contextualized, embodied knowing. In the third chapter, I focus on pastoral identity as the unifying, theological self-consciousness that informs the process of pastoral diagnosis in which the pastor or pastoral care specialist is the lens through which the process of diagnosis occurs. I presume that pastoral identity involves a complex integration of diverse types of knowledge at conscious and unconscious levels. It includes the formative influences of one's faith tradition as well as one's social location and embodiment. In this chapter I attend in turn to both "pastoral" and "identity" as concepts reciprocally modifying each other in the experience of pastoral identity. The former involves an evolving dynamic stability derived from the critical appropriation of a faith tradition. The latter is an evolving, intrinsic relationality necessarily shaped by such embodied particularities as gender, culture, class, race, and sexual orientation. In this chapter I encourage an appreciation for the complexity of pastoral identity and the importance of critical self-conscious reflection on such identity.

Part Two
Part two of this book focuses on three areas in which the practice of pastoral diagnosis can be enhanced. These concerns arise from the comparative analyses of the first two chapters. In chapters four and five I consider the critical issue of authority as it is envisioned and exercised in pastoral diagnosis. There is much confusion in this culture and in contemporary ministry about what power is and whether and how it may be exercised rightly. In chapter four I address what constructions of authentic power are legitimate and helpful for pastoral diagnosis. I assume authority is an emotional expression of power. It is an imaginative, dynamic construction of images of relative strength and need operative in every relationship. In this chapter I develop a relational understanding of authority. It locates the exercise of authority in the covenantal context of trust and joins love and justice as its norms. I propose strategies for developing images of strength in pastoral relationships that help to assure an appropriate exercise of power guided by these norms.

In chapter five I continue a focus on pastoral authority but here I turn to the structural and symbolic dimensions of it that are distinctive to ministry and add significant complexity to it. My concern in this chapter is to heighten awareness of the possibilities and difficulties that attend these distinctive features of pastoral authority. Structural features such as the public, communal, enduring, and multidimensional character of parish ministry[5] do affect how a pastor and parishioner experience the dynamics of authority. Similarly, pastors and pastoral care specialists are identified with the historical office of ministry which carries varied and complex meaning to persons and inevitably shapes their authorization of a representative of the church. This varies still further with geographical and congregational factors.

By symbolic authority I am referring to those signs, symbols, and behaviors mutually understood as mediating the nearness or presence of God. I give particular attention here to ritual practice as an important authorizing resource in ministry that has transformative possibilities because it is grounded in scripture's ethical vision for life in relation to God and one another. My concern is for the nature of power associated with such authority and accountability for it.

Alongside the exercise of authority, pastoral diagnosis relies on anthropological assumptions such as the nature and possibility of fulfillment or freedom as well as a description of the human predicament. In the comparative analysis of therapeutic paradigms with an illustrative ecclesial one, I noted the importance of clarifying how it is that sin and psychopathology limit human freedom differently and whether sin offers a distinctively useful and truthful contribution to understanding the human predicament. These questions are the focus of the sixth chapter. In this chapter I assume human experience is tragically structured. I engage in a critical reconsideration of classical understandings of sin and original sin and allow them to be informed by the precritical constraints psychopathology introduces for the exercise of human freedom. I demonstrate how sin and psychopathology do limit human freedom differently. Both are important for an adequate understanding of the human predicament and the possibility for the freedom for love.

In the seventh chapter I turn to revisions warranted in the area of the ethical values that inform the practice of pastoral diagnosis. Clarifying how the bondage of sin and psychopathology differ helps disclose the importance of focusing here on addressing the freedom for love as a distinctive description of human fulfillment. Freedom for love is not simply the absence of sin. It involves an intentional response to God's grace and an ongoing transformative process of disciplined participation in communal practices of worship and mission. Christian tradition envisions love as the goal of human freedom: love for God, self, and others that intends the mutual upbuilding of human community. In this culture and in North American churches there is considerable disagreement about what love is and what it requires. Two concerns focus this chapter. First, I explore the implications of recovering the threefold understanding of the command to love now often reduced to love of God and neighbor. I will use a theocentric ethical framework to reassert that suffering is not the fulfillment of Christian love but a means toward love's fulfillment as mutual respect and empowerment. I also seek to recover for diagnosis scripture's intrinsically relational concept of the self and of human freedom. This relationality is in contrast to the separative self encouraged toward autonomy closely identified with the individualism so valued by this culture. Second, given the importance of shaping normative images of the self and human agency that prevail in this culture, I offer for this more public conversation a theologically informed proposal drawing on process thought and emerging developmental theory. Asserting the ontological status of relationality for human experience, I review the power of love as a relational ethic to enhance various features of human being necessary for individual and communal flourishing.

In chapter eight I conclude this book by reflecting on pastoral diagnosis as powerful knowledge. This chapter relies upon several multifaceted dynamically related kinds of knowing which I describe as personal, trustworthy, and truthful. I explore the implications of these kinds of knowing for practitioners, helping relationships, and the pluralistic context in which diagnosis occurs.

My goal in this book is to encourage the practice of pastoral diagnosis as practical theological reflection. I hope the explorations and proposals of these various chapters demonstrate effectively the interpretive and constructive power of pastoral diagnosis as a theological resource for care in personal, congregational, and public spheres.

NOTES

1.   Wayne Oates, *The Religious Care of the Psychiatric Patient* (Philadelphia: Westminster Press, 1978); Oskar Pfister, *Christianity and Fear*, trans. W. H. Johnson (London: George Allen and Unwin, 1948); and Edgar Draper et al., "On the Diagnostic Value of Religious Ideation," *Archives of General Psychiatry* 13 (September 1965): 202–7.

2.   Stephen Ivy, "Pastoral Diagnosis as Pastoral Caring," *Journal of Pastoral Care* 42 (Spring 1988): 81–89; Stephen Ivy, "Pastoral Assessment: Issue and Directions," *Religious Studies Review* 16/3 (July 1990): 212–18; George Fitchett, *Spiritual Assessment in Pastoral Care: A Guide to Selected Resources* (Decatur, Ga.: Journal of Pastoral Care Publications, 1993); David C. Stancil, "The Spiritual Values Inventory," 1995 unpublished.

3.   Paul W. Pruyser, *The Minister as Diagnostician* (Philadelphia: Westminster Press, 1976).

4.   Miriam Siegler and Humphrey Osmond, *Models of Madness, Models of Medicine* (New York: Macmillan, 1974), 93–94. Siegler and Osmond, in reviewing a variety of models in which diagnosis occurs, assert the constancy of these three criteria (p.15).

5.   I am indebted to Wayne Oates, *Pastoral Counseling* (Philadelphia: Westminster, 1974) for his discussion of some of these variables.

CHAPTER ONE

§

Diagnosis:
Defining the Terms and Issues

Diagnosis has a critical role in care and healing. It is an evaluative process of discerning the nature of another's difficulty in order to provide an appropriate, restorative response.

The word *diagnosis* is derived from the Greek terms *dia* (through or by means of) and *gnosis* (knowledge attained through careful observation that is verifiable)[1] and suggests knowledge that is not simply one's opinion but understanding carefully discerned as true. In fact, the results of one's diagnosis have everything to do with the resources and perspectives with which one begins. Diagnosis is not a neutral process; it has both interpretive and constructive functions. Diagnosis reiterates the anthropological and philosophical assumptions of the practitioner and validates the usefulness of those assumptions for naming reality.

For example, the psychiatrist's diagnosis of schizophrenia presupposes the truthfulness of scientific and biological data on which it is based and rearticulates her reliance on it, her definition and value for health, and her authority in relation to the patient. A West African shaman may recognize similar symptoms as evidence of evil possession and prescribe rituals, medicines, and practices congruent with the worldview that shapes his diagnosis. By participating in this process, persons in the family and tribe of the "patient" deepen their trust in the truthfulness of the worldview in which they and the shaman stand. Both the psychiatrist and the shaman practice diagnosis in good faith. Their paradigms determine the radically different ways in which they interpret the difficulties and possibilities of those seeking their help. In turn their diagnoses reiterate the worldview of that paradigm, whether scientific or animist, and thus reassert the truthfulness of that way of seeing and being in the world.

Diagnosis is a process of naming the reality of another's experience. It extends the practitioner's claims for the authority of her or his way of understanding the world. Diagnosis is an exercise of power that requires a remarkable sense of accountability and care.

The interpretive and constructive power of diagnosis lies in three dynamically interdependent criteria inherent in the process of assessment. These criteria, which are often only tacitly held by the practitioner and those seeking help, include: anthropological assumptions, communally shared guiding values, and mutually understood dynamics of authority in the helping relationship.[2] For example, the shaman and her or his tribe share an anthropology that is inextricably relational and in which past relationships are experienced more simultaneously so that the ancestor's power and presence are quite real. The power of logical rationality is limited by the agency of spirits and forces beyond the reach of one's intellect. The shaman and his "patient" do not need to discuss their anthropology because this is the view of themselves they assume. When the psychiatrist recommends certain psychotropic drugs and hospitalization, she and the patient's family already share common values for the priority of health and a certain kind of rationality and functioning. The hierarchical authority of the psychiatrist in a Western, medical paradigm and of the shaman in an African, animist paradigm is clear; what they define as the problem is accepted as true.

Intriguingly, these three criteria can be defined quite differently and still together constitute the practice of diagnosis. In less dramatically different paradigms than the two mentioned here, there is a dynamic interdependence among these three criteria, and the relative importance assigned to each criterion may vary. A practitioner's authority (for example) may be exercised less hierarchically when anthropological assumptions are more egalitarian. Depending on their definitions and weight in their dynamic interdependence, however, these three criteria—of anthropological assumptions, guiding communal values, and the dynamics of authority in the helping relationship—may constitute different or even competing paradigms.

THREE MODELS OF THERAPY

This book compares carefully the assumptions informing three models of therapy often used by pastors and pastoral therapists: a medical-psychiatric model, a humanistic-growth model, and a transgenerational family systems model. A theory of therapy always rests on two previous sets of assumptions: a theory of personality and the underlying metaphysical level of philosophical and ethical assumptions grounding that understanding of human being in the world. Thus every theory of therapy includes, however tacitly, certain assumptions about such foundational matters as the nature of human being and fulfillment, life in community, the human predicament, our grounds for hope, guidelines for the normative exercise of freedom, assumptions about the nature of truth, and norms for the exercise of power in cultural structures including issues of race and gender. In the immediacy of the actual practice of therapy, the significance of such philosophical and ethical issues is often not easily apparent.

Sarah, the new client sitting before you, is an attractive woman in her early forties. She was referred by her pastor. She is on the faculty of the local university, where she teaches literature and her husband, Ben, an attorney, is with a law firm. They have two children, a daughter, Beth, age twelve, and a son, Isaac, age ten. Her parents, in their late sixties, have retired and recently moved to town. Her husband's family is in a nearby city.

Sarah reports that she is feeling caught by many competing demands and finds herself unable to cope any longer without help. Increasingly irritable at home, she cries too easily, does not sleep well, and has gained ten pounds over the past six months. She cannot concentrate as she needs to on her work and is worried about writing commitments now far behind schedule. Her husband's work keeps him from home until late many nights. Ben is unwilling to cut back, saying that she knew the law would be like this, and he is working at the same pace as his partners. She feels increasingly distant from him, and they are arguing more and more intensely. Because of sports and various lessons, the children's needs for attention and physical and emotional support have really escalated this year. Sarah has always been the one to be there for them and for Ben, but there is not enough of her to go around.

She had thought that her parents' suggestion to retire to the town might help, but now that is less clear, for they, too, have expectations of her. Her parents do offer some transportation and child care help, but they raise questions about the children's behavior and criticize her parenting and Ben's absence. They are slow in making friends in town and expect to be in touch or with Sarah often. Old tensions between Sarah and her mother have begun to show as Sarah realizes she is not measuring up to her mother's expectations. An argument between them several days ago convinced Sarah to get help.

Sarah has come seeking that help. She trusts that you have skills to hear her painful story and offer her a way at least to ease if not to resolve the difficulties and pressures she describes. How you respond therapeutically to Sarah and the story she has shared has everything to do with how you hear, interpret, and name her experience, that is, how you diagnose her difficulty.

Sarah will likely experience her therapist as caring and concerned. Therapists in all three models we will review would intend to lower her anxiety and improve her functioning. Their differences are more apparent only as attention is given to how they assess Sarah's needs, intervene in her situation, and define their short- and long-term goals for her.

These clinical psychologies each project particular philosophical and ethical positions. Neither a therapist nor her or his clinical theoretical approach can be value-neutral. They of course often use terminology that includes clinical or scientific language such as personality disorder, differentiation, or organismic valuing, but, as Don Browning suggests, such language projects religious and moral horizons whether or not this is acknowledged by the clinician or client.[3]

Recognizing the existence of these religious and moral horizons in clinical psychologies underscores the fact that diagnosis is not neutral. How practitioners name another's reality defines the ways they seek to assist that person and their goals for her or him. The power of diagnosis also includes reasserting the authority of the practitioner's worldview, which means not that the philosophical and ethical claims of a particular clinical psychology are "wrong" or inadequate, but that those who adopt any clinical approach need to do so critically with a keen sense of accountability for the interpretive power they are exercising.

This responsibility for careful and critical adaptation of clinical approaches is particularly important for pastors and pastoral therapists. It is now commonplace to acknowledge that in this highly pluralistic North American culture, psychological language and metaphors have transcended those of religion. We no longer easily describe an action as sinful, but we often loosely use such language as "sick" and terminology such as "compulsive" or "schizophrenic" in a nonclinical way. Such a shift bespeaks the interpretive power of various clinical, psychological approaches for shaping the self-understanding and worldviews of North Americans. Many who identify themselves as Christians do not perceive the religious and ethical horizons of their psychological jargon.

Pastors and pastoral therapists have a particular, if not unique, opportunity in the process of care and counseling to help parishioners and clients become more self-consciously aware of the religious and ethical horizons of the way they understand and want to resolve the difficulties leading them to seek care. To do so, however, will require that pastors and pastoral therapists engage in a mutually critical "conversation" with the clinical approach they have adopted. As theologians, Christian pastors have a responsibility to help those in their care learn to live with reverence, that is, to live in the world as those who understand themselves, their actions, and the world through the experience of a Christian religious faith.[4] While pluralistic, this faith does include explicit ethical and philosophical horizons rooted in scripture, its authoritative text. Scripture, however, does not provide the theoretical, clinical data of a psychological theory. Pastors need to value and become skillful in one or more of these clinical approaches. We recognize, however, that such approaches also include religious and ethical interpretations of human being and fulfillment. This means that pastors need to develop skills in critically engaging various clinical approaches to discern the religious and ethical horizons they intend *and* to allow for real conversation in which theological as well as psychological voices may learn from one another.[5] Then the diagnostic task of assessing and naming the difficulty of another will include critical theoretical and theological reflection on the tools we use.

A first step toward skill in pastoral diagnosis involves careful attention to the philosophical and ethical horizons we can discern in models of therapy frequently used by pastors and pastoral therapists. I will attend to three such models: medical-psychiatric, humanistic-growth, and transgenerational family systems approaches.

PHILOSOPHICAL AND ETHICAL ASSUMPTIONS
OF THREE THERAPEUTIC PARADIGMS

As pastors and pastoral therapists we need to develop skills in mutually critical conversation between our theological assumptions and the philosophical and ethical foundations of the various therapies we use. In a sense the process of pastoral diagnosis underscores our need to be multilingual conversationalists, for such conversations may include theological disciplines, ethics, philosophy, cultural anthropology, and theories of personality and therapy. As crosscultural studies have reminded us, when we only know one culture, we don't *know* any culture at all. Similarly, such multilingual conversations enrich our primary language of theological perspectives. Other disciplines may deepen and correct our theological understanding. They may also confirm the wisdom it offers at other points and invite theological critique of their alternative ways of understanding the experience of reality. Of course, for such conversations to be clear and helpful, they must share the same foundational focus. It will not do for pastors to pose questions at the level of philosophical assumptions about human fulfillment or life in community while therapists discuss more concrete behavioral tendencies and needs. The multilingual, mutually critical conversations required by the process of pastoral diagnosis mean that we need a strategy for getting beneath the operational language of therapeutic theories to disclose their often tacit philosophical and ethical foundations. Here the constitutive criteria of diagnosis provide one avenue for proceeding.

Diagnosis relies on three sets of assumptions more or less consciously held by the practitioner. These include: anthropological assumptions, communally shared guiding values or worldview, and mutually understood dynamics of authority in the helping relationship. While these categories obviously are broadly conceived, they constitute those concerns foundational for assessing an expressed need or difficulty and responding with the intent of healing or restoring the person or persons as participants in the community. For example, in the area of anthropology the following questions suggest the type of assumptions practitioners must make more or less self-consciously when evaluating a client or clients: What is the nature of human being, and what are its possibilities for fulfillment? What is the nature of human freedom, and what is its relation to the possibility for change? What is it about human being that leaves us vulnerable to brokenness? What does well-being look like by which we determine dysfunction? Who is responsible for brokenness or pain when it occurs? Who is responsible for healing? What is the relation of the individual to the community?

Clearly, the questions that disclose one's anthropological assumptions begin to impinge on those foundational values that shape one's view of the world, that is, "the way things are and ought to be." What priority do we give to the individual in relation to the community? How do we define fulfillment, and what priority does it have? What is the relation of freedom and accountability? To what source or sources of authority do we appeal? How do we know what is true and what is good? In what or whom do we hope?

The dynamics of authority in the helping relationship are closely related to the other two categories of anthropology and guiding values. These dynamics also include the practitioner's status and power as conferred by the culture. Here we need to ask, how is the person in need viewed by her- or himself, the culture, and the practitioner? To whom is the one seeking help accountable? What is her or his responsibility in relation to a process of recovery? What is the priority of health or adaptiveness in relation to the autonomy of the person seeking help? What is the status of the practitioner representing that priority relative to the status of those seeking help? What is the relationship between the practitioner's power and her or his accountability for it? To what or whom is she or he accountable? What is the role of the community in relation to those seeking help and to the practitioner?

While pastoral diagnosis requires shared conversation about such assumptions as these questions disclose, we will prepare for such conversation by posing some of these questions to the three therapeutic approaches we have named as a way to discuss key issues in their foundational assumptions. These will be important for mutually critical, shared conversations in chapters to follow.

Medical-Psychiatric Paradigm

Our search for the anthropological assumptions grounding this paradigm can begin with its carefully ordered diagnostic process. In its questions about Sarah's intrapsychic life, development over time, motivations, and relationships we begin to sense an understanding of human beings as highly complex biological and psychological organisms always responding to particular sociocultural realities. Sarah is pictured as a self struggling for control over her unconscious internal drives and the demands of her external reality. Pruyser describes this complex self as a "commonwealth or household"[6] to underscore that there is no autonomous ego but a constant dynamic interplay of drives generated from within Sarah's psyche and reality testing perceived from her external world. These drives are conflicting, for we find Sarah longing for positive change and more productive relationships yet undercut by her own pervasive sense of inadequacy, guilt, and fear.[7] Her motivations are conflicted and not as unitary as they may appear, for they represent a mixture of motives that include self-interested needs as well as care and responsibility. Sarah is self-conscious and decisional, but her conscious awareness does not include vast areas of her complex psyche. She is pictured as vulnerable and conflicted struggling to cope.

This vulnerability is not peculiar to Sarah but reflects the human predicament as a kind of original vulnerability that arises from the very intrapsychic complexity, developmental needs, and sociocultural external realities inherent in human life. We are a problem to ourselves and live in an environment that requires continuing adaptation. Symptoms arise when competing drives undo this dynamic equilibrium of the self.[8] "Health" will always be a contingent, relative possibility in the somewhat precarious equilibrium of the household of the self. The modest and always partial resolution of this predicament lies in efforts to reduce vulnerability to internal and external anxiety through strengthening the ego's ability to administer its household.

Strengthening the ego by enlarging its control through conscious awareness is the clue for enhancing Sarah's real but limited freedom. As her insight into and control over the needs and forces that drive her are increased, she will be able to change. Sarah's conscious awareness, however, will always be limited by the power and scope of the dynamic unconscious that includes her conscience and ideal goals for herself as well as primitive drives and needs.[9]

Hope for Sarah in this paradigm is related to its reliance on the empirical rigor of science in which psychology participates. The very comprehensiveness of the psychological examination Pruyser describes and the certainty that these categories of analysis are verifiable pervade his knowledgeable discussion. If Sarah will invest herself in this ther-

[handwritten note: Therapist as rep. of scientific expertise]

oms of distress can be
th future difficulties
disorder or enhanced
coping ~~. . . is a modest~~ one, ironically in part because the complexity of human being is so great. Hope does include Sarah's commitment, courage, and motivation, but it relies principally on the scientific truthfulness that grounds the therapeutic process. While Sarah is responsible for choosing a process of healing and investing herself in it, she is not accountable for her symptoms or the inability to cope with the stressors that have resulted in her chronic and now acute depression.

The dynamics of authority in the helping relationship are shaped by this paradigm's more hierarchical reliance on the therapist as a representative of the expertise of science. The client-therapist relationship may be cordial and mutually respectful, but the goal of insight presumes the knowledge of the therapist and the confusion and illusions of the client whose unconscious drives require the objectivity of another.

One thing striking in the diagnostic process of this paradigm is the focus on the individual. Clearly, it presumes that to be human is to be embedded in relationships, for identity itself includes the internalized experiences of significant parental and family relationships. Yet, in assessing relationships the therapist searches for the needs Sarah seeks to meet through them. The focus is on her. But the ideal is for the ability to engage in mutually satisfying, respectful, trusting relationships—sexual and nonsexual.[10] Individuals who have an adequate, honest self-awareness are better able to enter such relationships and experience empathy for the needs of others. In this paradigm, the ideal for human life is fulfillment in love and work in which one appropriately satisfies needs for relationship and competence.

The values that guide this paradigm begin with a priority for scientific validation through empirical evidence. As Sigmund Freud put it in his defense of the emerging explanatory power of science, the "criterion of truth [is] correspondence with the external world."[11] Persons are urged to put aside the need for the comfort of illusions resting on any other basis, such as religious trust in God's presence and power. This rigorous, rather stoic life which trusts only the logic and rationality of science does not disregard joy in relationships or aesthetic values, but it does presume that we never fully know ourselves or the full truth of our motivations. Rationality and objective self-awareness will best help us reach maturity. While there were no explicit indications of ethical questions to Sarah, we recognize in the conversation restraint from any appeal to other sources for guidance or obligations. Ethically, in this paradigm, our actions should be based on a realistic appraisal of our own and other's needs and motivations rather than on any more idealistic rationale such as love for one's neighbor.[12] We do not raise questions about institutional and cultural norms.

Humanistic-Growth Psychology Paradigm

In the humanistic-growth psychology paradigm there are real clues for discerning assumptions about human being in the initial interview with Sarah. The goal of the therapist to facilitate Sarah's trust in her own actualizing process and the direction of the process of change toward affective awareness and expression all suggest a very positive estimation of the basic nature of human beings as constructive and trustworthy.[13] Unlike the previous paradigm Sarah is not torn by conflicting drives; rather, she is understood to be motivated by a single, self-enhancing and species-enhancing drive that is organismically based.[14] She has an innate wisdom that comes through attention to her total sensory, affective, and cognitive self. Sarah is highly social and needs relationships of care. When she is alert to what she feels, she makes good, rational decisions.

Ideally Sarah will feel the courage to be her true self. She will be guided by her innate or organismic valuing process that allows her to function in ways fully open to her experience in the present, trusting herself and able to adapt quickly to various situations.[15] Rather than coping or adjusting, she will find ways to meet and enhance her needs because that will help actualize others. Health in this paradigm is not a contingent equilibrium but an expansive, normative ideal that Sarah may increasingly realize as she trusts her experience of herself. Carl Rogers described this ideal as the "psychologically mature person." Such persons are themselves inwardly free to value what enhances life for them and others.[16] He claims that given a climate of freedom and respect, all individuals across all cultures would choose such value directions. Thus the human organism is our best resource for a universal valuing process.[17]

How is it, then, that in this interview we find a woman who has little access to her own experience, finds what she can feel is frightening, and is primarily attentive to the needs and feelings of those around her? According to this paradigm Sarah is experiencing the fundamental estrangement from her own internal best wisdom to which all of us fall prey to some degree when we sacrifice valuing our own best wisdom, accepting instead the conditions of worth we perceive as required by relationships with others we need and want.[18] Sarah is not accountable for losing her sense of direction that is available when she is in touch with her intuitive wisdom, for her acquiescence arises from her need for affiliation and care. Nonetheless, she is responsible for entering therapy to recover the freedom to be herself that she has given up in so many ways.

It is hard to imagine a category more central to understanding this paradigm than that of freedom. In her interview Sarah describes careful attention to the expectations and needs of others, but she acknowledges pain in the realization that she does not know who she is or what she wants. The freedom therapists in this paradigm want for Sarah is well summarized in this quote from Rogers, who is describing here what he says is a central aspect of psychotherapy: "It is the experience of becoming a more autonomous, more spontaneous, more confident person. It is the experience of freedom to be one's self."[19] By virtue of seeking therapy Sarah has initiated the process of experiencing autonomy. As a scientist Rogers believed that objectively human behavior is in fact determined, that is, a predictable sequence of cause and effect. But with other existentialists he affirmed the value of a subjective sense of freedom that complements this scientific determinism, voluntarily fulfilling such actions as spontaneous choices.[20] This subjective experience of freedom to live fully in an emerging process accountable for one's choices is the expansive vision of freedom or autonomy in this paradigm.

In this paradigm such self-actualizing behavior is understood as compatible with a value for life in relationship. Clearly the focus is on individuals fulfilling their unique possibilities. Rogers believed that self-enhancing behavior was actualizing for others. The expectation for Sarah is that when she is more fully open to her own experience she will live more harmoniously with her family. This paradigm assumes that one of the deepest needs of people is for relationships and communication, and that these needs serve as a socializing mechanism that also restrains our aggressive tendencies.[21] This complementarity of self-actualization with its rational, internal self-regulation and the shared needs of the whole ecology of life suggests a vision of a natural harmony of unique individuals. When others in their defensiveness convey conditions of worth and care, life in community becomes hazardous. Paradoxically, the community is the locus of the human predicament and a context envisioned as mutually enhancing.

This existentialist vision of psychologically mature individuals free to be themselves living harmoniously with one another and the earth is supported by guiding values suggested in our review of the various categories. It is clear from the interview and assessment resources that individuals are given the highest value with each conceived as uniquely worthy and good. Autonomy as self-potentiation is the goal for each person. Each is the "architect" of her- or himself.[22] Ethically this value for the organismic valuing process innate in each person means that each person's values are authoritative and similarly directed. Human freedom ought to be self-directed, with one's judgments always evolving and particular to each event.

In this paradigm hope for resolving Sarah's predicament clearly lies in Sarah's recovery of her own best wisdom through recovering access to her organismic valuing process that will lead to a positive value of herself and self-enhancing choices in her behavior. The optimism of this paradigm includes a global scale to its vision for empowering persons freely to be themselves.

The dynamics of authority in helping relationships in this paradigm are necessarily quite egalitarian, for only Sarah is an expert on herself. The authority of the therapist lies less in any image of expertise or as a representative of an authoritative system of knowledge and much more in the authority of the relationship of trust, respect, and care she or he offers clients such as Sarah. In fact, change comes by virtue of this relationship.[23] Of course, therapists in this paradigm employ considerable skill in creating and maintaining such a relational environment. Their goal, however, is to help Sarah recover the authority of her own self-actualizing potential. They regard her as the only one who has the innate resources for changing her situation.

Family Systems Paradigm

When we ask about the nature of human being in this paradigm, we immediately sense a figure ground shift, for the emotional unit that is the focus of therapy is the family. Human beings are inextricably relational. In Murray Bowen's model we sense this shift in the questions posed to Sarah. Emotional difficulties are understood now as pointing to the family systems within which Sarah lives and loves, and her struggle is pictured as one of fusion with others. In this paradigm human beings are understood as motivated by two counterbalancing forces for togetherness and for individuality. Sarah represents what apparently is the predictable dilemma of an imbalance in favor of togetherness, which means she is more vulnerable to her emotional and feeling systems and less able to use her intellectual capacities for reason. On the basis of natural science and biology, Bowen postulated that human beings' phylogenetic history means that we share with other animate creatures an instinctual or emotional system that governs all living processes such as sleeping, mating, eating, and states of fear, contentment, and anxiety. Human brains have more recently developed a cerebral cortex which gives the capacity for rational reflection and decision making. This intellectual system is linked to the emotional one by a feeling system that allows conscious awareness of particular emotional states.[24]

The capacity to draw on one's intellectual system is related to the relative balance of togetherness and individuality and the quotient of anxiety that is higher when, as in Sarah's case, togetherness is heightened. When this happens access to rational capacities declines, and we are left to more primitive resources. Moreover, as the interview with Sarah suggests, each individual is deeply shaped by his or her multigenerational family process. Time and family emotional processes carry our inextricable relationality. The emotional process of previous generations in Sarah's and Ben's families significantly shape their marriage and their respective individual experience. The emotional past is in the present. Its influence depends on the degree of differentiation, that is, the separation in her emotional and intellectual functioning that Sarah can achieve.

Individuals' relation to community or other selves is clearly inescapable and here pictured as inherent to what it means to be human. We are systemic in an ontological sense, and this interrelatedness is so thorough that the whole is more than a sum of its parts. Our functioning is understood as influenced by this complex interrelatedness. Rather than a kind of linear causality, a circular communication process in which all are affected is preserved here. Hence, the therapist asks about all the significant relationships Sarah experiences and places her experience in this complex web of relationships. Sarah's initiation of therapy and probable changes in patterns of relating will affect all in the family systems in which she lives. Part of what the clinician discussed in this interview was the triangles in which Sarah participated. In this model the smallest *stable* relationship system involves three rather than two.[25] As tension rises in Sarah's relationships with Ben, we find that instead of resolving it she becomes more involved with the children, and he with his work. Relations of individuals to others are clearly complex and significantly affected by phylogenetic and generational legacies that influence an individual's ability to use her or his intellectual capacities.

Ideally in this model persons become what Bowen described as "well differentiated," meaning that their intellect can function separately from their emotional system.[26] From the interview with Sarah this ideal emerges in the concern for the amount of energy she uses for loving and being loved with a focus on pleasing others and meeting their needs. Bowen sometimes used the phrase "solid self" to describe an optimal balance of differentiation. Solid selves are not emotionally fused or reactive to others but have clear access to their intellectual, reasoning capacities.

> The solid self is made up of clearly defined beliefs, opinions, convictions, and life principles. These are incorporated into self from one's own life experiences, by a process of intellectual reasoning and the careful consideration of the alternatives involved in the choice. In making the choice, one becomes responsible for self and the consequences.[27]

Ideally persons like Sarah will learn to be more autonomous in relationships and more logical in the various decisions they encounter.

This capacity to be a "solid self" able to distinguish feelings from reason and rely on the latter is only partially realized by anyone. This model understands that there are real limits imposed on all individuals precisely because of our phylogenetic and generational legacy; that is, our predicament is less intrapsychically located than external and historical. Each person, necessarily shaped in a particular family crucible, has certain limits and possibilities by virtue of his or her multigenerational and nuclear family emotional processes. As Bowen conceptualized our predicament, levels of differentiation match in marriages, and the amount of undifferentiation will impair one or more of any children in that marriage. This can be modified by ties with extended family and levels of anxiety in this nuclear family.

Bowen thought that the wife or mother, as primary caretaker of the children, is the key in projecting this undifferentiation and husbands or fathers acquiesce. The mother's anxiety over the needs of the child is the culprit.[28] Often one child is more impaired than other siblings. A child's distance from the family process improves their differentiation. This projection process is transgenerational so that all are complicit in this impairment. The consequence is greater emotional fusion manifested in what Bowen described as a "pseudo self" in which persons pretend to be other than they are to meet what they perceive as the expectations of others or of groups. There is no internal or logical consistency in this self's beliefs, opinions, and behavior.[29] The degree to which our pseudo self reigns is directly related to the degree of undifferentiation a person experiences. The clinician's assessment that Sarah's capacity for distinguishing her intellectual and feeling self is a rather undeveloped 45–50 on the scale of differentiation (1–100) suggests that she is beginning to recognize the relative dominance of her pseudo self.

The question becomes, how free is a person like Sarah to improve her level of differentiation and what form does freedom assume in this model? From the analysis of her interview we recognize that change is possible and even anticipated given the nascent resources for differentiation Sarah demonstrates. This suggests, of course, that there are real limits to Sarah's freedom—the same phylogenetic and multigenerational limits noted earlier. The possibilities vary directly with the level of differentiation one "inherits" from one's nuclear family. Bowen suggests that change will be only minimal but any increase in differentiation will have significant results.[30] While not responsible for the multigenerational context into which she was born, Sarah has certainly demonstrated responsibility in seeking help. Her ability to carry through and begin to correct the imbalance in togetherness and individuality depends not only on her own courage and current capacity for differentiation, but also on the therapist's ability to relate to her objectively modeling rational, nonreactive processing of actions needed. Increasing Sarah's freedom lies in increasing her access to her own capacities for reasoned decision making. In a sense, freedom and the ability to transcend feelings with reason appear quite similar in this model. Sarah's movement out of emotional fusion will allow similar movement for others in her family system.[31]

Hope for persons like Sarah lies in her investment in a therapeutic process that will increase her ability to use her reason and thus reduce the impairment from the legacy of her multigenerational family process. That is, hope lies in her ability to distinguish between thinking and feeling processes and to rely on the former.

As suggested earlier, the therapeutic relationship is crucial for the possibility of change. In the Bowen model, the dynamics of authority in that relationship are relatively hierarchical, even though Bowen preferred to describe himself as a coach who supervised a family. All conversation is directed to the therapist, who may educate or train counselees as they reconstitute relationships with their families of origin. In this process therapists model emotional objectivity and careful reason in the face of distress such as Sarah's.

The guiding values for this model clearly lie in the objective logic of the natural sciences. Bowen trusted in the facts of emotional functioning that he believed were predictable and universal. Clearly rationality as distinct and untainted by feelings as possible is of primary value. Paradoxically, while this theory claims an inextricable relationality for human life, its value for the "solid self" who is well differentiated, autonomous, and self-directed suggests a high regard for individuality in the midst of the groups in which one functions. It always presents fusion rather than individuation as problematic. Ethically, Bowen describes the well-differentiated person as principled and responsible, but he does not suggest any criteria for such principles other than internal logical consistency and reasoned reflection on one's life experience.[32] This suggests a prizing of an individual's ability to reason independently when scientific facts do not provide direction.

Summary

This initial exploration of foundational assumptions in these three psychological theories discloses that in fact there are important similarities and dissimilarities among them. Certainly, each has a real value for the individual and her or his freedom as autonomy even in the context of a family. Similarly, each is apparently unquestioning of cultural, structural assumptions regarding the exercise of power in marriage and family relationships. Each highly values truth as scientifically verifiable, although they differ in their estimation of a client's capacity for objective, rational thought. They also differ, sometimes significantly, in their understanding of the nature of human being, human fulfillment, the human predicament, the nature of human freedom, and the possibility for change. The following table may assist in a comparative analysis.

CONCLUSION

I began this chapter with the assertion that the process of diagnosis is never neutral but, rather, rests on assumptions about the nature of human beings, guiding values, or worldview, and the dynamics of authority in helping relationships. Reiterating these assumptions in the process of diagnosis gives it interpretive and even constructive power, although these philosophical and ethical assumptions are often unspoken beneath the more operational language of therapy. Pastors who recognize that scripture does not provide the psychological data for a theory of therapy need to develop skills in critically adapting the therapeutic theories they use. Such adaptation requires skills in engaging respective points of continuity and discontinuity at the level of foundational theological and theoretical assumptions. As a prelude to such critical conversation, we have explored one such approach and "uncovered" important philosophical and ethical assumptions grounding three theories frequently used by pastors. We turn now to the particular concerns pastors and pastoral therapists bring to the process of diagnosis and the critical conversation that it requires.

NOTES

1. *Theological Dictionary of the New Testament,* vol. 1, ed. Gerhard Kittel, trans. Geoffrey Bromiley (Grand Rapids, Mich.: Eerdmans, 1964–76), 690–91.

2. Cf. T. T. Patterson, *Management Theory* (London: Business Publication, Ltd., 1967) and Miriam Siegler and Humphrey Osmond, *Models of Madness, Models of Medicine* (New York: Macmillan, 1974), 93–94. Siegler and Osmond, in reviewing a variety of models in which diagnosis occurs, assert the constancy of these three criteria (p. 15).

3. Don S. Browning, *Religious Thought and the Modern Psychologies: A Critical Conversation in the Theology of Culture* (Minneapolis, Minn.: Augsburg Fortress, 1988), 8.

Table 1.1

COMPARATIVE ANALYSIS OF PHILOSOPHICAL AND ETHICAL ASSUMPTIONS INFORMING DIAGNOSIS
IN MEDICAL-PSYCHIATRIC, HUMANISTIC, AND FAMILY SYSTEMS PARADIGMS

	Medical-Psychiatric	Humanistic-Growth Psychology	Transgenerational Family Systems
1. Nature of the Human	Human being as a bio-psycho-social phenomenon; motivated by conflicting drives; mastery and constancy in the environment; developmentally shaped by intrapsychic, interpersonal, and sociocultural forces both conscious and unconscious; relational; and capacity for self-transcendence.	Human being as a bio-psycho-social phenomenon; motivated by a single drive toward self-fulfillment; inherently good, trustworthy, and constructive in orientation; innate organismic wisdom; socialized maturity; relational; and capacity for self-transcendence.	Human being as a bio-psycho-social phenomenon; motivated by conflicting forces for togetherness and individuality; linked phylogenetically with other animate beings by instinctual/emotional system that governs living processes and has additional capacity for intellectual and affective responses; inextricably familial and relational.
2. Nature and Possibility of Fulfillment	Honest self-awareness that allows for mutually satisfying and respectful relationships; appropriately meeting needs for relationship and competence through love and work; health as a contingent ideal relative to cultural norms for adaptive behavior vis-à-vis internal, interpersonal, and sociocultural forces.	When given freedom and respect to be one's self (as in therapy), able to maximize self-actualizing potential as fully functioning person open to new possibilities, flexible, responsive to the moment and caring for self and others; health as an expansive, normative ideal.	Lies through capacity for objective reasoning allowing more freedom from instinctual impulses; takes the form of differentiation as a "solid self"; clear about particular identity and capable of being more autonomous in relationships; responsible for self and the consequences.

3. Nature and Possibilities of Human Freedom	Real though limited by the power and scope of the dynamic unconscious and conflicting drives; negotiated within the entire economy of genetic, physical, intrapsychic, interpersonal, and sociocultural life; increased by insight into intrapsychic and interpersonal needs and drives; experienced as adaptive mastery of the environment.	Real and unlimited as a subjective experience of self-potentiation to complement objectively ordered world of determined events; achieved through convergence of organismic and self-actualization; includes accountability for one's choices.	Real though limited by phylogenetic, multigenerational, and nuclear family limits; lies in access to human capacity for reasoned decision-making that reduces anxiety and increases autonomy in relationships; change toward increased autonomy is possible through a therapeutic process that increases differentiation from family of origin; not accountable for phylogenetic or family legacy but responsible for seeking help.
4. Human Predicament	Originates in vulnerability to contingencies of psychical, physical, and historical existence for which one is not accountable; continuing reality because of the precarious equilibrium of the ego so only modest and partial resolution ever possible; complicit in personality dysfunction as cumulative deficit expression of personality-environment interaction; requires assistance of others for healing.	Universally experienced estrangement from wisdom of organismic valuing process in exchange for perceived conditions of worth in important relationships; deepening self-alienation; origin and locus of problem outside of self; not accountable for problem but accountable for seeking recovery.	Originates in vulnerability to the phylogenetic and generational legacies that define limits and possibilities for increasing balance of differentiation in counterbalancing forces of togetherness and individuality; family projection process principally carried through mother's anxious care impairs autonomy of one or more children creating greater balance of pseudo self or emotional fusion in the children; all share complicity in multigenerational process.

Table 1.1   *continued*

COMPARATIVE ANALYSIS OF PHILOSOPHICAL AND ETHICAL ASSUMPTIONS INFORMING DIAGNOSIS
IN MEDICAL-PSYCHIATRIC, HUMANISTIC, AND FAMILY SYSTEMS PARADIGMS

	Medical-Psychiatric	Humanistic-Growth Psychology	Transgenerational Family Systems
5. Individual in Relation to the Community	Priority given to the individual; recognizes significance of relationships as inextricably tied to individual identity and fulfillment; relationships are necessarily ambiguous; and community is the context for value though individually appropriated.	Priority given to individual's self-fulfillment; expectation that self-enhancing behavior is species-enhancing; needs for relationship are socializing; locus of self-alienating conditions of worth; vision of natural harmony of self-enhancing, unique individuals.	Family rather than individual is emotional unit for diagnostic focus; humans relational in ontological sense; triangles not dyads smallest stable relational unit; togetherness however, if not balanced by individuality, is problematic; autonomy in relationships is ideal.
6. Nature and Possibilities for Hope	Primarily located in the empirical rigor of science; also requires and is related to client's resources and motivation; limited to modest goals of enhancing control of drives and needs and enhancing coping skills.	Global scope to optimism based in organismic wisdom of self-actualizing process available to all; confidence in and reliance upon the client's capacity for self-actualization in context of trust and respect such as therapy.	Principally lies in capacity for rational thought which lowers vulnerability to emotional reactivity and increases autonomy in relationships because reason allows one to distinguish between thinking and feeling and choose the former; therapeutic modeling of reason and objective nonreactive processing.

7. Guiding Values or Worldview	Primary worth of individual; rigorous and exclusive trust in empirically verified, scientific facts; objective self-awareness through insight; ethical criteria shaped only by rational appraisal of needs and motivations.	Rigor of science; primary worth, goodness, value, and potential of each individual; freedom as autonomy; ethical criteria lie in assumption of universally common, positive direction to organismic valuing process innate in each individual.	Primarily lie in objective logic and predictability of natural sciences; prizing of individual autonomy in relationship; prizing of rationality; suspicion of affective dimensions; ethical criteria are internal consistency and rational reflection on experience.
8. Dynamics of Authority in the Helping Relationship	Hierarchical with reliance on therapist as an objective representative of the expertise of science; mutual respect.	Client as expert on her/himself; therapist's authority lies in authority of relationship of trust and care; therapist as companion facilitating client's journey of recovery of self and self-actualization.	Somewhat hierarchical with all conversation directed through therapist who coaches or supervises process of differentiation; emotional objectivity and nonreactive processing in therapeutic relationship are essential; goal of helping family or individual define their problems and use their resources to deal with those problems.
9. Diagnosis	Crucially important; shaped by classificatory approach; seeks to understand ecology of client's intrapsychic, interpersonal, and contextual experience in behalf of constructive responses for more adaptive mastery of the environment.	Repudiates classificatory model as unnecessarily and inappropriately hierarchical; use of processive assessment techniques to discuss placement on continuum of openness to change and spontaneity of feeling and experience.	Crucial, initial and continuing; family units as focus; seeks to assess levels of differentiation and family emotional process in behalf of lowering anxiety and increasing differentiation and autonomy.

4.   I am indebted to David Hester for this insight regarding the importance of living with reverence. See his convocation address, "Fear of God and the Beginning of Knowledge: Wisdom and Church Education," Louisville Presbyterian Theological Seminary, Louisville, Ky., September 3, 1991, for an elaboration of this point.

5.   Browning, *Religious Thought*, 14–17.

6.   Pruyser, *The Psychological Examination: A Guide for Clinicians* (New York: International Universities Press, 1979), 20.

7.   Sigmund Freud, "Anxiety and Instinctual Life," in *New Introductory Lectures on Psychoanalysis*, trans. and ed. James Strachey (New York: W. W. Norton, 1966), 95.

8.   Sigmund Freud, "Dissection of the Psychical Personality," in *New Introductory Lectures*, 51.

9.   Cf. Sigmund Freud, *The Ego and the Id*, trans. Joan Riviere, rev. and newly ed. J. Strachey (New York: W. W. Norton, 1962).

10.   Pruyser, *The Psychological Examination*, 219.

11.   Freud, "Weltanschauung," in *New Introductory Lectures*, 155.

12.   Cf. Sigmund Freud, *The Future of an Illusion*, ed. James Strachey (New York, W. W. Norton, 1989).

13.   Carl Rogers, "A Therapeutic View of the Good Life: The Fully Functioning Person," in *On Becoming a Person* (Boston: Houghton Mifflin, 1961), 194.

14.   Carl Rogers, "Toward a Modern Approach to Values: The Valuing Process in the Mature Person," in *Person to Person: The Problem of Being Human* (Lafayette, Calif.: Real People Press, 1967), 27.

15.   Rogers, "A Therapeutic View," 186ff.

16.   Rogers, "Toward a Modern Approach to Values," 25–27.

17.   Ibid., 27.

18.   Ibid., 19.

19.   Rogers, "Learning to be Free," in *Person to Person*, 47.

20.   Ibid., 52.

21.   Rogers, "A Therapeutic View," 194.

22.   Rogers, "Learning to be Free," 47.

23.   Rogers, "Some Hypotheses Regarding the Facilitation of Personal Growth," in *On Becoming a Person*, 31.

24.   Murray Bowen, "Theory in the Practice of Psychotherapy," in *Family Therapy in Clinical Practice* (New York: Jacob Aronson, 1985), 356.

25.   Ibid., 373.

26. Ibid., 363.
27. Ibid., 365.
28. Ibid., 381ff.
29. Ibid., 365.
30. Ibid., 371.
31. Ibid.
32. Ibid., 365.

CHAPTER TWO

§

Pastoral Diagnosis: Defining the Issues

Sarah, the client whom we met in the previous chapter, is also a parishioner with her family at First Presbyterian Church in the midwestern city in which she lives. In this chapter we will explore the way in which an ecclesial paradigm and a congregational context may shape her pastor's practice of pastoral diagnosis. We will use illustratively the theological commitments of a Reformed denomination here and those of other denominations in later chapters.

In this postmodern culture in which many Christians have a rather inarticulate theological worldview, pastoral diagnosis assumes a new level of importance. Sarah's pastor cannot assume that Sarah has an informed understanding of the resources of her faith for her current crisis. Because diagnosis is not neutral, pastoral diagnosis has a significant role to play in the process of constructing or strengthening a theological worldview. How a predicament is named shapes the strategies and the goals toward which a process of care proceeds. It is important to identify theological resources for assisting pastors in the process of critically adopting therapeutic theories for pastoral use.

The phrase *ecclesial paradigm* here refers to a Christian theological worldview that describes a distinctive way of being in and seeing the world. The origin and life-giving center of this paradigm is the redemptive love of God made known in Jesus Christ. That love has a transforming effect for believers that engenders a historical, corporate experience at conscious and precritical levels in which people respond to one another and their world with love and acts of faithfulness. While the process of transformation is ongoing and fulfillment of the love it intends is always partial, it does shape the foundational philosophical and ethical assumptions of believers who choose to stand in this paradigm.[1] As with the therapeutic paradigms we explored, pluralism characterizes the ecclesial paradigm. Beyond the common affirmation of the Lordship of Jesus Christ, nuanced and dramatic differences exist among traditions within this paradigm.

CONGREGATIONAL CONTEXT

"Congregational context" refers to particular ecclesial communities that are shaped by acts of worship and mission in response to a common affirmation of the Lordship of Jesus Christ. Congregations are a highly pluralistic genre of extraordinary dynamic and systemic complexity that include racial, ethnic, cultural, sexual, political, personal, and theological differences. They represent another level of pluralism and significant particularity within the various traditions of the ecclesial paradigm. Congregations mediate the foundational assumptions of a theological tradition, but they do so in interaction with their particular social, historical, and political contexts so that their witness and faith are shaped dialogically with their environment. Recognizing the particularity of a congregation's theological identity is significant for the task of pastoral assessment. Similarly, pastors need to be conscious of the many structural and sociocultural dynamics that shape the congregation's life and faith. These structural dynamics include the ways Sarah's pastor knows and relates to her.

In this case Sarah belongs to a relatively large Presbyterian congregation of six hundred members. It is the oldest Presbyterian church in the presbytery and has some influence in the life of this small midwestern city by virtue of its history and the fact that many members hold influential professional or managerial positions in the city. For example, Ben's senior colleagues and other faculty and administrators from the university attend First Church. The congregation's ethos is somewhat conservative or traditional, but the leadership wants to be on the "correct" side of issues. Thus change is supported but through civic and ecclesiastical structures already in place.

Most of the congregation is white and language about people and God is mostly inclusive. The church uses the NRSV and a new hymnal. Only in the last decade, however, have women had more than token representation in the worship life and governance of the congregation. Most of the twelve women on the forty-two-member session are older and did not work outside the home. With the growing number of dual career families in the congregation, several middle-aged women with established careers have been elected, as has one person of color.

Worship is formal in tone and the sermons and liturgy are informed by a rather complex understanding of the local and global social context and human emotions. A strong flavor of individualism prevails, however, that interprets God's power, providence, and grace in ways that do not fundamentally challenge the status quo in personal or civic structures. The congregation considers itself warm and especially congenial for families. Two young adult couples in the congregation with school-age children recently experienced divorces, which has elicited more talk about "the family" under siege and concern about whether emerging family patterns are fair for children.

Several years ago this congregation called a woman as an associate pastor. Ann, now forty-five, is married to a CPA and has two children. Sarah sought her out because she knew her through several types of contacts at church.

Ann knows Sarah and her family in multiple ways. She leads Beth's confirmation class, and her son is in the same soccer league as Isaac, so they meet at games occasionally. She knows Sarah's parents through the new member orientation classes as well as through a home visit and their occasional participation in older adult activities. Ann works with Ben on the Session and has been with Sarah and Ben as a couple for fellowship activities. She has gotten to know Sarah best through the "faith and fiction" discussion group in which Sarah participated until this year when she withdrew citing family scheduling difficulties.

Ann's relationship with Sarah is complex. She knows and relates to three generations of Sarah's family. When she preaches, teaches, serves as liturgist, or leads programs, Ann assumes professional, public, and symbolic roles. When she and Sarah have talked about their children and juggling careers and family obligations during a soccer game or at social occasions, her role is more that of a friend. Of course, even in these informal contexts, Ann symbolizes the congregation and the faith in which Sarah trusts. Sarah knows Ann's views, values, faith, and even some of her struggles through the public roles and more personal conversations they have shared. Ann's multiple relationships and roles with Sarah and her family will endure beyond this time of crisis in Sarah's life. Her assessment of Sarah's situation will include a rich knowledge of Sarah and her family as well as the religious beliefs and values that help shape Sarah's worldview and sense of herself. Of course, Ann will need to listen carefully for Sarah's way of appropriating those beliefs and values in her self-understanding, relationships, and worldview, and for how such beliefs and values offer resources for healing and constructive changes.

The process of diagnosis in the ecclesial paradigm and particular congregations introduces contextual, relational, and explicit philosophical concerns that are avoided by therapeutic paradigms. Even this brief summary of the congregational context in which Sarah worships and reflects on her faith is suggestive for the ways it mediates particular perspectives of the ecclesial paradigm that may inform her sense of herself, her world, and relationships. This congregation appears to have a civic orientation to mission[2] that seeks change through existing structures and does not call those structures and systems into question. The congregation does not demonstrate any significant investment in structural change and seems to keep its focus inward on educational and supportive activities. The congregation seems to value intellectual rigor and evidently reflects the culture's reliance on individualism. Gender roles and rules also seem traditional beneath some minor accommodations to change. Worshipping, learning, and serving here likely will reinforce Sarah's traditional gender role assumptions and her reticence in valuing her affective experience and needs. It is also likely that her faith and the culture's values will not clash often. Sarah's relationship with her pastor, Ann, demonstrates the distinctive way pastoral relationships exist over time in public and private spheres, with symbolic as well as structural dimensions of authority alongside occasions of more egalitarian exchanges, including shared confessional concerns and often bridging more than one generation.

HISTORY OF PASTORAL DIAGNOSIS

It is helpful to put Ann's process of pastoral diagnosis in historical context.[3] Indeed, paying attention to the distinctive ways in which the ecclesial paradigm shapes diagnosis and pursuing the critical conversations that pastoral diagnosis requires between ecclesial and various psychological paradigms are modern concerns. For generations pastoral diagnosis has been practiced as theological reflection on the contingencies of human experience in order to discern the truthfulness and usefulness of the ecclesial paradigm for providing healing and constructive responses for believers. In fact, such theological discernment was practiced by Pharisees before the common era.[4] From its inception, diagnosis in Judaic and later Christian contexts has included explicit confessional dimensions in the sense of shared religious beliefs and values. It has also presumed, on the basis of those beliefs and values, an ethical horizon for life choices and a broad focus on the whole of life rather than a compartmentalization of religious experience. Healing is presumed to include more than merely restoration; it also extends to providing resources for faith and discipleship.

In the early life of the church, diagnosis was practiced as discernment with catechumens. Later it was directly linked with the penitentials. Gregory the Great's *Pastoral Care*, written in the sixth century, is a brilliant and classic example of pastoral diagnosis as an assumed and essential part of care and guidance.[5] Spiritual direction in the Roman tradition illustrates assessment used in relation to discernment and guidance. Later the Reformers moved away from the casebook approach of the penitentials but continued to link assessment with discipline in the sense of both correction and guidance. Their focus became repentance witnessed in the transformed life. Calvin's letters, Richard Baxter's *The Reformed Pastor*, and Jonathan Edwards's *A Treatise Concerning Religious Affections*, illustrate the continuity of this concern in pastoral care and pastoral diagnosis.[6]

By the early part of the twentieth century, Anton Boisen's case study approach suggested a significant transition in the use of pastoral assessment.[7] The scientific method and psychological diagnosis were available to him alongside his concern for understanding the religious experience of persons who were mentally ill. Boisen moved pastoral diagnosis from its congregational context to clinical settings. In such contexts clarity about the nature and purpose of diagnosis was not sustained. Religious experience was increasingly the object rather than the context of diagnosis. As access to therapeutic paradigms increased, pastors found them helpful and adopted them. The perceived usefulness and truthfulness of pastoral diagnosis diminished in the relativizing consequences of modernity, and the broad life-encompassing scope of pastoral diagnosis narrowed to the clinical usefulness of religious ideation. Its ethical horizon shrank back in submission to the increasing reign of individualism with its concomitant relativization of previously held norms. In fact, from the early 1950s through the mid-seventies, many pastors uncritically adopted the humanistic paradigm which disparaged any process of diagnosis and encouraged value neutrality by the practitioner. Of course, the idea of such neutrality is clearly naive to postmodern sensibilities.

During this period only a few voices called attention to the theological integrity of pastoral practice,[8] but by the mid-seventies they sparked a now wide consensus that intends to recover a theological center for pastoral care. Pluralism is now recognized as the context rather than the problem for ministry. Paul Pruyser and Seward Hiltner urged pastors to recognize the significance of diagnosis for reasserting the distinctive usefulness and truthfulness of the ecclesial paradigm in a pluralistic context,[9] while others have explored the distinctive ways in which the ecclesial paradigm and the pastoral office affect the process of diagnosis.[10]

Currently a number of different approaches to pastoral diagnosis coexist,[11] most of which recognize that pluralism requires that diagnosis must involve a critical conversation with behavioral sciences and psychological paradigms. This means that Ann's process of pastoral diagnosis, unlike that of her historical counterparts, involves the use of other perspectives that augment her theological resources. She will use a theory of therapy and perhaps developmental approaches as she assesses Sarah's predicament. Her assertion that the ecclesial paradigm is useful and truthful and its ethical perspectives compelling is not so simple for her as was the advice of John Calvin, Richard Baxter, or Jonathan Edwards in their time. The difficulty lies not so much in the advent of these therapeutic theories and the skill they require as in the collapse of the interpretive hegemony once enjoyed by the ecclesial paradigm. Ann cannot simply assert a theological claim with Sarah, nor can she presume Sarah's informed and confident trust in the theological assumptions of the faith she professes weekly. Ann will probably need to help Sarah construct or recover a theologically informed self-understanding as a part of the process of pastoral care. Ann's theological awareness in framing her diagnosis of Sarah's difficulties will determine whether and how her care for Sarah contributes to Sarah's theological self-understanding.

A REFORMED PERSPECTIVE

It is important for pastors like Ann to be keenly aware of the theological assumptions informing their work. As we noted earlier, the ecclesial paradigm, because it includes various traditions with subtle or nuanced differences, is itself pluralistic. In order to proceed with our own goal of illustrating the kind of critical conversation required by pastoral diagnosis, we will analyze a recent "A Brief Statement of Faith" adopted by the Presbyterian Church (U.S.A.) and used in the congregation Ann serves, and we will employ the same categories used earlier with several therapeutic paradigms. In later chapters we will explore how different theological traditions may modify the critical conversation this analysis suggests.

The Presbyterian Church (U.S.A.) stands within the Reformed tradition that began to emerge in the sixteenth century. It is a confessional tradition; that is, it is guided not only by scripture but also by the gathered confessional documents of Reformed communities of faith over the course of the tradition's four-hundred-year history as well as by the Apostles' and Nicene Creeds. Each is understood as representing that era's effort to allow their faith to interpret their historical context, so the confessions are understood as partial and occasional. Reformed confessions also seek first to be catholic in scope, then Protestant, and finally to represent the particular emphases of Reformed perspectives. This "A Brief Statement of Faith" is included in a *Book of Confessions* which has constitutional status in the PC(U.S.A.). It complements previous confessions collected in this volume and, pertinent for our case, changes the Scots Confession's prohibition of women in offices of ministry. Such differences among the confessions demonstrate the rather fluid character of this tradition beyond core perspectives identified with Reformed faith. In its *Book of Order* the PC(U.S.A.) identifies these core perspectives as Reformed:

> Central to this tradition is the affirmation of the majesty, holiness, and providence of God who creates, sustains, rules, and redeems the world in the freedom of sovereign righteousness and love. Related to this central affirmation of God's sovereignty are other great themes of the Reformed tradition:
>
> (1) The election of the people of God for service as well as for salvation;
>
> (2) Covenant life marked by a disciplined concern for order in the Church according to the Word of God;

(3) A faithful stewardship that shuns ostentation and seeks proper use of the gifts of God's creation;

(4) The recognition of the human tendency to idolatry and tyranny, which calls the people of God to work for the transformation of society by seeking justice and living in obedience to the Word of God.[12]

We will elaborate on these in our analysis of a contemporary Reformed confession.

"A Brief Statement of Faith," adopted in 1991, articulates a Reformed perspective for this time and context. It is included here in full:

A BRIEF STATEMENT OF FAITH
PRESBYTERIAN CHURCH (U.S.A.)

1	In life and in death we belong to God.
2	Through the grace of our Lord Jesus Christ,
3	the love of God,
4	and the communion of the Holy Spirit,
5	we trust in the one triune God, the Holy One of Israel,
6	whom alone we worship and serve.
7	We trust in Jesus Christ,
8	fully human, fully God.
9	Jesus proclaimed the reign of God;
10	preaching good news to the poor
11	and release to the captives,
12	teaching by word and deed
13	and blessing the children,
14	healing the sick
15	and binding up the brokenhearted,
16	eating with outcasts,
17	forgiving sinners,
18	and calling all to repent and believe the gospel.
19	Unjustly condemned for blasphemy and sedition,
20	Jesus was crucified,
21	suffering the depths of human pain
22	and giving his life for the sins of the world.
23	God raised this Jesus from the dead,
24	vindicating his sinless life,
25	breaking the power of sin and evil,

26   delivering us from death to life eternal.
27 We trust in God,
28   whom Jesus called Abba, Father.
29 In sovereign love God created the world good
30   and makes everyone equally in God's image,
31   male and female, of every race and people,
32   to live in one community.
33 But we rebel against God; we hide from our Creator.
34   Ignoring God's commandments,
35   we violate the image of God in others and
            ourselves,
36   accept lies as truth,
37   exploit neighbor and nature,
38   and threaten death to the planet entrusted to
            our care.
39 We deserve God's condemnation.
40 Yet God acts with justice and mercy to redeem
        creation.
41   In everlasting love,
42   the God of Abraham and Sarah chose a
                covenant people
43   to bless all families of the earth.
44   Hearing their cry,
45   God delivered the children of Israel
46   from the house of bondage.
47   Loving us still,
48   God makes us heirs with Christ of the covenant.
49   Like a mother who will not forsake her nursing child,
50   like a father who runs to welcome the prodigal home,
51   God is faithful still.
52 We trust in God the Holy Spirit,
53   everywhere the giver and renewer of life.
54   The Spirit justifies us by grace through faith,
55   sets us free to accept ourselves
                and to love God and neighbor,
56   and binds us together with all believers
57   in the one body of Christ, the Church.
58   The same Spirit
59   who inspired the prophets and apostles
60   rules our faith and life in Christ
                through Scripture,
61   engages us through the Word proclaimed,

62	claims us in the waters of baptism,
63	feeds us with the bread of life and the cup of salvation,
64	and calls women and men to all ministries of the Church.
65	In a broken and fearful world
66	the spirit gives us courage
67	to pray without ceasing,
68	to witness among all peoples to Christ as Lord and Savior,
69	to unmask idolatries in Church and culture,
70	to hear the voices of peoples long silenced,
71	and to work with others for justice, freedom, and peace.
72	In gratitude to God, empowered by the Spirit,
73	we strive to serve Christ in our daily tasks
74	and to live holy and joyful lives,
75	even as we watch for God's new heaven and new earth,
76	praying, "Come, Lord Jesus!"
77	With believers in every time and place,
78	we rejoice that nothing in life or in death
79	can separate us from the love of God in Christ Jesus our Lord.
80	Glory be to the Father, and to the Son, and to the Holy Spirit. Amen.[13]

ANALYSIS OF PHILOSOPHICAL
AND ETHICAL ASSUMPTIONS

To ask about the nature of the human in the ecclesial paradigm immediately confronts us with the consequences of affirming the reality of transcendence as the God made known through acts of history and especially incarnationally through Jesus of Nazareth. A Reformed perspective gives particular emphasis to the power and majesty of God and the proclamation of God's sovereign reign over human life and history. God's initiative and God's saving power are the context in which to understand what it means to be human. As the opening line of this confession suggests, human beings have always to do with this living God. The language of Creator implies that human beings are first of all creatures—creations of this living God. Human life—embodied, gendered, racially diverse, affective, and relational—takes on a profound intentionality and value as a reflection of God's image and purpose.

Ann understands Sarah as uniquely valuable. Sarah's whole life—her hopes, fears, sexuality, intelligence, and relationships—are important, for Ann presumes that God is actively present in Sarah's life. Moreover, there is an ethical horizon to human life in this paradigm because humankind is inextricably linked with the purposes of its Creator, the Holy One of Israel revealed most fully in the life and ministry of Jesus of Nazareth. This assertion of God's incarnation in one who modeled radically self-giving love and demonstrated its power to challenge and transform human lives and systems means that justice and love become the criteria for the human vocation of worship and service. Ann listens to Sarah's pain and hopes to ease it, but she also has the larger goal of helping Sarah construct a more adequate self-understanding that will enhance her discipleship.

Ann listens to Sarah knowing that the goodness God intends for creation and creatures in relationships of love and care is distorted through the conflicting drives experienced by humans. This conflict arises from the capacity for self-transcendence and the anxiety that accompanies creatureliness in historical existence. Such self-transcendence allows one to be in trusting relation to the Creator and Redeemer of life, but it also elicits the anxiety that accounts for sin as the refusal to trust and turning from God in rebellion or shame. The consequence is a progressively profound alienation.

The context for human life as described in this paradigm includes a certain original vulnerability to suffering and alienation, for, as this confession suggests, creaturely anxiety occurs in a "broken and fearful world." God's promise to save is not a promise to keep safe. The anxious need for reassurance that she was loved and valued which Sarah described as prompting her readiness to live up to the expectations of her parents and, later, of others reflects a complex interaction of family dysfunction, cultural pressures, and her own complicity over time in the alienating consequences of sin. This alienation, profoundly destructive in individual lives, also pervades the systems and structures of culture and church. For example, the gender assumptions that Sarah holds and that contribute to her loss of self are apparently more entrenched in the congregation where she worships than in the culture at large. What is particularly distinctive in this paradigm's understanding of the human predicament is the assertion that this alienation, called sin, is so thoroughgoing that human beings cannot free themselves from its bondage. Therapy, rational thought, wealth, or political might will not work. The human predicament is so profound, we require a savior.

In this confession we find the assertion that in Jesus of Nazareth God knows and has shared the depths of human pain and suffering and triumphed over it. But sin is an enduring reality with which believers struggle in this life. That is, Ann and Sarah understand themselves as forgiven sinners. They are forgiven, but they continue to struggle with the conflicting drives of trust and the refusal to trust that anxious fear elicits. This paradigm asserts that only God's Spirit can free us from sin's destructive effects because, once chosen, sin continues to limit human freedom to live with trust. Certainly Ann hears Sarah describe progressive alienation in the shame and pride she experienced.

As Sarah's story demonstrates, sin affects our relation to ourselves and others. It begins as a refusal to live in right relation to God. Therefore, the alienation it describes is best understood as idolatry— the effort to control, contain, or replace God. Because of the Reformed emphasis on respect for God's majesty and power, theologians in this tradition have long emphasized the rebellion of pride as the primary sign of sin in human life and community, briefly noting the tradition's corresponding possibility of hiding associated with shame.[14] More recently, as women were recognized as theologians in this tradition they noted, as does this confession, that sin may as often mean shame's refusal to be a self and preferring to live through another—the sin of hiding.[15] In either case sin demonstrates an anxious human dis-ease with creaturely dependence and an effort to save oneself.

This paradigm characterizes sin as an abuse of human freedom; that is, sin is understood as chosen though already thoroughly pervasive in church and culture. Human freedom is real but distorted or limited by sin. Sarah is accountable for the choices she has made, but Ann also recognizes how other sociological and psychological factors and systemic evidences of sin contributed to Sarah's refusal to trust. Sarah is now no longer as free to live with trust in God and to choose to love her neighbor as herself. There is, this confession suggests, a paradoxical tension between human freedom for love and the bondage of sin. The latter arises by the pretense of self-sufficiency, which results, ironically, in increased alienation. The bondage of true freedom lies in a willingly chosen commitment to love oneself, God, and neighbor. Sin is a continuing reality, but this freedom can be increasingly recovered by trusting in God's Spirit to renew and transform one's life.

This means that Ann and Sarah regard change as possible if Sarah chooses to trust in God's promises and to open herself to new behavior. Such freedom is inherently ethical, for it is fulfilled by the choice to live with love as defined by God's justice and compassion. This love binds believers to all in the human community as neighbors. In this paradigm, then, human freedom is disciplined by one's willing commitment to love neighbor and self.

There is an iconoclastic character to such freedom because its criteria are defined not by culture or individual hopes and needs but by the love and justice that characterize the presence and power of God. That means that as Ann listens to Sarah's experience and pain, she has a critical principle by which to assess all the factors that are complicit in Sarah's bondage. That principle also guides her efforts to help Sarah exercise her freedom more faithfully so that they do not merely reflect cultural or congregational norms.

The significance of human freedom in this paradigm becomes even more apparent when we consider that the ideal for human life centers in the freedom for love. This is freedom willingly disciplined by God's love and justice through that care for self, others, God, and creation which mirrors God's regard for life and the created order. This possibility comes only through the initiative of God's Spirit, who loosens the bondage of sin to create the freedom for choosing the bonds of love. As Ann listens to Sarah she recognizes that what seems problematic for her is caring for herself as much as she cares for others. An imbalance on either side of this equation renders love inauthentic.

Ideally, Sarah will come to trust experientially that God's love includes her, and that sense of being loved and valued will shape her care of others and creation. Such love has transforming intentions systemically and structurally as well as personally. Ann's hope for Sarah is that as she begins to believe she is loved and valuable in God's eyes, she will increasingly recognize that the gift of this love invites her to acknowledge her connections with and responsibilities toward those whom God also loves and the creation that she and others are called to tend. The ideal for human life does include this commitment to service. Its roots lie in the sense that historically God has called believers to witness to the transforming power of God's love. Human life is purposive, and its purpose is to extend God's love and justice.

This ecclesial paradigm also clearly affirms the value of such service in the ordinariness of daily life. Because the incarnation asserts that no person or occasion is insignificant, together Ann and Sarah will discern God's presence in Sarah's daily life. The reference in the PC(U.S.A.)'s "A Brief Statement of Faith" to living "holy and joyful lives" is particularly helpful in elaborating on the human vocation to worship and service as mentioned earlier in the document. Ideally, as believers come to feel deeply that life is lived in God's care, their lives will be characterized by praise, gratitude, and reverence for God and all God has created. Alongside such reverence for life and creation pastors such as Ann look for evidences of joy. Surely Sarah and her family system possess little of that now. Such joy is not a blind optimism that refuses to recognize the reality of pain and sin, but rather a profound expression of trust in God's care and wonder and delight in the gift of daily life in relationships of mutual care.

As our analysis of the ideal for human life suggests, this ecclesial paradigm asserts that human life is inherently relational and that the whole of creation is interwoven. The paradigm also attributes a positive value to such interdependence by the call to live as one community. Each life is equally valued, and differences of gender and race are seen as reflecting the richness of God's image rather than distortions of it. Ann is aware that Sarah's pain and self-understanding reflect long-standing patriarchal distortions in culture and church that undermine the value of women, but she also recognizes that appropriate love for self is crucial for life in community because it requires mutual care and respect for one another. As we noted concerning the ethical dimensions of the ideal for human life, the freedom for love in this paradigm underscores that life in community is an ethical and intentional claim on all believers. The many comments about mutual care and responsible care for one another in "A Brief Statement of Faith" suggest that this faith tradition assumes that life in community is no simple possibility. Faithfulness rather than perfection is Ann's hope for her parishioners. While Ann is not surprised by the difficulties in Sarah's life and family, she does believe that community can be a locus of healing and care by the grace of God's Spirit who can transform the alienation of sin that divides and distorts bonds of care. It is in and through relationships that we experience God's care and healing most often.

The nature and possibilities for hope in this paradigm, like its assessment of the human predicament, are quite radical. Hope is located beyond the capacities of the self in the saving promises of God which, for believers, have transforming power even in the present. Sarah and Ann have faith in God as Creator and Redeemer who kept covenant with the people of Israel and, through Jesus of Nazareth, demonstrated God's convincing power to save. This faith means that Sarah and Ann face this present pain with a certain confidence that their resources for dealing with it go beyond their best efforts and the various resources of culture. They trust that the sustaining and transforming presence of God's Spirit is available to them. As this confession suggests, this hope in God's transforming love does not guarantee the end of fear and brokenness in the world. Nevertheless, the life and resurrection of Jesus of Nazareth does mean that the power of such experiences is limited and must finally yield to the power of God's love. Believers may face them with courage and energy. Sarah and Ann also trust that forgiveness for the evidences of sin in their own lives comes not because they earn such release but because God's love is actively transforming the present. It is important to realize that this confidence in God's saving activity invites believers to join in this ministry of redemptive transformation rather than allowing a sort of quietism. Human energy, intelligence, imagination, and love are important without being the limits of hope. Ann will use the best therapeutic resources available to her, and she will encourage Sarah to identify and begin to make changes in her life, but she will do so trusting that all these efforts rest in the life-giving energy of God's Spirit.

The guiding values of this paradigm are ordered by the assertions of lines 1–6 in "A Brief Statement of Faith," for they claim the sovereignty of God who is Lord of creation and redemption. Thus all of life is subject to the values associated with God as disclosed primarily through scripture as well as in tradition and experience. This means that as Sarah seeks to orient her life and determine changes, she will test her direction by the guidance of scripture, finding there the norms of love and justice for human life and relationships. More than that, Sarah's regular participation in worship suggests that she makes some use of means of grace such as worship, preaching, the sacraments, and prayer.

Clearly this ecclesial paradigm values freedom that is disciplined by obedience to the norms of scripture, which do not merely convict and restrain but also guide. Of particular importance is this paradigm's value for human life: it regards life as a gift to celebrate and share with gratitude, the incarnation as affirming God's value for all human life, and Jesus' ministry as signalling a particular concern for the vulnerable. Because God chooses to act in history, this paradigm affirms the significance of faithful action in this time and place: it holds one accountable for the exercise of freedom and links the stewardship of gifts for faith and practice. The human vocation is our service as well as our praise. The principal ethic guiding this faithful activity or service is love as defined by the life and ministry of Jesus of Nazareth. Love and justice are inextricably joined in this paradigm because of the character of God's saving presence both with the people of Israel and in the ministry of Jesus of Nazareth. The broad commitments of freedom, justice, and peace suggest the impetus that this paradigm gives to believers to join in God's redemptively transforming action at structural as well as personal levels. It is for this reason that Ann is attentive to the way Sarah's pain has narrowed the sphere of her world and her concerns. She will help Sarah expand the horizons of her care as she helps her recover the freedom for love that God intends.

Of course this vision of transformation, personally and structurally, rests in a value for and reliance upon a community of faith. It allows for no hierarchy among believers, but rather assumes that the gifts of all are needed. Further, this paradigm clearly has an abiding respect for the radicality of personal as well as structural sin. So we find a pervasive assertion that all behavior is tainted by self-interest and all behaviors and structures require the critique of faith. Repentance is a continuing process; thus this paradigm values faithfulness and recognizes perfection as impossible. Ann assumes that Sarah is complicit in the pain and familial dysfunction she describes. In recognition of the difficulty sin brings to life in community, this paradigm underscores the value for community life of power shared in ways that enhance all. It also values difference as enriching rather than as the occasion for domination. Precisely because love is difficult, justice, mercy, freedom, and peace take priority.

Because of this ecclesial paradigm's respect for the activity of God's spirit in calling persons to offices of ministry, both real and symbolic authority are operative in ministerial relationships. It is important to realize that the focus lies in the office and functions of ministry; it does not elevate the person of the minister. Thus Sarah respects Ann's authority as one whose gifts in worship, preaching, care, teaching, and administration are evidence of her call to ministry and whose call is also confirmed by others in the denomination and congregation. Ann's authority lies in her skills and wisdom and in her office. Sarah knows that Ann, like herself, is also subject to the Lordship of God and requires God's gracious forgiveness. The dynamics of authority in this paradigm are at once leveled by the shared need for grace for all believers and unbalanced by Ann's real and symbolic authority and power as one to whom the office of religious leadership is entrusted. Ann's authority is not at the expense of Sarah's value and worth or of her autonomy. Sarah, too, is gifted for ministry in the Body of Christ by virtue of her baptism. Historically, in this ecclesial paradigm the offices of ministry continue the covenantal relationship of care suggested by the confession's biblical similes of God as faithful, nursing mother, and attentive, compassionate father. Ann's authority lies in her ability to be a trustworthy channel of God's gracious care.

Throughout this analysis we have noted the kinds of evidence Ann uses to assess Sarah's well-being in relation to this paradigm's image of a Christian life as participation in God's redeeming transformation. The confession's consistent use of "we" suggests the significance of participation in the life of the congregation's worship and service. Ann pays attention to whether and how Sarah participates with other believers and to the relative freedom Sarah experiences from sin's bondage and for love. Has she confronted her sin and has she been able to receive forgiveness? Does she experience joy and gratitude for life lived in God's care? How does she tolerate the failures and struggles of others? Is Sarah's freedom for love disciplined by obedience to God's Word so that in her own life and her involvements in behalf of others she extends the good news of God's love, justice, freedom, and peace? Does Sarah confront and resist those forces in culture and church that destroy and deform human life? Does she extend God's care not only to herself but especially to those marginalized and to the planet? Through questions such as these Ann assesses Sarah's appropriation of her faith. The life of faith is here understood as a continuing process of repentance, renewal, and sanctification, that is, growth in faith in the sense of its depth and power in shaping the quality and practice of one's life. Sarah's participation in God's redeeming transformation will always be partial, but it can be enhanced through her deepened involvement in the worship and service of the community of faith. For this reason Ann's pastoral diagnosis is shaped not by a vision of perfection but by a vision of one who strives to serve Christ and lives with reverence and joy in daily life.[16]

Our analysis of a Reformed ecclesial paradigm is summarized in Table 2.1, which enables us to see important points of comparison with the psychological paradigms analyzed earlier.

Table 2.1
COMPARATIVE ANALYSIS OF PHILOSOPHICAL AND ETHICAL ASSUMPTIONS INFORMING DIAGNOSIS
IN MEDICAL-PSYCHIATRIC, HUMANISTIC, FAMILY SYSTEMS, AND REFORMED ECCLESIAL PARADIGMS

	Medical-Psychiatric	Humanistic-Growth Psychology	Transgenerational Family Systems	Reformed Ecclesial Paradigm
1. Nature of the Human	Human being as a bio-psycho-social phenomenon; motivated by conflicting drives; mastery and constancy in the environment; developmentally shaped by intrapsychic, interpersonal, and sociocultural forces both conscious and unconscious; relational; and capacity for self-transcendence.	Human being as a bio-psycho-social phenomenon; motivated by a single drive toward self-fulfillment; inherently good, trustworthy, and constructive in orientation; innate organismic wisdom; socialized maturity; relational; and capacity for self-transcendence.	Human being as a bio-psycho-social phenomenon; motivated by conflicting forces for togetherness and individuality; linked phylogenetically with other animate beings by instinctual/emotional system that governs living processes and has additional capacity for intellectual and affective responses; inextricably familial and relational.	Human being as creation of a loving God—a spiritual-bio-psycho-social phenomenon; reflecting God's image in relationships of responsibility and care for the whole created order motivated by conflicting drives for trusting God's loving care to live with love and refusing such trust in self-protecting, alienating behavior; created good yet in context of vulnerability; self-transcending and therefore anxious; inherently relational; bound by sin.

2. Nature and Possibility of Fulfillment	Honest self-awareness that allows for mutually satisfying and respectful relationships; appropriately meeting needs for relationship and competence through love and work; health as a contingent ideal relative to cultural norms for adaptive behavior vis-à-vis internal, interpersonal, and sociocultural forces.	When given freedom and respect to be one's self (as in therapy), able to maximize self-actualizing potential as fully functioning person open to new possibilities, flexible, responsive to the moment and caring for self and others; health as an expansive, normative ideal.	Lies through capacity for objective reasoning allowing more freedom from instinctual impulses; takes the form of differentiation as a "solid self"; clear about particular identity and capable of being more autonomous in relationships; responsible for self and the consequences.	Freedom for love of self, others, and God that also leads to participation in God's redemptive transformation of structures and systems; a posture of reverence for all of life and joy in living; a commitment to faithfulness in the daily vocation of worship and service in which love and justice are joined. Such fulfillment comes through the initiative of God's Spirit and in this life remains partial.
3. Nature and Possibilities of Human Freedom	Real though limited by the power and scope of the dynamic unconscious and conflicting drives; negotiated within the entire economy of genetic, physical, intrapsychic, interpersonal, and sociocultural life; increased by insight into intrapsychic and interpersonal needs and drives; experienced as adaptive mastery of the environment.	Real and unlimited as a subjective experience of self-potentiation to complement objectively ordered world of determined events; achieved through convergence of organismic and self-actualization; includes accountability for one's choices.	Real though limited by phylogenetic, multigenerational, and nuclear family limits; lies in access to human capacity for reasoned decision-making that reduces anxiety and increases autonomy in relationships; change toward increased autonomy is possible through a therapeutic process that increases differentiation from family of origin; not accountable for phylogenetic or family legacy but responsible for seeking help.	Real though limited and distorted by sin for which each is responsible; it can be partially recovered by trusting in God's Spirit to renew and transform life. It arises as one willingly chooses the discipline of bonds of love for self, others, and God. Iconoclastic because its criteria are God's justice and love rather than cultural or individual hopes.

Table 2.1 *continued*
COMPARATIVE ANALYSIS OF PHILOSOPHICAL AND ETHICAL ASSUMPTIONS INFORMING DIAGNOSIS
IN MEDICAL-PSYCHIATRIC, HUMANISTIC, FAMILY SYSTEMS, AND REFORMED ECCLESIAL PARADIGMS

	Medical-Psychiatric	Humanistic-Growth Psychology	Transgenerational Family Systems	Reformed Ecclesial Paradigm
4. Human Predicament	Originates in vulnerability to contingencies of psychical, physical, and historical existence for which one is not accountable; continuing reality because of the precarious equilibrium of the ego so only modest and partial resolution ever possible; complicit in personality dysfunction as cumulative deficit expression of personality-environment interaction; requires assistance of others for healing.	Universally experienced estrangement from wisdom of organismic valuing process in exchange for perceived conditions of worth in important relationships; deepening self-alienation; origin and locus of problem outside of self, not accountable for problem but accountable for seeking recovery.	Originates in vulnerability to the phylogenetic and generational legacies that define limits and possibilities for increasing balance of differentiation in counterbalancing forces of togetherness and individuality; family projection process principally carried through mother's anxious care impairs autonomy of one or more children creating greater balance of pseudo self or emotional fusion in the children; all share complicity in multigenerational process.	Originates in the anxious inability to trust God's promises of care in a context of vulnerability to contingencies of psychical, physical, and historical existence and is a continuing difficulty throughout life. While one is not responsible for vulnerability to these contingencies, believers are responsible for their refusal to trust God's promises and the ensuing, progressively alienating consequences of sin's bondage that distort and limit human freedom and all the systems and structures of human life; fundamentally an idolatrous turn from God, it most often takes the form of pride or shame; so profound only God's grace is sufficient to save.

5. Individual in Relation to the Community	Priority given to the individual; recognizes significance of relationships as inextricably tied to individual identity and fulfillment; relationships are necessarily ambiguous; and community is the context for value though individually appropriated.	Priority given to individual's self-fulfillment; expectation that self-enhancing behavior is species-enhancing; needs for relationship are socializing; locus of self-alienating conditions of worth; vision of natural harmony of self-enhancing, unique individuals.	Family rather than individual is emotional unit for diagnostic focus; humans relational in ontological sense; triangles not dyads smallest stable relational unit; togetherness however, if not balanced by individuality, is problematic; autonomy in relationships is ideal.	Human beings are inherently relational; created for interdependent relationships of mutual responsibility and care; life in community makes ethical claims on each. Community is normative ideal never fully realized because of distortions of sin but the locus of God's healing and care.
6. Nature and Possibilities for Hope	Primarily located in the empirical rigor of science; also requires and is related to client's resources and motivation; limited to modest goals of enhancing control of drives and needs and enhancing coping skills.	Global scope to optimism based in organismic wisdom of self-actualizing process available to all; confidence in and reliance upon the client's capacity for self-actualization in context of trust and respect such as therapy.	Principally lies in capacity for rational thought which lowers vulnerability to emotional reactivity and increases autonomy in relationships because reason allows one to distinguish between thinking and feeling and choose the former; therapeutic modeling of reason and objective nonreactive processing.	More radical than sin, hope lies in the saving love of God which, when trusted, has the power to transform present realities and heal but will be fully realized beyond this life; related to but not limited by human resources; universal in scope.

Table 2.1   *continued*
COMPARATIVE ANALYSIS OF PHILOSOPHICAL AND ETHICAL ASSUMPTIONS INFORMING DIAGNOSIS
IN MEDICAL-PSYCHIATRIC, HUMANISTIC, FAMILY SYSTEMS, AND REFORMED ECCLESIAL PARADIGMS

	Medical-Psychiatric	Humanistic-Growth Psychology	Transgenerational Family Systems	Reformed Ecclesial Paradigm
7. Guiding Values or Worldview	Primary worth of individual; rigorous and exclusive trust in empirically verified, scientific facts; objective self-awareness through insight; ethical criteria shaped only by rational appraisal of needs and motivations.	Rigor of science; primary worth, goodness, value, and potential of each individual; freedom as autonomy; ethical criteria lie in assumption of universally common, positive direction to organismic valuing process innate in each individual.	Primarily lie in objective logic and predictability of natural sciences; prizing of individual autonomy in relationship; prizing of rationality; suspicion of affective dimensions; ethical criteria are internal consistency and rational reflection on experience.	Reliance on the sovereign love of God whose will for human community is revealed in scripture and most fully in the life of Jesus of Nazareth; the love and justice of these sources are normative for life in human community; each life is sacred though ethical criteria give particular value to the vulnerable; rationality is in the service of faithful participation in God's love and justice and may be distorted by sin; because love is difficult justice, freedom, and peace are priorities for action.

8. Dynamics of Authority in the Helping Relationship	Hierarchical with reliance on therapist as an objective representative of the expertise of science; mutual respect.	Client as expert on her/himself; therapist's authority lies in authority of relationship of trust and care; therapist as companion facilitating client's journey of recovery of self and self-actualization.	Somewhat hierarchical with all conversation directed through therapist who coaches or supervises process of differentiation; emotional objectivity and nonreactive processing in therapeutic relationship are essential; goal of helping family or individual define their problems and use their resources to deal with those problems.	Complex: leveled by need for grace shared by all, unbalanced by real and symbolic authority located in office of ministry; authority derived from ministry of Jesus of Nazareth; authority is functional and warranted by gifts for ministry; authority lies in trustworthy exercise of relational power.
9. Diagnosis	Crucially important; shaped by classificatory approach; seeks to understand ecology of client's intrapsychic, interpersonal, and contextual experience in behalf of constructive responses for more adaptive mastery of the environment.	Repudiates classificatory model as unnecessarily and inappropriately hierarchical; use of processive assessment techniques to discuss placement on continuum of openness to change and spontaneity of feeling and experience.	Crucial, initial and continuing; family units as focus; seeks to assess levels of differentiation and family emotional process in behalf of lowering anxiety and increasing differentiation and autonomy.	Crucially important; shaped by norm of Christian life as participation in God's redeeming transformation through freedom for love and vocation of worship and service; seeks to assess believer's deepening commitment to the practices and disciplines of faith.

CRITICAL CONVERSATIONS
AMONG THE PARADIGMS

Our analysis of the philosophical and ethical assumptions that inform psychological paradigms often used by pastors and an ecclesial paradigm now allows us to begin the kind of critical conversation required by pastoral diagnosis. Our concern will be to note points at which the respective assumptions challenge one another so that pastors such as Ann will be more alert to the need to adapt therapeutic resources in behalf of the theological integrity of their practice. In like manner they may also find insight from a psychological paradigm that revises theological perspectives. The "conversations" that follow are not exhaustive, but they do suggest the kind of critical dialogue needed for theological integrity in pastoral practice.

Medical-Psychiatric and Ecclesial Paradigms
The medical-psychiatric and Reformed ecclesial paradigms have much in common. Each recognizes the complexity of human being and holds that human experience includes conflicting drives or needs. Each also appreciates the bondage of human freedom and the difficulty of historical existence in a "broken and fearful world." Both paradigms regard courage as a necessary virtue. Even these similarities require clarification. Our conversation will focus on important differences in understanding and responding to the human predicament and corresponding issues in the nature of hope. However, we may need to draw in other categories briefly as well.

Pastors who use the medical-psychiatric paradigm value its appreciation of the complex, conflicted nature of human experience and the contingent character of historical existence. This paradigm recognizes the continuing vulnerability of human experience to internal or external difficulties. In psychodynamic approaches the human predicament is posed as serious and chronic due to this vulnerability—physical and psychical as well as historical; that is, finitude itself is our problem. It is obviously unresolvable, although with the best technical, scientific, and medical resources, one can learn to master some difficulties and develop strengths for coping with others. There is an isolating stoicism beneath this approach which pictures anxious human beings trying to master internal conflicts in an environment that is at best indifferent. Scientific rationality stands as the sole resource. In such an environment there is no larger purpose or meaning for human life to guide action and provide criteria for critiquing personal and cultural norms.

A Reformed ecclesial paradigm understands the human predicament differently. It regards the refusal of finitude (and absolutization of some mundane good) rather than finitude itself as our problem. This may appear to be a subtle difference, but it gives pastors like Ann a very different way to understand the anxious, complex vulnerability of persons such as Sarah. The broken and fearful world to which the Reformed "A Brief Statement of Faith" refers is not approached stoically as fate's design but as sin's distortion of the life in community that God intends. While it is now a fearful and painful place, it is not arbitrary, indifferent, or hostile. Ann and Sarah are not safe from the internal and external dis-ease of historical existence in such a world, but neither are they pictured as finally alone before the winds of fate. Sarah is first of all a creation or creature of God. Her life in relationships of care and responsibility reflects the image of the one who called her into life. There is, then, an inherent ethic and purposiveness for life that precedes personal and cultural preferences and rests in God's life-giving and just love. Faith, in this worldview, will not protect Sarah from the contingencies of historical existence or intrapsychic pain, but it does afford her a sense of belonging, value, and purpose.

Ironically, reframing the human predicament as the refusal to trust in God's love means that the bondage Sarah experiences is more radical in this paradigm. The alienation of sin is more thoroughgoing and enduring than the dysfunction of psychopathology. Sarah cannot recover the freedom for love through human resources. Change or relief from sin's bondage is possible, but only through faith in God's love. Ann recognizes that Sarah's distress represents an interaction of sin and psychopathology. Change is difficult with both; but just as the ecclesial paradigm has a more radical estimate of human bondage, it also has a more radical claim on hope. The medical-psychiatric paradigm offers a cautious optimism which relies on human imagination and intelligence alone to help Sarah restore a better balance in her psyche and interpersonal life. On the other hand, the ecclesial paradigm asserts that God's life-giving love is at work not only to help heal the pain Sarah is experiencing but to create in her and the human community commitments to just and mutual love. It claims resources for healing and change that contradict a stoic individualism but that acknowledge the continuing historical reality of pain and suffering, not because that is the way the world is but because sin has so distorted the structures and systems of human life. One resource for the hope offered by the ecclesial paradigm is the ecclesial community as the locus of God's gracious love, although God's redemptive involvement in the world is not limited to such communities.

What we find in these estimates of the human predicament are different assertions about what is true. One paradigm allows the limits of rationality to draw the parameters of hope while another asserts that love most fully revealed in the ministry, death, and resurrection of Jesus of Nazareth defines the possibilities of hope.

But this profound difference does not mean the two paradigms have nothing to offer each other or that Ann would be ill advised to draw on the resources of the medical-psychiatric paradigm. Ann need not concur with this paradigm's limited hope and stoic individualism to be instructed by other insights and challenges it offers. It does enlarge her theological perspectives on the bondage Sarah experiences, for sin and psychopathology limit human freedom differently and interactively, as we will later pursue in detail. This paradigm's careful analysis of the intrapsychic vulnerability of human being and the complexity of interpersonal experience helps Ann recognize the ambiguity surrounding sin's rebellion. The bondage Sarah has "chosen" of living through others and avoiding sharing or being accountable for her own gifts is not a simple act of will; rather, it reflects the distortions of early familial experience that have limited Sarah's sense of herself and her resources for being herself. These limits have continued into her adult life and affect her marriage. Sin and psychopathology interact, for Sarah has made choices that have deepened or extended her experience of alienation and loss of self and perhaps fear of being herself.

The analysis of intrapsychic and interpersonal vulnerability must be put in a broader context, for Ann is aware that Sarah's choices and distorted sense of self mirror the distortions of patriarchal structures and sexism. The absence of any criteria for critiquing cultural assumptions in the medical-psychiatric paradigm is problematic and one of the points at which the ecclesial paradigm properly can challenge its adequacy. It can help discern the distortions in Sarah's experience, but it does not offer a broader critique of the context in which such distortions arise. The ecclesial paradigm's appreciation for structural and systemic evil and original sin which insinuates itself in the fabric of human life and relationships gives Ann a corrective for the more narrow psychodynamic view of the human predicament.

Ethically Ann is also aware that her hopes and concerns for Sarah extend beyond the vision of this therapeutic approach. She wants more for Sarah than relief from depression, improved self-esteem, and better skills for coping with the demands of intimate relationships. She also wants Sarah to experience a deeper level of change that arises from a renewed or possibly new experience of God's love which invites her into the freedom for love of herself and others. It is a mutual love that creates joy as well as commitment to justice. Because Ann views the alienation of sin as more profound than that of psychopathology, she knows that claiming such freedom is a lifelong process that Sarah can begin by acknowledging the reality of sin's bondage and the reality of forgiveness that frees her and sustains her in her efforts to love. The ecclesial paradigm provides Ann with resources to join healing with the new life of deepened faithfulness or discipleship.

Humanistic-Growth and Ecclesial Paradigms
Ann may also choose to respond to Sarah from a humanistic-growth psychology therapeutic approach. Certainly this psychological paradigm and her ecclesial paradigm have elements in common. Each regards human beings as having intrinsic value and potential for fulfillment and appreciates the importance of self-esteem. Both paradigms value the whole person, including affective and cognitive dimensions of the self. Of course even some of these similarities require clarification. In this critical conversation we will focus on differences in the ways these two paradigms understand human freedom and the nature of fulfillment, although we may bring in dimensions of other categories.

Since the popularization of this psychological paradigm, pastors have appreciated its value for each individual and her or his potential and gifts. They have seen continuities between the freedom for life that accompanies God's gracious love and the freedom experienced in the therapeutic context of unconditional regard, empathy, and congruence espoused by this approach. Yet, this humanistic paradigm understands human nature quite differently from several key positions in Ann's ecclesial perspective. Individuals in this paradigm are envisioned as having a single, organismically based drive toward self-actualization. This drive also discloses an innate moral wisdom and goodness that will blossom if unfettered by externally imposed constraints, for, as Rogers says, if we are free to be our true selves we will create a harmonious culture. Self-love and self-enhancement indirectly afford harmony in the human community. The dis-ease experienced by persons like Sarah is imposed from the expectations of others and her desire to meet their needs or expectations.

Ann's ecclesial paradigm locates Sarah's dis-ease as emerging from the anxiety of the conflicting needs within herself for authentic relationships of mutual care and trust and the anxious self-securing need for control in the face of human vulnerability. Ann believes that human beings are created with the capacity to use their freedom for love, but not with innate moral goodness, nor is truth defined by an individual's affective experience. Rather than the underlying harmony envisioned in the humanistic paradigm, here the capacity for self-transcendence, the finite limits of embodiment, the inevitability of conflicting needs in community, and the contingencies of historical existence disclose an anxious vulnerability as the context for human experience. This paradigm also states that, however difficult, relationality rather than individualism defines human being while Ann assumes that love is no simple possibility, it is only through involvement in just and caring relationships that we experience human wholeness.

The implications of these differences in the two paradigms emerge with particular clarity in their definitions of the nature of human freedom and fulfillment. Rogers' assertion of an underlying natural harmony congruent with individuals' organismic valuing process means that ideally freedom is subjectively experienced as unlimited. It is a matter of self-potentiation with the goal of autonomy. Criteria for its fulfillment and practice are idiosyncratic.

In contrast, the Reformed ecclesial paradigm posits freedom as more than a subjective reality and understands freedom within an inherently relational context as a norm for life fulfilled by the freedom for love that mirrors God's love and justice; thus its criteria are not idiosyncratic. Rather, this freedom is disciplined by bonds it willingly embraces. The ethic that guides freedom in this paradigm is not self-enhancement but love that serves. Here freedom is also more vulnerable. In the humanistic paradigm Ann would understand Sarah's self-described loss of self as an exchange of authenticity for the seeming security of others' care. Sarah can choose to change her behavior and through therapy recover the freedom to be her true self. But in the ecclesial paradigm Sarah's need for security reflects anxiety that inevitably leads her to refuse her relationship of trust with God and to exchange the freedom for love that God intends for actions that appear to offer her more security. This existential anxiety that leads to sin is an enduring reality for Sarah. God's Spirit can help Sarah recover her freedom for love, but her dependence on God's help to sustain her in such freedom is lifelong. In this paradigm Ann recognizes that Sarah's predicament requires changes in her behavior and sense of self that will help her secure that identity in a more profound understanding of her life lived in God's care and loving acceptance. Moreover, she will assume that through helping Sarah to recover a more authentic experience of love in relation to God, herself, and others, her freedom to be herself will flourish. That is, self-fulfillment arises through relationships of mutual care and responsibility and service. The freedom for love envisiond by this ecclesial paradigm is relational and disciplined.

While these differences are striking, the growth-humanistic paradigm has helped correct an imbalance in the Reformed ecclesial paradigm's inattention to care for one's self. We see evidence of this influence at two points in the Reformed confession analyzed here: the inclusion of self-acceptance alongside love for God and neighbor as consequences of God's grace, and the broadening of sin to include shame's hiding alongside pride's rebellion.

Pastoral Theologies

Marie McCarthy casts this theological problem of recovering adequate self-regard as finding an appropriate relation of eros, agape (self-sacrificial love), and mutual regard.[17] Ann's Reformed ecclesial paradigm has a long history of privatizing self-sacrificial love in Christian ethics. Reinhold Niebuhr is a good example of this subordination of equal regard for self and neighbor to self-sacrificial love. Regarding mutuality as an inadequate norm because it was vulnerable to the sinful calculations of reciprocity, Niebuhr described mutual regard as a partial fulfillment of the ultimate goal of self-sacrificial love symbolized in the cross of Jesus Christ.[18]

Humanistic psychology has encouraged cultural interest in self-esteem and self-actualization. Yet, this perspective does not encourage reciprocity; rather it describes care for others as a natural derivative of adequate regard for self and holds the development of adequate self-regard as the priority.

This perspective has prompted theologians to recover earlier dimensions of Christian tradition articulated in Augustine's doctrine of caritas which synthesized value for self-affirmation, regard for others, and self-sacrifice.[19] Theologians Louis Janssens and Gene Outka have recovered the biblical emphasis on equal regard of self and neighbor,[20] with Janssens reversing the role of self-sacrificial love from the ideal of Christian love to a transitional means toward mutual regard.[21] Reformed ethicist Beverly Harrison notes that this shift helps reduce the idealization of martyrdom and self-sacrifice that often encouraged exploitation of the marginalized, and that it refocuses attention on the radical character of Jesus' love for others in his life and ministry.[22] Evidence of this shift is suggested in the extended attention given to Jesus' ministry in the statement of faith analyzed here.

Certainly Ann recognizes in Sarah precisely Harrison's concern, for Sarah has uncritically adopted the ideal of self-sacrifice and needs to recover this new normative emphasis on equal regard. This ecclesial perspective, however, does more than merely bolstering Sarah's self-esteem and self-actualization; it also pays attention to the disciplined choices and negotiations that life in community requires.

Humanistic psychology's emphasis on the deficit in self-regard reportedly experienced by so many in this culture accompanies feminist theologians' recovery of the Christian tradition's long-standing recognition that sin is not exhausted by the experience of pride. Sin is not only the assertion of too much self but may also manifest itself as too little self or the refusal to be a self by abdicating the responsibilities that accompany human freedom.[23] The sin of hiding aptly describes the way many refuse to acknowledge and develop their gifts or choose to live through the accomplishments of others, undervaluing the significance of their vocation and daily experience.

This recovery of a broadened definition of sin assists Ann, for much of Sarah's dilemma seems to lie in her decision to exchange the pursuit of her authentic self and needs for meeting the expectations and needs of others. Sarah acknowledges her complicity in this sin of hiding, but she needs to hear the gracious word of God's care and acceptance of her rather than pride's antidote of adequate regard for the other. Without this broader definition of sin and grace, Ann's ecclesial resources would only have deepened Sarah's bondage.

Once again it is clear that humanistic perspectives that encourage adequate self-regard and recognize it as a problem for many have contributed to the recovering of undeveloped resources in the Christian tradition. Yet, the absence of proposals in humanistic perspectives for adequately balancing this self-regard with the responsible use of freedom for others means that its proposals are not adequate in themselves. Not only is balance or mutuality lacking; this perspective also fails to provide criteria beyond organismically derived and therefore idiosyncratic values to guide persons' exercise of their freedom for self-actualization. Ann does want to help Sarah recover a more adequate sense of self-esteem and to encourage her in self-affirmation to balance her care for others; yet, she also recognizes that all choices introduce limits. The natural harmony that Rogers asserts as underlying human behavior is not verified by historical existence. Sarah will need criteria to guide her efforts toward neighbor love as equal regard.

Transgenerational Family Systems and Ecclesial Paradigms
Many pastors find a transgenerational family systems therapeutic approach helpful. If Ann chooses to use it, she will certainly be aware of its complementarity with her ecclesial paradigm. Both perspectives value the complex interconnectedness of human relationships. They recognize the transgenerational character of each person's strengths and weaknesses and the complicity of many in this emotional process. Both paradigms acknowledge change as a difficult and complex process involving more than the individual's will; they also value the importance of differentiation in a person's ability to take responsibility for his or her freedom. Of course, even these similarities require elaboration.

This critical conversation between the two paradigms focuses on four categories of analysis: the nature of the human, human fulfillment, the human predicament, and ethical concerns within guiding values. A difficulty immediately apparent to Ann as a Christian pastor is the dualism espoused by this family systems theory. It is a problem painfully familiar to Christians, for Christian tradition has been battling the consequences of this spiritualistic dualism since its origins.[24] This hierarchical priority for the human spirit as rationality over the physical body has had an enduring influence in Western thought. It involves a distrust of physical senses and emotions in favor of supposedly objective or pure rationality. Bowen articulates this perspective when he describes the evolutionary advance of the

cerebral cortex as that resource which may allow humans to transcend the instinctual behavior rooted in their phylogenetically-based
emotional process. Bowen's therapeutic goal of differentiation is, in
part, an index of an individual's ability to transcend emotional and
affective influences to make reasoned decisions. The "solid self"—
Bowen's ideal for maturity in human life—is able to distinguish feelings from reason and rely on the latter. This solid self is described with
the attributes of rational control: clearly defined beliefs, opinions,
convictions, and life principles achieved through a process of intellectual reasoning.[25]

Not surprisingly, this reliance on a spiritualistic or mind–body
dualism invites its historical partner, patriarchal dualism, for in the
mind–body hierarchy femininity has been associated with the body,
sensuality, and emotionality, while masculinity has valued the soul,
the rational mind, and objective distance from the distractions of
emotions and passion.[26] Bowen's "solid self" has attributes identical
to those identified with masculinity by this patriarchal culture: autonomy, rationality, self-sufficiency, principled action, and goal-directed-
ness. As Deborah Luepnitz notes, in Bowen's approach the healthy or
mature adult is a healthy male.[27] Those attributes which characterize
the upper levels of Bowen's Scale of Differentiation do indeed reflect
such a gender bias to the extent that they distrust emotion and value
reason and a kind of critical distance and self-determination.[28] Persons
described as poorly differentiated, on the other hand, are more influenced by feelings and value relationships that include love and
approval.[29] To be sure, there is real value to be gleaned from Bowen's
scale and his insight about the relationships between an adequate
sense of self and authenticity in beliefs and relationships. As a number of researchers have suggested, gender informs one's epistemology
and style of moral reflection.[30] The ways in which maturity or health
are measured need to reflect a complementarity of the values and
attributes described by Bowen as hierarchically arranged. Jean Baker
Miller suggests that the image of distance implicit in differentiation
may distort the actual processes involved in maturation, which, she
notes, are skills for enhancing the increasing complexity of the self-in-
relation.[31] Bowen's scale of differentiation is also indifferent to the
inequity of power that accompanies the sexist dualism it replicates. It
does not include any acknowledgment of the cultural and historical
context of the self-in-relationships.

Ironically, this family systems approach, by virtue of the spiritualistic dualism it embraces, also promotes the individualism that accompanies this philosophical orientation. While Bowen asserts the importance of a balance in the human drives for individuation and togetherness, he gives such priority to individuation or differentiation that, in the end, his ideal "solid self" seems isolated rather than systemically interconnected. In avoiding enmeshment, he also seems to have lost the relationality integral for human being. Bowen's value for differentiation is so stressed that it distorts the reality of selves dynamically and reciprocally influencing one another.[32] The consequence, says van den Blink, is the danger of encouraging a solipsistic individualism rather than a self-in-relation.[33]

All three of these concerns for the dualistic distortions in this approach call for response from Ann's ecclesial perspective. While the spiritualistic dualism subordinating body to mind has plagued Christianity from the earliest centuries, the incarnation, which figures so prominently in "A Brief Statement of Faith," as well as its assertion of life as God's creation, refute any subordination of physicality. As ethicists James Nelson and Beverly Harrison note, embodiment is a central value in Christian tradition.[34] It asserts that all of human experience is valuable. In fact, as Harrison points out, embodiment is our means to experiencing our connectedness. Truncating affective experience from intellectual insight renders human beings vulnerable to ethical distortions such as patriarchy, economic exploitation, and sexual violence that arise from objectifying rather than connecting with others.[35] Differentiation is valuable not as an end in itself but as a means to becoming a self-in-relation. Such relationality includes the self-in-relation to God. Dualism encourages internal alienation that distorts spirituality. Ann's larger goal of helping Sarah recover or construct a sustaining sense of God's presence will involve helping her recover an awareness of and value for her own embodiment.

This ecclesial paradigm values Bowen's insight regarding the two human drives of individuation and togetherness and the importance of differentiation for persons' responsible exercise of freedom. Yet, it gives particular attention to the importance of togetherness. As suggested earlier, in this paradigm the freedom arising from differentiation or individuation is for service in behalf of the whole community. As "A Brief Statement of Faith" asserts, creation presumes community as normative; to be created in the image of God is to be created for relationship (lines 29–32). The "Brief Statement" also asserts that just as sin distorts community, redemption restores the possibility for relationality with God and one another. Letty Russell uses the terms *partnership* and *stewardship* to describe the intent of this paradigm regarding relationality. Her point is that the relationality presumed here has a normative intent. This partnership creates a freedom for service—the stewardship of gifts and resources for the human community.[36] The "Brief Statement" suggests that the criteria for such stewardship include justice, freedom, and peace; listening for those on the margins; prayer; witnessing to God's love; and critiquing barriers to that love in church and culture (lines 67–71). Russell is underscoring the ethical dimensions of relationality as partnership. It is not a simple contractual arrangement but presumes the goal of care.

Of course, human experience is always temporal. We are created in generations and are called to care for each other through these generations.[37] Yet, care is not confined to family alone. Part of the radicality of this paradigm's notion of relationships lies in its redefinition of *neighbor.* The Hebrew Scriptures enjoin care for strangers and sojourners as well as widows and children (Lev. 19:33-34; Deut. 10:18-19). Jesus of Nazareth expanded the definition of *neighbor* and *care* in his ministry by breaking down all such divisions as family, class, ethnicity, physical ability, and even ethical acceptability (see, e.g., Matt. 25:35; Luke 10:29-37). It is clear that should Ann choose to use Bowen's transgenerational family systems paradigm, she would need to revise its priority for individuation so that it reflects the stewardship of care.

While Ann recognizes that Sarah has not adequately dealt with what Bowen describes as differentiation, she also values the commitment to connectedness and nurture that Sarah seeks to offer and receive. Certainly she concurs with Bowen that only a pseudo-mutuality and inauthentic care can emerge from a needy, inadequate sense of self. However, the autonomous, self-directed solid self that Bowen describes as the fulfillment of differentiation does not value care, mercy, advocacy, and justice which the ecclesial paradigm includes in its characterization of relationality. The norm of neighbor-love in the ecclesial paradigm offers a correction to this patriarchal model of maturity. As Beverly Harrison suggests, love is a relational and tender but awesome source of power, and love's work is that of communication, care, and nurturance. It is "tending the bonds of community."[38]

This activity has been seen as women's work and discounted as too mundane and undramatic, too distracting from the serious business of world rule. Those who have been taught to imagine themselves as world builders have been too busy with master plans to see that love's work *is* the deepening and extension of human relations. This urgent work of love is subtle but powerful.[39]

The patriarchal ideal of self-reliance cuts off connectedness, while this ecclesial paradigm describes mutual love as the ideal for relationality. As Harrison notes, the life and ministry of Jesus demonstrate the radical character of love as a way of being in the world that "deepens relation, embodies and extends community [and] passes on the gift of life."[40]

In this ecclesial paradigm Ann finds resources for valuing Sarah's gifts for nurturance and her longing for nurturance and care, as well as means of correcting the way in which her inadequate sense of self now distorts those gifts and needs. This paradigm, unlike the family systems perspective, offers a partnership and claims that gender and the exercise of power are relevant issues for relationality. As noted earlier, the mind–body dualism that Bowen's theory embraces easily accommodates the even more enduring dualism of patriarchy and the transgenerational family systems theory does not recognize persons' social and historical context.

To be sure, for most of its history the structures and teaching of the ecclesial paradigm have also reflected patriarchal distortions. The fact that "A Brief Statement of Faith" twice asserts the equality of women and men (lines 30–31, 64) indicates that it wants to identify these distortions as such and to repudiate them. But, as James Poling notes, whenever power is organized in any institution such as the family, there is a potential for abuse that extends across generations.[41] It is in the family particularly that patriarchal assumptions have distorted the mutuality of partnership into a hierarchical arrangement of domination. Celia Allison Hahn describes this as a division of the biblical mandates for dominion and procreation.[42] Dominion became the work of men, whose place is the public sphere, and procreation is associated with women, who are relegated to the private sphere. Similarly, power became associated with self-assertion and vulnerability became a sign of weakness rather than the strength of receptivity. In patriarchal terms, power is linear. But from ecclesial perspectives in which love is normative, the value of connectedness requires a recognition that ideally power is relational and, as such, it encourages communion and enlarges freedom. Power is organized within the web of relationships in which human life is sustained. "Our ability to act in effective ways depends on our connections with other persons, and with the institutions and ideas that form the basis of our experience."[43]

When we reflect on Sarah's story, we recognize that she is describing a process of renouncing mutuality in her marriage until the marriage increasingly resembles Hahn's description of public and private spheres. Despite Sarah's responsible professional career, she has allowed herself to be defined in the marriage by procreation alone. She overfunctions in keeping the family's connections, and, by her report, Ben has underfunctioned as a parent, as a son, and as a sibling. According to her description Ben uses power more unilaterally than relationally. Of course, this distortion is not unprecedented but reflects the contextual patriarchal ideology that has affected both Sarah's and Ben's gender identities and roles. At present, neither is as free to use their power relationally as this ecclesial paradigm envisions. Ann's assessment of this family's dilemma from an ecclesial perspective will recognize the influence of patriarchy in Sarah's distorted experience of herself and her perception of herself in relationships. The inadequate sense of self that Sarah describes is rooted both in a culture that does not value women and their gifts equally and in a particular family history that replicated those distortions. The absence of any theory of gender or power in the transgenerational family systems paradigm deprives it of any means of critiquing patriarchal inequities; thus its practitioners may unwittingly replicate cultural ideological biases.

Not surprisingly, the transgenerational paradigm defines the human predicament solely in terms of commitment and does not regard the assertion of too much self as a difficulty. There is no guard against the exploitation of power over others and little value for power used for deepening connections. The ecclesial model's recognition that human motivations can be abusive or exploitative is an invaluable corrective for the naiveté of this family systems paradigm. It recognizes that the internal logical consistency of reasoned ethical principles is not an adequate criterion for guiding human behavior, nor does it provide accountability for one's actions. The ecclesial paradigm paradoxically affirms the power of love's possibilities and the need to respect the distortions of power that human freedom allows.

A transgenerational family systems paradigm does remind this Reformed ecclesial paradigm to value its relational understanding of the self, the complexity of change, and the complicity of generations in the strengths and limits of an individual's agency. While Bowen's theory does not provide any critique of the values carried across generations, it does insist that all behavior is shaped within a dynamic field of relationships. In such a field human agency is never completely free. Bowen's theory helps pastors such as Ann appreciate the enduring strength of familial emotional patterns, and its insistence on the importance of differentiation testifies to the fact that individual freedom is complex.

In this critical conversation we have identified important points of complementarity and raised important correctives relevant to the process of diagnosis. It is clear that the dualism in the transgenerational family systems paradigm is particularly problematic for this Reformed ecclesial paradigm because it overvalues rationality at the expense of affective resources and overvalues individuation at the expense of connections. It also uncritically adopts patriarchal values and expressions of power, for it has no recognition of cultural and historical context. On the other hand, the systemic appreciation for the complexity of life within and across generations is an important reminder to this ecclesial paradigm that its focus on accountability for human freedom must acknowledge the enduring web of relationships that complicate human agency.

SUMMARY

This brief foray into critical conversations between an ecclesial paradigm and several therapeutic approaches does suggest the importance of pastors critically adapting such approaches. We found large areas of complementarity and commonality, as well as differences significant for the process of diagnosis. Each therapeutic approach poses challenges that help strengthen or correct ecclesial perspectives, and, conversely, the latter poses important challenges and correctives to each therapeutic paradigm.

Even this initial exploration of the sort of critical conversations required by pastoral diagnosis suggests the need for further reflection on the three constitutive criteria for diagnosis earlier identified as guiding values or shared ethical assumptions, anthropological assumptions, and dynamics of authority in the helping relationship.

Significant differences in the nature and possibility of freedom in these four paradigms point to the importance of further exploration of the distinctive ethical horizon of pastoral diagnosis. Accountability for the stewardship of freedom as well as the definition of its fulfillment regularly emerge as tensive points in these comparative analyses. The relation of the individual to the community is also a prominent point of difference to be pursued further. Issues such as gender and the exercise of power disclose the need to assure that the process of pastoral diagnosis includes critical assessment of the influence of culture and the congregational context.

Alongside these ethical concerns we will also explore further the way sin and psychopathology limit human freedom differently and interactively, with corresponding implications for the nature of hope. This analysis has demonstrated how each of the psychological paradigms explains the origin and duration of psychopathology or dysfunction differently. They disclose the original vulnerability of human beings that arises simply by way of our embodied historical existence. Existential vulnerability emerges through our capacity for self-transcendence, while the alienation arising from our fearful response to our vulnerability to relational and historical contingencies gives rise to sin. At the concrete level these two dimensions of vulnerability yield a tragic blur, but it is important for pastors to be able to discern one from the other without reducing the significance of either. The victimization of psychopathology occurs within the milieu of sin, but the insights of psychosocial analyses are necessary for pastoral diagnosis.

The dynamics of authority in the helping relationship are clearly more complex in the ecclesial paradigm. Resources for informing that complexity, however, were minimal in the statement of faith we analyzed. More attention to the structural and symbolic dimensions of this authority will be required, along with an examination of transferential issues. While a later chapter will be devoted to issues of authority, these several critical conversations suggest the importance of exploring how the person of the pastor affects the process of diagnosis. We turn now to that discussion.

NOTES

1. Emil Brunner, *The Misunderstanding of the Church* (Philadelphia: Westminster Press, 1953), 6, 10–12.

2. William James, *Varieties of Religious Experience* (New York: Modern Library, 1936).

3. For helpful reviews of the history of pastoral assessment, see Seward Hiltner, "Toward Autonomous Pastoral Diagnosis," *Bulletin of the Menninger Clinic* 40 (September 1975): 574–78; Wayne E. Oates, *The Religious Care of the Psychiatric Patient* (Philadelphia: Westminster Press, 1978), 87–110; and Paul Pruyser, *The Minister as Diagnostician* (Philadelphia: Westminster Press, 1976), 31–33.

4. Don S. Browning, *The Moral Context of Pastoral Care* (Philadelphia: Westminster Press, 1976).

5. St. Gregory the Great, *Pastoral Care*, trans. Henry Davis, S. J. (Westminster, Md.: Newman Press, 1950).

6. See Jean Calvin, *Letters of Jean Calvin,* ed. Jules Bonnet (Philadelphia: Presbyterian Board of Education, 1858); Richard Baxter, *The Reformed Pastor*, ed. Hugh Martin (Richmond: John Knox Press, 1956); and Jonathan Edwards, *Religious Affections*, ed. John E. Smith (New Haven: Yale University Press, 1959).

7. Anton Boisen, *Out of the Depths* (New York: Harper and Brothers, 1960).

8. For examples of this concern, see Daniel Day Williams, "What Psychiatry Means to Theological Education," *The Journal of Pastoral Care* 18 (Fall 1964): 129–31; Wayne E. Oates, "Do Pastoral Counselors Bring a New Consciousness to the Health Professions?" *Journal of Pastoral Care* 26 (December 1972): 255–57; Charles V. Gerkin, "Is Pastoral Counseling a Credible Alternative in the Ministry?" *Journal of Pastoral Care* 26 (December 1972): 257–60; and Harmon L. Smith, "Language, Belief, Authority: Crisis for Christian Ministry and Professional Identity," *Pastoral Psychology* 23 (April 1972): 15–21.

9. Pruyser, *The Minister as Diagnostician,* and Seward Hiltner, "Toward Autonomous Pastoral Diagnosis."

10. Harville Hendrix, "Pastoral Counseling: In Search of a New Paradigm," *Pastoral Psychology* 25 (Spring 1977): 157–72; Ralph L. Underwood, "Personal and Professional Integrity in Relation to Pastoral Assessment," *Pastoral Psychology* 31 (Winter 1982): 109– 17;

George Fitchett, *Spiritual Assessment in Pastoral Care* (Decatur, Ga.: Journal of Pastoral Care Publications, 1993); Stephen Ivy, "Pastoral Diagnosis as Pastoral Caring," *Journal of Pastoral Care* 42 (Spring 1988), 81–89.

11. Stephen Ivy, "Pastoral Assessment: Issue and Directions," *Religious Studies Review* 16/3 (July 1990): 212–18.

12. *The Constitution of the Presbyterian Church (U.S.A.), Part II, Book of Order* (Louisville, Ky.: The Office of the General Assembly, 1991), G-2.0500.

13. Presbyterian Church (U.S.A.), "A Brief Statement of Faith," in *The Book of Confessions* (Louisville, Ky.: Office of the General Assembly of the Presbyterian Church, 1991).

14. Reinhold Niebuhr, *The Nature and Destiny of Man*, 2 vols. (New York: Scribner's, 1949).

15. Valerie Saiving, "The Human Situation: A Feminine View," in *Womanspirit Rising*, ed. Judith Plaskow and Carol Christ (San Francisco: Harper, 1979), and Susan Nelson Dunfee, *Beyond Servanthood: Christianity and the Liberation of Women* (Lanham, Md.: University Press of America, 1989).

16. For a fuller discussion of a Reformed understanding of the character of a life of faith and enhancing growth in such a life, cf. Theology and Worship Ministry Unit, Presbyterian Church (U.S.A.), *Growing in the Life of Christian Faith* (Louisville, Ky.: Distribution Management Services, 1989).

17. Marie McCarthy, "The Role of Mutuality in Family Structure and Relationships: A Critical Examination of Select Systems of Family Therapy from the Perspective of Selected Options in Contemporary Theological Ethics," Ph.D. diss., University of Chicago, 1985.

18. Niebuhr, *Nature and Destiny of Man* 2: 48.

19. David Tracy, "The Catholic Model of Caritas: Self- Transcendence and Transformation," in *The Family in Crisis or in Transition*, Concilium 121 (New York: Seabury, 1979), 100–111.

20. See Louis Janssens, "Norms and Priorities in a Love Ethic," *Louvain Studies* 6 (Spring 1977): 207–28, and Gene Outka, "Universal Love and Impartiality," in *The Love Commandments*, ed. Edmund Santurri and William Werpehowski (Washington, D.C.: Georgetown University Press, 1992), 1–103.

21. Janssens, "Norms and Priorities in a Love Ethic," 228.

22. See Beverly Harrison, "The Power of Anger in the Work of Love" in Carol S. Robb, ed., *Making the Connections* (Boston: Beacon Press, 1985), pp. 3–21.

23. See Judith Plaskow, *Sex, Sin and Grace* (Lanham, Md.: University Press of America, 1980); Plaskow and Christ, eds., *Womanspirit Rising;* Susan Nelson Dunfee, "The Sin of Hiding," *Soundings* 65 (1982): 316–27.

24. James Nelson, *Embodiment* (Minneapolis: Augsburg, 1979), 45.

25. Murray Bowen, "Theory in the Practice of Psychotherapy," in *Family Therapy in Clinical Practice* (New York: Jacob Aronson, 1985), 365.

26. Nelson, *Embodiment*, 46.

27. Deborah Luepnitz, *The Family Interpreted* (New York: Basic Books, 1988), 42–43.

28. Bowen, "On the Differentiation of the Self" in *Family Therapy*, 474–75.

29. Ibid., 473–74.

30. Cf. Carol Gilligan, *In a Different Voice* (Cambridge, Mass.: Harvard University Press, 1982); and Mary Belenky et al., *Women's Ways of Knowing* (New York: Basic Books, 1986).

31. Jean Baker Miller, "The Development of Women's Sense of Self," in *Women's Growth in Connection*, ed. Judith Jordan et al. (New York: Guilford Press, 1991).

32. A. J. van den Blink, "The Helping Response," Ph.D. diss., Princeton University, 1972, 227.

33. Ibid., 357.

34. Nelson, *Embodiment*; James Nelson, *Between Two Gardens* (New York: Pilgrim Press, 1983); and Harrison, "The Power of Anger in the Work of Love" in Robb, ed., *Making the Connections,* pp. 3–21.

35. Harrison, "The Power of Anger in the Work of Love" in Robb, ed., *Making the Connections*.

36. Letty Russell, *The Future of Partnership* (Philadelphia: Westminster Press, 1979), 25–27.

37. John Patton and Brian Childs, *Christian Marriage and Family* (Nashville: Abingdon, 1988), 32.

38. Harrison, "The Power of Anger in the Work of Love," 12.

39. Ibid.

40. Ibid., 18.

41. James Newton Poling, *The Abuse of Power* (Nashville: Abingdon, 1991), 87.

42. Celia A. Hahn, *A Sexual Paradox: Creative Tensions in Our Lives and in Our Congregations* (New York: Pilgrim Press, 1991), 129ff.

43. Poling, *Abuse of Power*, 24.

CHAPTER THREE

❦

Pastoral Identity:
A Resource for Diagnosis

We now turn our attention to pastoral identity, because pastoral diagnosis has everything to do with the practice of ministry. Diagnosis is both particular and an ongoing process. It projects the development of strategies and interventions in light of insights it discloses. Through diagnosis, Sarah's pastor, Ann, is involved in a highly interpretive process of naming reality through the lens of a particular theological worldview or paradigm. This underscores the significance of the theological clarity and intentionality of Ann's diagnostic lens because it will affect the theological integrity of her practice of ministry.

But in reality diagnosis may not be reduced to the application of clear and orthodox ideas. Diagnosis is a unity of being and doing; it does not offer an utterly objective perspective from which Ann can perceive Sarah and her family's predicament, but, rather, it involves a highly dynamic, collaborative, and contextualized knowing. It is collaborative because Ann and Sarah together develop a narrative of the predicament of Sarah and her family, using insights that arise through the dynamics of their shared experience as well as from Ann's particular skills. Sarah brings to this occasion the history of her multifaceted relationship with Ann, her assumptions about ministry, her relationship to this congregation, and her appropriation of her faith tradition. Ann brings to this moment not only her history with Sarah but also her relationships with three generations of Sarah's family, the congregation's norms and expectations, the influences of the public sphere relevant to Sarah's situation, their common theological tradition, and her own appropriation of Christian faith in her particular cultural-historical context. Of course, in this collaborative process, Ann, as pastor, has responsibility for facilitating and guiding the conversation to assure both the hospitality and narratival integrity the gospel intends.

Clearly the relational process of pastoral diagnosis, no less than any other form of ministry, is significantly shaped by the dynamic web of relationships, structures, and systems in which the pastor and parishioner live. Because pastoral diagnosis is so highly relational, Ann's person—the unity of her doing and being—is crucial. Her knowing is a unity of her embodied, affective, intellectual, spiritual, relational, priestly-professional, and cultural-historical self. Finally, it is Ann who is the hermeneutical lens on which her practice of pastoral diagnosis relies. While these factors are always at work in shaping Ann's identity, we are concerned with her self-conscious assimilation of such influences in behalf of the theological and spiritual integrity of her ministry. We are concerned with her pastoral identity.

Pastoral identity describes the ways in which one's faith tradition and personal appropriation of that tradition shape or organize one's identity and function in the practice of ministry. As suggested earlier, this integration of varied influences toward a unity of being and doing occurs at more than conscious levels. *Formation* is a term often employed to describe the intentional process of developing and articulating a theological self-consciousness. Heightening such self-consciousness of one's pastoral identity contributes to congruence between one's faith and vision for ministry and one's practice of it. Diagnosis in general and pastoral diagnosis in particular is always shaped by the practitioner's appropriation of her or his professional identity with the values and assumptions this entails.

PASTORAL

With its ministerial connotations, the word *pastoral* derives its meaning from two theological categories: ecclesiology and Christology. Ecclesiology is important because it contributes to our understanding of the nature and mission of the church and thus requires us to attend to the influence of the historical particularity of our tradition on our self-understanding. Christology will likely correspond to our ecclesiology; it illuminates whether and how our style of relating to others is congruent with our understanding of the incarnation of God in Jesus of Nazareth. Of course, one dimension of Christology is the recognition of the shaping role of cultural-historical contexts for pastoral identity and ministerial practice. Here we will focus on Ann, Sarah's pastor, to explore the ways in which ecclesiology and Christology shape her pastoral identity.

Christology

Clearly ecclesiology and christology inform one another, for the church seeks to be an embodiment of God's love in Christ in the world. While the Reformed family of the Christian church is diverse, the recent confessional statement cited earlier, "A Brief Statement of Faith," offers significant clues for uncovering Ann's Christology.

> We trust in Jesus Christ,
>> fully human, fully God.
> Jesus proclaimed the reign of God:
>> preaching good news to the poor
>>> and release to the captives,
>> teaching by word and deed
> and blessing the children,
>> healing the sick
>>> and binding up the brokenhearted,
>> eating with outcasts,
>> forgiving sinners,
>>> and calling all to repent and believe the gospel.
> Unjustly condemned for blasphemy and sedition,
> Jesus was crucified,
>> suffering the depths of human pain
>> and giving his life for the sins of the world.
> God raised this Jesus from the dead,
>> vindicating his sinless life,
>>> breaking the power of sin and evil,
>> delivering us from death to life eternal.[1]

Four themes emerge with particular relevance for shaping Ann's pastoral identity: Jesus' status as fully human and fully God, his role of proclaiming the reign of God, his suffering, and his resurrection. The framers of this document reversed the usual location of the assertion of Jesus' human status so that it comes first. While each assertion significantly modifies the other, this reversal underscores this document's emphasis on the significance of Jesus' faithfulness in its historical context and of God's value for life and the created order. God's love has assumed human form in order to encounter the possibilities and the limitations of historical existence. As Marjorie Suchocki put it, "Jesus reveals the nature of God as love, and the nature of God's love."[2] In "For the Time Being" by W. H. Auden, Gabriel announces to Mary, "Love's will on earth may be, through you, / No longer a pretend but true."[3] In Jesus we encounter the actuality of God's intention for right relation with God and one another.

"A Brief Statement of Faith" gives remarkable emphasis to the scope and substance of Jesus' embodied proclamation of the reign of God. With Calvin, it asserts the saving significance of Jesus' obedience present throughout the course of his ministry rather than simply in his death.[4] In his classic description of various theological and ethical stances regarding Christianity's posture toward culture and its transformation, H. Richard Niebuhr describes Reformed faith as conversionist in style.[5] This conversionist posture is rooted in an understanding of incarnation that affirms the goodness of creation and human life, understands sin as its distortion, and looks to God's transforming presence in the midst of historical existence. With its focus on the significance of Jesus' life and ministry, the "Brief Statement" underscores the radical reversal of status and privilege envisioned in the reign of God. The poor, women, children, the disabled, and the deformed receive the particular care of Jesus. As the prophet Micah foretold, correct worship and justice are reciprocally joined. "God's nature is revealed as a love that is just," and measured not simply by its benefits for the elite or even the majority but for the protection of the least.[6] By its attention to Jesus' life and ministry, this confessional document is especially helpful for shaping the priorities and practice of Reformed clergy like Ann.

The radicality of Jesus' love proved fatal. He wasn't crucified because of blasphemy or sedition, but because the love he embodied so threatened the pretense of control and security that pervade the religious and political spheres. His crucifixion, sanctioned by religious and secular authorities alike, illustrates the thoroughgoing bondage of sin and demonstrates God's identification with our experience of alienation, loneliness, emotional and physical pain, and betrayal. Along with the broader tradition, Reformed faith has embraced a whole variety of options for understanding the atonement. Here it simply confesses "God's loving response to our betrayal."[7] These items inform Ann's self-understanding as one who announces and seeks to embody a love that we long for and paradoxically fear because of the risks it entails. Moreover, in her ministry with those who suffer, she embodies the presence of One who knows the depths of human suffering.

Ecclesiology

The resurrection proclaims the triumph of God's love over the forces that threaten to deform or destroy human life. Hope in the sovereignty of God's transforming love is a present reality. The life-giving power of God's love is now unambiguous even if it is only partially realized in historical life. Moreover, the freedom for love that triumphs in the resurrection belongs not only to Christ, but through him to us so that we too are freed not from the world but to live in it, challenging and overcoming the structural, relational, and personal bondage of sin as participators in God's redemptive transformation.[8] Thus suffering is not an end in itself; God's love has a transforming intention and effect. This is good news capable of grounding Ann's ministry, because the love she announces and seeks to embody can be trusted.

The resurrection not only empowers Ann's ministry, it also gives rise to the church. Ann's understanding of the nature and mission of the church will correspond to the emphases of her Christology. While her ecclesiology will not be confined by her Reformed heritage, it will reflect the themes and predispositions of this heritage. So once again we find significant clues for Ann's ecclesiology in "A Brief Statement of Faith."

> We trust in God the Holy Spirit,
>> everywhere the giver and renewer of life,
> The Spirit justifies us by grace through faith,
>> sets us free to accept ourselves and to love God
>> and neighbor,
>> and binds us together with all believers
>> in the one body of Christ, the Church.
> The same Spirit
>> who inspired the prophets and apostles
>> rules our faith and life in Christ through Scripture,
>> engages us through the Word proclaimed,
>> claims us in the waters of baptism,
>> feeds us with the bread of life and the cup of salvation
>> and calls women and men to all ministries of the Church.

> In a broken and fearful world
> the Spirit gives us courage
>> to pray without ceasing,
>> to witness among all peoples to Christ as Lord and
>> Savior,
>> to unmask idolatries in Church and culture,
>> to hear the voices of peoples long silenced,
>> and to work with others for justice, freedom, and peace.
> In gratitude to God, empowered by the Spirit,
>> we strive to serve Christ in our daily tasks
>> and to live holy and joyful lives. . . .[9]

These lines pose for us the historical particularity of Ann's tradition. As the basis of her theological worldview, Reformed faith sets a context for Ann's knowing, but it does not confine her ideas in some deterministic way. Rather, it may function more as predisposing Ann to particular values and priorities in ordering her energies and commitments as a pastor.

Such predispositions are evident in the above lines. Life begins in and is sustained by God, whose sovereignty is evidenced in the power of God's love. The church is a community of forgiven people. Forgiveness is not simply a freedom from sin but more profoundly a freedom for love, a disciplined freedom in which, paradoxically, believers willingly commit themselves to the norms and vision of the body of Christ—a local and global commitment. Ecclesial existence as described in these lines is both gift and task. It is only possible through an experience of God's Spirit freeing one for love; yet, in historical existence it is never more than partially realized. Ann's ministry involves interpreting the power of this vision for life, forming persons in this way of being, and empowering believers for faithfulness to God's redemptive transformation in personal, relational, and public spheres of life.[10] The vision of ecclesial existence serves as a critical principle that corrects and guides her ministry.

The authority for Ann's ministry is derivative. That is, it requires her faithfulness to continuity with God's redemptively transforming presence in the world as witnessed to in scripture, in its contemporary proclamation in word and sacrament, and in daily praxis of God's vision for justice, freedom, and peace.

Ministry inevitably requires the three roles of interpretation, formation, and advocacy or empowerment. These roles function interdependently, interpreting the significance of experience through the lens of faith and carefully encouraging the formation of an identity shaped by such a Christian worldview. The believer's faithful witness in the public sphere is their goal. These three roles help us discern the operative structure of Ann's ecclesiology. In "A Brief Statement of Faith" the words *rules* and *engages* demonstrate how Ann's tradition gives primacy to the authority of scripture and its continuing interpretive and transformative power. Indeed, this tradition asserts that the Spirit itself rules and engages us through the scripture and the word proclaimed.[11] While preaching is considered a mark of the church in Reformed faith, the broader term *proclamation* suggests that Ann's responsibility for nurturing[12] appropriations of this transformative word in others extends to the constructive possibilities of conversations such as those she will have with Sarah. Certainly, her pastoral identity is further shaped by the power and authority that accompany her responsibility as one charged with the task of interpretation.

Growing in the life of Christian faith is a lifelong task. It encompasses the formation of affective, spiritual, moral, and intellectual dimensions of identity that thereby reflect one's faith commitments. Ann's understanding of her responsibilities in the formation of those entrusted to her care is shaped by three emphases noted in the "Brief Statement": the significance of life in community, the sacraments, and the disciplines that enhance the deepening of faith commitments. The essence of ecclesial existence—the vision and the present empowerment of the reign of God—functions not only as a critical principle for Ann's ministry as noted above but also as a developmental principle.[13] Ann is aware that ecclesial existence is mediated through the authenticity of life in community. There is a dialectical dynamic between ecclesial vision and its historical form in congregational life together.[14]

Formation entails the hard work of giving concrete form to the freedom for love in a community's life together. In describing self-acceptance as well as love of God and neighbor, "A Brief Statement of Faith" helps Ann recover the tradition's threefold love commandment. Both the inclusion of the concern for self-acceptance and its placement alongside the concerns for love of God and neighbor provide important guidance in contemporary culture and wisdom for listening to Sarah's predicament.

That ecclesial existence paradoxically intends both freedom and obligation has local and global implications for Ann's nurturing of life in community. The community that Ann pastors has a defined membership; yet, at the same time, they are part of a worldwide community. In both cases this means the toleration of real differences and respectful dialogue. The same is true in the community's witness to the love of God in Christ. In Ann's tradition boundaries are important for assuring self-definition, but they are not intended to exclude or isolate. In fact, it is important to reach beyond those boundaries to hear the concerns of those silenced by various oppressive forces. God's Spirit is not confined in its redemptive transformation to the efforts of the ecclesial community.

Ann's vision for life in community is guided by an inclusive principle. While the document addresses such a principle only for those in ordained ministry, in a tradition long corrupted by the exclusion and/or domination of women the import of this commitment for the entire community is clear. The freedom for love and for life in community that God intends is inclusive.

In Ann's tradition, the sacraments are a tangible form of the proclamation of God's word, sharing in its power by proclaiming the power of new being which, although unambiguous, is only partially realized in historical existence.[15] They mediate the ecclesial community's temporality of memory and hope. As one privileged to administer the sacraments, Ann comes to baptism keenly aware of the dynamic power her tradition grants to this sacrament as conveying God's initiating and gracious love. Baptism marks the beginning of a lifelong formation in response to God's "claiming" of one for life in a community shaped by its commitment to love's praxis. Communion conveys God's sustaining presence; it encourages believers in their ministry and boldly asserts the Spirit's continuing transforming power that is available to believers.

Especially important for Ann's sacramental self-consciousness in ministry is the dialectical relation between the sacraments and concrete forms of the new life they intend: the courage to pray and witness, to confront idolatry, to risk solidarity with those who are powerless and disregarded, and to work for justice, freedom, and peace. The sacramental and the concrete shape and enliven each other. In fact, holiness is a fulfillment of daily, concrete, communal living—not separate from but arising through engagement in the world.

Ann's understanding of her role in advocacy and empowerment for public ministry is shaped by her tradition's strong affirmation of the actuality of God's sovereignty and God's positive regard for creation in human life and history. Reformed Christians link God's love, power, and justice to inform their theology of ministry. Since the "Brief Statement" presumes God's present power to engage and transform culture and church, the conversionist perspective on the church's role in culture is evident here. God's Spirit "engages," "claims," "feeds," and "calls," and gives courage to believers to "witness," "unmask," "hear," "work," and "serve." The relational power of love, not the coercive power of might, marks the Spirit's empowerment.[16] The importance of vocation as a daily obligation of service in behalf of God's vision for justice, freedom, and peace is an important conversionist, Reformed theme that will shape Ann's ministry of formation and interpretation. Ann's vision for her congregation's ministry is shaped by this commitment to create approximate embodiments of God's justice and love. The congregation's proclamation of God's love in Christ must engage the changing dynamics of culture and church as a contemporary embodiment of that love and justice.

These Reformed themes and values formally articulated in a confessional, constitutional document of Ann's denomination are operative in shaping the ethos and norms of her theological worldview. They shaped her theological education and her ordination vows and are part of her weekly liturgical practice. That is to say, they have an enduring influence at assumptive and explicit levels. Of course, the particularity of congregational contexts, clergy mentors, and the influence of historical, cultural situations will create variations in emphasis.

IDENTITY AND IDENTITY DEVELOPMENT

Pastoral identity reflects our internal and external relations to a particular theological tradition and perspective.[17] In that sense the role of our tradition, while never fully available to consciousness, is pervasive in its influence. Our theological tradition seems to contribute to our identity in the way Erik Erikson describes as "inner-continuity and social sameness"[18] over time. A phenomenon that Joretta Marshall describes as a "stabilizing" function[19] that provides a theological compass as we conceptualize and articulate theologically informed responses in ministry. One's theological tradition is also stabilizing in the dynamically evolving process of the formation and maintenance of one's own identity as a Christian and a pastor. Because pastoral diagnosis is a hermeneutical process heavily dependent on the pastor as an interpretive lens, there is no doubt about the importance of an internalized integration of one's theological foundations for one's pastoral identity.

Stability must not be confused with static. Ideally, the stabilizing influence of Ann's theological norms and values will be dynamic, much like a gyroscope keeps moving bodies on course. There are several dimensions characterizing the dynamism of tradition in pastoral identity. Within tradition itself, for example, we used Niebuhr's terms to describe the conversionist ethical posture predictable among Reformed Christians who emphasize the transforming role of the church in culture. If Ann were a Lutheran pastor, she would likely reflect that tradition's more paradoxical approach to church and culture in which the two spheres are separate. She would feel the tensions of her dependence on God in Christ and trust in the promise of life eternal while seeking to be a good citizen in a sinful culture. Were Ann an Episcopal priest, she would likely reflect what Niebuhr describes as a Christ-above-culture perspective, valuing the church's role as interpreter of divine law ordering present life and valuing culture as a resource to extend faithfulness.

Beyond such diversity within the tradition, there is surely a tensive dynamic between the local theology of a particular congregation and its relation to the tradition in which it stands.[20] Ann's pastoral identity is shaped by the dynamics of the congregations in which her faith took shape as well as in the ongoing interactions she has in the congregation she is called to lead. She negotiates her particular faith commitments in relation to the congregation's prevailing style of appropriating its tradition. Its civic orientation is only one of several ways for the congregation to enact its conversionist heritage so that the dynamism of stability is evident here as well. And finally, in conversation with Sarah, Ann's integration of her tradition is a compass that guides their discussion rather than a map that prescribes it.

Recent research has demonstrated persuasively that identity is not simply a matter of linear stability but a highly dynamic, evolving, and intrinsically relational[21] process.[22] In writing on the development and maintenance of pastoral identity Marshall distills three dimensions within a dynamic, evolving understanding of identity and develops these in relation to pastoral identity.[23] She proposes that pastoral identity requires fluidity to prevent stagnation (as our discussion of the dynamism of stability suggests) and a continuing engagement with others that serves to renew and enlarge self-understanding. In this third dimension, Marshall asserts that pastoral identity is stretched and challenged by events and people who engage us through raising ideas or presenting situations that require the construction of theological responses. This engagement with real difference introduces novelty alongside sameness and, ideally, prevents stability from lapsing into stagnation.

Identity development is highly interactive—essentially relational. It reflects what is happening between people, and one could say that it also reflects what is happening in the subtle and explicit transmission and construction of culture as well. Certainly ecclesial identity is socially mediated. In addition to disclosing relationality as the basis for our experience of self and development (self-in-relation),[24] researchers at the Stone Center suggest that development may be understood less as a matter of increasing autonomy and more as a matter of increasing complexity in relationships that also enhance one's own capacities and agency.[25] Relationality is the means of identity formation; at the same time, increasingly complex relationality becomes a goal of identity formation. These assertions certainly inform our understanding of pastoral identity as stabilizing, fluid, and constructively engaging.

Some examples may help illustrate the implications of understanding pastoral identity as a highly dynamic interaction of these three dimensions. When Ann encounters Sarah's suffering, she may well hear Sarah's struggle with a tradition and culture that seem to endorse an increasing loss of herself in relation to the well-being of her children, husband, and parents. That is, sacrificial love (*agape*) is presented as the end rather than a means to love as mutual care.[26] She knows that Reformed faith is complicit in the Christian tradition's sacralization of suffering as redemptive (atonement). Sarah's predicament confronts Ann with the distortions created by this focus. This situation illustrates well how pastoral identity relies upon a stabilizing, dynamic appreciation for scripture and tradition as well as a readiness for constructive engagement of the tradition. Clearly, responsible praxis requires maintaining a tensive balance between a tradition's stabilizing, dynamic, and creative possibilities. Ann's pastoral praxis with Sarah illustrates a theological sensitivity to issues of power-in-relation and an openness to theological and theoretical reflection that challenges patriarchal distortions in earlier Reformed resources.

Ann may well turn to Reformed feminist theologians Beverly Harrison and Delores Williams,[27] who argue that what is redemptive in the person of Jesus is his choice to love radically in a way that privileged the status and worth of those marginalized and oppressed by culture and religion. Jesus was killed because of the way he loved, and we are called not to martyrdom but to keep faith with God's liberating call for justice, freedom, and peace. Along with her tradition's recovery of the threefold character of the command to love, which includes the loving acceptance of self, Ann may well find that Sarah's situation commends a constructive revision of her understanding of atonement. This illustration suggests how critical it is for Ann's pastoral identity to be sufficiently stable to receive the challenge presented by Sarah's suffering and to allow Ann to respond creatively and constructively. It also makes clear the constructive possibilities of pastoral diagnosis when informed by this dynamic, interactive understanding of pastoral identity. We will consider the ethical implications of recovering a threefold character of the command to love in more depth in a subsequent chapter.

One other illustration may be useful. Sarah's marital predicament certainly suggests the constraining effects of stereotypical gender roles that she and her husband, Ben, embody. Despite her tradition's complicity in extending the effects of patriarchy, Ann also finds in it corrective resources such as God's equal valuation of women and men and empowerment of both for discipleship. Her conversionist ethic urges her to engage Sarah and Ben toward change. Because she understands God's Spirit to be at work beyond the bounds of the church, she is able to pursue research that offers theoretical resources for critically adapting the family systems model, which she will use to frame her response to Sarah and Ben, to include attention to issues of gender.[28] In this instance Ann's pastoral identity provides a compass by which she may diagnose theological distortions in Sarah and Ben's situation, critically adapt resources available in culture, and offer constructive and redemptive expressions of care.

The interpretive and constructive roles of pastoral diagnosis certainly are clear as we reflect on these two brief illustrations. Moreover, they demonstrate pastoral diagnosis as practical theological reflection. Pastoral diagnosis is shared, disciplined, theological reflection on experience informed by critical correlation of theological/biblical resources and behavioral science resources. Its goal is to mediate the transformative, redemptive love of God so as to empower for discipleship. Pastoral diagnosis requires an internalized, integrated theological self-consciousness described above as pastoral identity.

EMBODIMENT

The integration of theological self-consciousness occurs within one's particular, embodied experience. Pastoral identity is not simply the critical, intellectual appropriation of theological tradition; just as God's love became incarnate in the life and ministry of Jesus, so pastoral practice is also always embodied—that is, it is particular, historical, gendered, and so forth. Pastoral diagnosis requires not only our self-conscious awareness of the intellectual convictions that guide our practice but also a holistic appreciation for the many factors that shape our embodied particularity. Attention to pastoral identity illustrates well the need to reject the spiritualistic dualism of our Hellenistic heritage, which dichotomizes rationality or spirit over body and names the affections as problematic for true "objective" knowing and action.[29] Rather, as Beverly Harrison reminds us, our affections and intellect are dynamically and integrally related.

> [A]ll our knowledge, including our moral knowledge, is body-mediated knowledge. All knowledge is rooted in our sensuality. We know and value the world, if we know and value it, through our ability to touch, to hear, to see. **Perception** is foundational to **conception**. Ideas are dependent on our sensuality. Feeling is the basic bodily ingredient that mediates our connectedness to the world. When we cannot feel, literally, we lose our connection to the world. All power, including intellectual power, is rooted in feeling. If feeling is damaged or cut off, our power to image the world and act into it is destroyed and our rationality is impaired. But it is not merely the power to conceive the world that is lost. Our power to value the world gives way as well. If we are not perceptive in discerning our feelings, or if we do not know what we feel, we cannot be effective moral agents. This is why psychotherapy has to be understood as a very basic form of moral education. In the absence of feeling there is no rational ability to evaluate what is happening. Failure to live deeply in "our bodies, ourselves" destroys the possibility of moral relations between us.[30]

Harrison reminds us that the integrity of ministerial practice—truthful seeing and justice as right relations—depends on honoring the dynamic interactions of affections and intellect. The healing and transformation intended by ministry relies on our awareness of our embodied experience as well as on our intellectual heritage and formation. Harrison rightly insists that feelings—the capacity for empathy—provide our connection with the world and with one another. When feelings are denied then discernment is distorted. As the incarnation makes clear, embodiment and relationships are the locus of the power to love. This does not mean we do as we feel. Rather, the moral question, "What do I do with what I feel?" can only be answered properly when we are able to feel deeply.[31]

In a later chapter we will explore more fully the implications of this relational foundation for more adequate ethical guidance in pastoral diagnosis. The remainder of this chapter will address several pertinent dimensions of pastoral identity as embodied knowing. These include gender, spirituality, power, epistemology, and social location. While embodiment does not determine our theology and experience of God, it is formative for our practice of ministry.

Gender

Gender is an especially significant, formative experience in identity, including pastoral identity. It is absolutely intrinsic to our self-understanding. Numerous studies demonstrate that from the moment of birth, infants' experience is shaped differently by their gender because our responses to them are shaped by complex tacit and explicit codes for gender roles. After age eighteen months, our identity (as selves-in-relation) is engendered. From that point on our understanding of our gender role increases in complexity as our exposure to formative relationships and institutions multiplies. As Ellyn Kaschak puts it, "gender is achieved" and "practiced" throughout our lives.[32] That is, while gender has biological roots, its meaning and function is socially constructed and, in turn, pervasive in its shaping of all our experience.

> Under ordinary circumstances, to have a body means to be alive, to move, to act, and to interact. In this society, however, literally everything about **how**, **when**, and even **if**, we do any to these activities is gendered. Any question about the physical is meaningless until it is gendered. Conversely, everything about it is meaningful once gen-

dered. The meaning is located contextually, not in the act or attribute itself, and . . . is communicated interpersonally. . . .[33]

Biological reality is given meaning in one's relational, cultural, and political context. Political, because gender is deeply embedded in our understanding and experience of the mediation of power interpersonally and socially. It is also true that "no experience of power, sexual or other, is intrinsic to a person or to a relationship, but rather that our experiences of power-in-relation are socially constructed."[34]

Historically, the prevailing definition of the relationship of gender and power lies in the joining of the spirit/mind-over-body dualism discussed earlier and the sexist dualism that funds the oppressive practice of patriarchy.[35] Pervasive in intellectual thought and extended through distortions of Jewish and Christian anthropology, this double dualism posits the subordination and inferiority of women (reduced to bodily experience) and the superiority of men (reduced to rationality). This stereotyped association of maleness and rationality coincides with an ascetic definition of spiritual purity. Unfortunately, once in place, such stereotyped constructions of gender roles and corresponding constructions of inequality of power are self-perpetuating through their internalization. In culture generally and the Christian church specifically, a history of relational, economic, and political marginalization, subordination, and oppression has ensued for all women with particularly invidious results for women of color.

As these reflections on the social and political construction of gender suggest, it is impossible to practice ministry untouched by their implications. Moreover, because Christian ministry is guided by the radically inclusive vision for the love that Jesus' ministry embodied, "[t]heologically, and ethically our questions must include what it means for any of us to know her [or his] sexual 'identity' in the relational praxis of transformation."[36] In assessing the predicament of persons such as Sarah and Ben, pastors such as Ann cannot be indifferent to the political and social constructions of their self-understanding as woman and man. And equally importantly, Ann must be aware of the ways in which her personal and professional identity are informed by the politics of gender. She must also attend to the ways gender rules and roles shape the dynamics of her relationship with Sarah and Ben.

Particularly important in her self-awareness is the way these rules and roles are extended through our verbal and nonverbal communication. Popular discussions of differences between women and men focus on women's predispositions toward nurturing complex webs of relationships and sustaining intimacy and care. Men are described as predisposed to be concerned for establishing and sustaining their status as independent, competent individuals. These orientations elicit quite different communicational styles and behavior. Some suggest that the differences are sufficient to make an analogy of crosscultural communication appropriate,[37] though in a context in which persons seem to be speaking the same language.

An appreciation for the interplay of gender and language is important for the practice of ministry in at least two ways. First, pastors such as Ann need to be mindful that their communication is "coded" by the culture's prevailing assumptions regarding gender. Extra care in conversation and interpretation is required. But, secondly, it would be naive to ignore the fact that communication mirrors and extends the inequities of power-in-relation described earlier in our discussion of the politics of gender and patriarchy. The differences often observed in men's and women's conversation are not as benign as the crosscultural analogy suggests, as if these are simply "natural" differences descriptive in function. Rather, the analogy of majority and minority culture communication more accurately discloses the pervasive effects of inequities of power, for the male style of functioning is more highly regarded and rewarded. As Rachel Hare-Mustin has observed, we may better account for this apparent dualism by attending to who has more power in the interaction rather than assuming a "natural" gender difference.[38]

Earlier we described ministry as the praxis of transformation toward the fulfillment of God's vision for radically inclusive community organized by mutual love. Our discussion of the ways in which the politics of gender insinuate themselves into structures of communication underscores the significance of critical self-consciousness in our own communication and in the process of interpretation so central to pastoral diagnosis. Without such awareness, one easily becomes complicit in reiterating the inequities "encoded" in the politics of communication.

Spirituality and Sexuality

Having explored the assertion that we may only know ourselves and our world through our gendered identity, it is a simple yet startling extension to say that we only know God through the embodied lens of gender.[39] Spirituality and sexuality are profoundly intertwined. Christian spirituality is rooted in a sense of connectedness with God's life-giving Spirit. It involves a sense of meaning and the possibility for life that is larger than one's own efforts through participation in God's redemptive transformation. The centrality of God's incarnation in Christian tradition gives further validation to the significance of embodiment for one's experience of God's presence.

The internalization of engendered rules and roles shapes our capacity to imagine and receive God's presence and indeed to imagine God. Certainly the pervasive influence of patriarchy's sexist dualism, joined with the mind/spirit-over-body dualism in Christian tradition, has introduced profound limitations in the interaction of spirituality and sexuality, especially through the stereotyped roles for women and men prescribed by such dualisms. As James Nelson has observed, the social construction of masculinity within the sphere of patriarchy has meant that many men have learned that masculinity requires a distrust of their affective selves, which results in a difficulty with the vulnerability of intimacy that relationality and spirituality require and a corresponding distance in their experience of God.[40] Sexuality and gender roles are linked with performance. Not surprisingly, male images of God emerge as judgmental, severe, and relatively inaccessible, not unlike a predominant image for fathers. Women often describe their experience of being reduced to their affective selves and of distrusting their intellects, a difficulty with claiming an adequately defined self-in-relationship that authentic intimacy and spirituality require, and a corresponding distance in their experience of God, whom years of tradition suggest is the author of their subordination.

Feminist theologians have helped disclose the pervasive consequences of such distortions in the interaction of sexuality and spirituality. Valerie Saiving observed that women's predictable experience of sin was not that of pride's self-assertion over against the well-being of others but the "underdevelopment or negation of the self."[41] Saiving has pointed out that there is no generic or neutered approach to spirituality. Judith Plaskow explored such differences with an appreciation for the significance of social and political construction in the interplay of spirituality and sexuality.[42] She disclosed patriarchy's narrowing of the tradition's understanding of sin's effects as if the assertion of too much self or pride exhausted sin's consequences. Rather, pride seems to be sin's likely form among those privileged in a particular culture. Sin's fearful turn may also result in the refusal to risk being a self and in living instead through the accomplishments of others or avoiding accountability altogether. Plaskow identified the correspondence of definitions of grace and sin, noting the dramatically different form of grace when the sins take the shape of hiding from the risks and responsibilities of being a self. Her discussion of the dramatically different ways in which sin and grace are often experienced among women and men (given current constructions of gender rules and roles) helps us recognize the importance of attending to the interaction of sexuality and spirituality.

Surely, any person of faith will be concerned with the distortions in his or her spiritual life that patriarchy presents, but the possibility of such distortions is of special concern to women and men clergy. Clergy are representatives of an institution deeply complicit in extending such distortions, and they have myriad opportunities to shape the faith and religious experience of believers. As pastors respond to persons like Sarah and Ben, their self-awareness informs their ability to discern these same distortions in their own faith experience. Pastoral diagnosis is a hermeneutical process—vulnerable to complicity in extending unexamined biases and capable of helping construct new alternatives. For example, numerous are those women whose struggle to risk being a self—hidden by living through the achievement of others—was misdiagnosed and affirmed as selfless giving. Affirmed in fact was their experience of sin. A more perceptive appreciation for the complexity of sin's forms in such women's experience would clarify that grace would issue in the encouragement to discern and develop one's own gifts for discipleship rather than as a selfless corrective to pride.

Of course, gender and sexuality are not simply a source of distortion in their interaction with spirituality. The distinctive embodiment and gendered experiences of women and men give each particular insights into the remarkable complexity of the presence of God. Once sexuality is understood as God's gift and intrinsic to experience, we may recognize its revelatory possibilities as a window for understanding more about the nature of God. James Nelson, for example, encourages men to find analogies between their experience of an erect phallus and a quiescent penis[43] and a balanced spirituality of active achievement and quiet receptivity. Valuing vulnerability alongside forceful strength provides new insight into God's exercise of power in relationship with us.

Sexuality and Epistemology

Pastoral identity assumes a supporting theory of knowing or epistemology because it is a way of integrating knowledge of ourselves, knowledge from sources deemed authoritative, and reflection on daily experience. Realizing that previous research did not include women, Belenky et al. recently conducted extensive inductive research among women cutting across racial, class, and educational lines to discern the possible influence of gender on epistemology,[44] and in so doing they found differences not disclosed by earlier research on young adult men. For example, some women relied more on an empathic style of analyzing other's ideas, which seems to support other developmental data disclosed from women's experience that differentiates women and men according to women's continuity with a female primary caregiver while boys establish identity through separation from her.[45] Perhaps a more striking difference in the comparative research focused especially on the presence of a way of knowing which they entitled "silence" to describe the debilitating consequences of experiencing one's self as mindless and voiceless.[46] Not surprisingly, women in this perspective were victims of particularly oppressive situations. But it is sobering to note that all of the women with whom they spoke described a struggle to believe they were capable of thinking creatively. This mirrors the spiritualistic dualism of mind over body discussed earlier. It suggests how pervasively destructive the consequences of such stereotypes can be as women as well as men internalize their assigned roles. Certainly the confidence with which one embodies pastoral identity will vary in relation to the authority one grants one's own experience and ideas.

It is likely that the differences that emerge in this comparative study of the influence of gender on epistemology are largely the consequence of sexism and sexual and physical violence all too common among women, that is, the internalization of subordination. Nevertheless, for our purposes this research by Belenky et al. confirms that self-concept does interact with one's assumptions regarding the nature of truth, knowledge, and authority. How one knows and trusts that something is true and authoritative has everything to do with how or whether one authorizes one's own experience, and that experience is always gendered.

Recent literature has disclosed the complexity and difficulties of masculine identity in this culture.[47] Ann is also a pastor for Ben,

Sarah's husband. For too long "gender issues" have been used to signal attention to women's experience with the unintended effect of suggesting that problems are solely located there and obscuring the need for attention to difficulties posed for men in a patriarchal context. Both men and women have particular (and partial) ways of knowing and valuing what we know. Sexist dualism also constrains and distorts the full expression of male experience. While girls learn to sacrifice their authentic selves to stay in relationship, boys learn early on to disconnect from relationships to preserve their separate selves and to value themselves comparatively and competitively according to their achievements.

Ben's challenge appears to be the converse of Sarah's, for she describes him as having internalized the importance of a separate, achieving, emotionally self-sufficient identity. To the extent that this is so, he is vulnerable to underdeveloping the empathic skills that help sustain important relationships and nurture emotional intimacy in such relationships—what psychiatrist Stephen Bergman poignantly describes as a "self-in-spite-of-relationship."[48] He is also vulnerable to overdeveloping his commitments to success in his work, allowing it to define him at the expense of his intrapersonal and interpersonal experience and commitments.

Ben is a "successful" man in a culture that encourages men to use an epistemology that values emotional distance and logical rationality often exercised competitively. Such an epistemology discloses different aspects of reality and values experience differently from Sarah's more ecological or connected knowing. Each is partial and in need of the other's correction. Of course, the distanced or disconnected rationality Ben has learned dominates in this culture. Obviously, it is well for Ann to listen for clues about Ben's experience, knowing that it is likely to be different from her own. Even more important is the recognition that the task of diagnosis requires each of us to pay keen attention to the strengths and limitations of our predisposed epistemological styles.

Ethics

Ethical reflection is an aspect of epistemology and a central dimension of both pastoral identity and pastoral diagnosis. Here too we see that embodiment is a formative factor, for women and men often approach ethical dilemmas with different ethical motivations. Men often define justice according to a principled, objective determination of rights and rules to achieve a fair resolution. Women often define justice according to the responsibility for care within networks of relationships. From the perspective of many men moral problems arise as competing rights. For many women moral problems arise as conflicting responsibilities. Carol Gilligan proposes that these two modes of ethical reflection represent the consequence of a social construction of gender related to current childrearing practices that presume the primary influence of the mother.[49] She also asserts that a more truthful hermeneutic for ethical reflection combines the two perspectives because each alone is partial. On the other hand, Rachel Hare-Mustin insists that a danger of this apparent dichotomization is its indifference to the relative differences in power which account better for associating these two styles than does gender.[50] She suggests that when women are in the more powerful position, such as with children, they may well adapt so-called masculine perspectives. She goes on to note that only one of these styles—rationality—is rewarded societally.[51]

The influence of inequitable divisions of power in any discussion of gender roles and rules is certainly relevant for our discussion of pastoral identity and pastoral diagnosis. It suggests the need for a kind of bifocal vision in one's self-conscious pastoral identity. Predictably, there are different styles of behavior and conceptualization for women and men which have emerged over generations. Because all of us are affected by these, we must not be indifferent to their influence. But because pastoral identity and pastoral diagnosis have a transformative goal that repudiates the sexist inequities symptomatic in these social constructions, we also must keep clear about how we use our self-awareness. These differences are not benign; therefore, through one lens we must know how to function within the rules and roles that present patterns represent, while through the other we must be alert for ways of transforming the inequities evidenced by these differences.

Social Location
Social location is a shorthand way of referring to economic, educational, racial, cultural, sexual orientation, and gender differences that help define our particular, historical, embodied existence. The historical particularity of Jesus especially draws attention to the issues of social location in part because he was certainly not indifferent to the effects of marginalization, oppression, or privilege that correspond to

the above categories. Our discussion of the role of self-concept and self-authorization in the process of knowing leads easily into a discussion of social location because its categories of economic, educational, racial, cultural, sexual orientation, and gender differences have everything to do with the experience of empowerment that accompanies the development of one's own sense of authority. As Carter Heyward expresses it, "no experience of power, sexual or other, is intrinsic to a person or to a relationship, but rather . . . our experiences of power-in-relation are socially constructed."[52] Pastoral identity is inevitably and variously shaped by the social construction of power. For example, pastors such as Ann now realize that interpretation of scripture will be partial if they take into account only Euro-American perspectives. Feminist, womanist, liberationist, gay and lesbian, and "two-thirds-world" voices have demonstrated how social location influences the experiences and questions we bring to texts. Of course, in one sense the particularity of perspective is necessary for understanding. But if we fail to recognize our particularity as also partial, it becomes distorting rather than a contribution toward our fuller understanding.

Certainly womanist theologians such as Jacquelyn Grant and Delores Williams are disclosing the influence of race in shaping faith and self-concept.[53] A good illustration of how social location informs theological reflection critically and constructively is found in Williams's discussion of the convergence of Black women's history of relentless oppression especially in surrogate roles for white men and women. Their experience, she proposes, suggests that Jesus' surrogacy on the cross is not experienced as redemptive but that Jesus' redemptive force lies in the way he lived, embodying a vision for right relations in community.[54]

Socioeconomic Class
Judith Orr pursues the shaping force of social location from the perspective of socioeconomic class and the experience of women.[55] She describes the inadequacy of defining class through simple statistical definitions and focuses instead on economic and relational power in the sphere of work. She notes that "the socio-economic class of women is determined by a network of power relations shaped by employment, fertility, and marriage."[56] Her research suggests that a working-class social location shapes one's experience differently from middle-class

expectations. "Both at work and in the world, a common experience in working-class life is that one's actions will not produce predictable results, that one doesn't control one's own life."[57] A critical difference for middle-class women is the experience of more economic control and power-in-relation in the work spheres. Thus from within a working-class experience, Orr suggests that God's interventions in behalf of restoring justice, dignity, and equality are of special importance. Social location dynamically shapes both self-concept and spiritual needs. The task of pastoral care in such contexts

> is not, as it is with the middle class, helping persons interpret or discover the unity and meaning of life in the midst of periodic life crises, nor to enhancing one's sense of identity, autonomy, and self-fulfillment. Rather, it is confronting the ongoing crisis of inequality, enhancing cooperative skills for conflict resolution, and effecting change in institutions to meet human need, thereby overcoming deficits in one's sense of integrity, dignity, and self-respect.[58]

The socioeconomic determinants of power-in-relation shape pastoral identity through their influence on our own self-concept and the expectations and hopes through which we experience God's presence and power. The practice of pastoral diagnosis will certainly be affected by our predominant experience of socioeconomic class and requires skill in discerning the influence of class in the lives of those we seek to help. Sarah's dilemma, with the competing demands of marriage, family, extended family, and profession, reflects middle- and upper-middle-class expectations of these institutions. As her pastor, Ann will assess such influences in light of the middle-class framework she and Sarah share. Her dilemma also illustrates the unspoken constraints these expectations pose for women when marital and parenting roles fail to accommodate the complexity of competing demands. The construction of gender and power in relation to Ben, previously adequate, no longer is sufficient. Ann's analysis of Sarah's dilemma needs to include sensitivity to Sarah's middle-class expectations for relative autonomy and accompanying responsibility as well as her expectation of more mutuality with her spouse in their construction of their respective roles. Ironically, Sarah's relative privilege in the sphere of work leaves her less prepared for her experiences at home. An ability to discern how social class colors this couple's experience deepens Ann's appreciation for the alienation that is emerging in their marriage and for the origins of Sarah's depression. Ann's perspective is bifocal, for the rules and roles of the middle class are familiar while her theological vision urges an alternative construction.

Racial/Cultural Identity

Culture, the final category of social location to which we will attend, is understood as foundational for identity formation. It is the socially mediated matrix of values, beliefs, customs, religion, and basic life assumptions into which each human is born.[59] Our attention to culture is closely related to Orr's research and our earlier reflections on the social construction of power-in-relation because, predictably, the experience of one's cultural identity is from within a majority or minority status. This is so because the matrix of cultural identity includes racial, economic, and/or other identifying factors related to the exercise of power and control. Crucial for the self-awareness required by pastoral identity and pastoral diagnosis is the recognition of the influence of one's culture in one's self-understanding, including one's relative power in the larger context arising from one's cultural/racial identity.[60]

In their book *Counseling the Culturally Different*, Derald Wing Sue and David Sue argue persuasively that the social construction of power across cultures especially to reduce the significance of difference when it represents the distinctive experience of a minority is a critical factor in effective analysis of crosscultural communication.[61] They note that racism and other forms of subjugation are a serious, insidious distortion in the process of identity development. Identity development is further complicated by the corresponding internalization of a subjugated identity among those so identified (Table 3.1). They also describe the possible path of those who know the privileges of majority status but choose to reject its accompanying subordination of the status of persons who differ. This path of revised identity development proceeds through conformity, dissonance, resistance and immersion, introspection, and integrative awareness (though retreat is possible throughout the first three stages)[62] (Table 3.2). Their proposals help us recognize the way in which one's particular racial and cultural identity development informs one's sense of self-esteem and power or agency. Movement through identity development toward a mutually empowering racial and cultural identity is not to be presumed; rather, it is fraught with the possibility of retreat.

Table 3.1
RACIAL/CULTURAL IDENTITY DEVELOPMENT

Stages of Minority Development Model	Attitude toward Self	Attitude toward Others of the Same Minority	Attitude toward Others of Different Minority	Attitude toward Dominant Group
Stage 1: Conformity	Self-depreciating	Group-depreciating	Discriminatory	Group-appreciating
Stage 2: Dissonance	Conflict between self-depreciating and appreciating	Conflict between group-depreciating and group-appreciating	Conflict between dominant-held views of minority hierarchy and feelings of shared experience	Conflict between group-appreciating and group-depreciating
Stage 3: Resistance and Immersion	Self-appreciating	Group-appreciating	Conflict between feelings of empathy for other minority experiences and feelings of culturo-centrism	Group-depreciating
Stage 4: Introspective	Concern with basis of self-appreciation	Concern with nature of unequivocal appreciation	Concern with ethnocentric basis for judging others	Concern with the basis of group-depreciation
Stage 5: Integrative Awareness	Self-appreciating	Group-appreciating	Group-appreciating	Selective appreciation

From Donald R. Atkinson, George Morten, and Derald Wing Sue, *Counseling American Minorities: A Cross Cultural Perspective*, 3d ed. Copyright © 1989 Wm. C. Brown Publishers, Dubuque, Iowa. All rights reserved. Reprinted by permission.
*Cf. Derald Wing Sue and David Sue, *Counseling the Culturally Different*, 2d ed. (New York: John Wiley & Sons, 1990), 97

Table 3.2
MAJORITY GROUP'S IDENTITY DEVELOPMENT
[Adapted from Sue and Sue, *Counseling the Culturally Different*, 2d ed. (New York: John Wiley and Sons, 1990), 114–16]

Stages of Majority Development Model	Attitude toward Self	Attitude toward Others of the Same Majority	Attitude toward Minority Group or Marginalized
Stage 1 Conformity Stage	Self-appreciating Minimal self-awareness as majority gender/race	Group-appreciating Acceptance of majority's superior status	Group-depreciating Stereotypical ideas operative/acceptance of inferior status Denial and compartmentalization
Stage 2: Retreat Possible Dissonance State	Conflict between self-appreciating and self-depreciating Recognize previously compartmentalized experiences that challenge stereotypes Growing recognition their behavior inconsistent with values Guilt, shame, anger, depression, ambivalence, fear, and rationalization may arise	Conflict between group-appreciating and group-depreciating Fear of ostracism for ideas re: group's behavior and anger may emerge Guilt and shame	Conflict between group-depreciating and group-appreciating Feelings of embarrassment, shame, guilt, perhaps rationalized helplessness to effect change

		Self-depreciating	Group-depreciating	Group-appreciating
Stage 3: Retreat Possible	Resistance and Immersion Stage	Guilt, anger, negative feelings re: majority identity	Anger at feeling "taught false information and systemic oppression so pervasive	May develop "paternalistic protector role" or "over-identification" with minority group (then realize not one of them)
Stage 4	Introspective Stage	Concern with developing new internal basis for self-appreciation	Recognition racism not exhaustive Recognize need for further reflection and action by this group Concern for developing basis for modified group appreciation	Concern with a basis for group appreciation
Stage 5	Integrative Awareness	Modified self-appreciating Accepts responsibility for complicity Nonexclusivist identity Not immobilized by guilt	Modified selective group appreciating posture Increased awareness of structural/systemic political influences Commitment to effect change	Group-appreciating Recognition of real diversity

Decisive for the experience of positive agency is persons' location of responsibility and control vis-à-vis their actions and experience. Responsibility without control, for example, is debilitating. But recognition that responsibility is limited by social and economic structures and systems through which control is exercised externally may allow a different analysis of one's own agency and a better sense of self-in-relation to the limits and possibilities for change.[63]

Pastoral identity is invariably shaped by racial/cultural identity. Effective pastoral diagnosis arises through keen appreciation for both the formative and distorting power of cultural identity.

Sexual Orientation

The stigmatization and marginalization of gay and lesbian persons in this culture warrants attention to the particularity of their experience here. The identity development process described above is suggestive for the importance attending to the dynamic process of moving within the continuum between "the closet" and a self-identified gay or lesbian identity. Illustrative of resources developed for this purpose is the schema Vivienne Cass has developed from her own therapeutic practice, which suggests different perspectives or interpretations of lesbian women's experience that they may bring to a process of developing an integrated lesbian identity.[64] Cass proposes six such perspectives: identity confusion, identity comparison, identity tolerance, identity acceptance, identity pride, and identity synthesis. Kristine Falco's *Psychotherapy with Lesbian Clients: Theory in Practice* is similarly helpful in considering the challenge a homosexual social location poses for pastoral diagnosis.[65] Our concern is to encourage the congruence of emotional, physical, sexual, and spiritual internal needs and relational experience.[66]

Homophobia and heterosexism complicate the experience of those seeking care and those who offer it. Heterosexual caregivers would do well to locate themselves in the Majority Group's Identity Development process (Table 3.2). As with other issues posed by real difference and one's internal process, it may be necessary to refer persons addressing gay or lesbian issues if one cannot authentically encourage the process of developing an integrated gay or lesbian identity. Even if one is able to ally with another to facilitate this process, theological debates in many Christian communions about the status of homosexuality as a sin pose a particular challenge for pastoral diagnosis because the pain we encounter is in part the making of the institutions we represent. Spiritual and theological issues are often explicitly present in the issues to be assessed and then addressed. The heterosexual caregiver's ability to acknowledge her or his own complicity in the sin of heterosexism and prior work in addressing consequences of homophobia in his or her emotional life are crucial here as they are for North American Caucasians in dealing with those who experience racism in this culture.

CONCLUSION

We have described pastoral diagnosis as a highly interpretive process of naming reality through the lens of a particular theological worldview or paradigm. But our attention to pastoral diagnosis as a relational process has quickly underscored that diagnosis—rather than an objective, universal, and static knowledge—is a highly dynamic, collaborative, and contextualized knowing in which one's tradition has a formative but not a deterministic role.

We have given particular attention to pastoral identity because the kind of knowing required in diagnosis necessarily involves unity of a pastor's being and doing. The pastor's self-conscious assimilation to a dynamic unity of her or his embodied, affective, intellectual, spiritual, relational, priestly/professional, and cultural/historical self is the hermeneutical lens of pastoral diagnosis.

We have used pastoral identity to conceptualize the way one's faith tradition and personal appropriation of that tradition shape or organize one's identity and function in the practice of ministry. We have used the terms *pastoral* and *identity* to explore the mutual, dynamic, critical interaction of tradition and identity formation. We gave particular significance to Christology and ecclesiology in relation to the term *pastoral*. Insights regarding the intrinsic relationality of the self as a self-in-relation shaped our reflections on identity development. Embodiment served as an overarching theological concept for exploring the influence of particular, historical, affective experience such as gender, spirituality, and social location on our identity.

As illustrations of Ann's ministry with Sarah underscored, pastoral diagnosis is a process of practical theological reflection on experience that correlates theological and biblical resources and behavioral sciences in behalf of redemptive transformation. The theological integrity of pastoral diagnosis requires our attention to the formation of pastoral identity as an internalized, integrated theological self-consciousness. To the extent that this is so, we are better equipped to mediate in the process of diagnosis the constructive and redemptive possibilities of Christian tradition.

NOTES

1. Presbyterian Church (U.S.A.), "A Brief Statement of Faith," in *The Book of Confessions* (Louisville, Ky.: Office of the General Assembly, 1991), items 7–26.
2. Marjorie Suchocki, *God, Christ, Church* (New York: Crossroad, 1982), 99.
3. W. H. Auden, "For the Time Being," in *Collected Longer Poems* (New York: Random House, 1969), 145.
4. John Calvin, *Institutes of the Christian Religion*, 2 vols., trans. Ford Lewis Battles (Philadelphia: Westminster Press, 1960), 2.16.5.
5. H. Richard Niebuhr, *Christ and Culture* (New York: Harper & Row, 1951), 190–229.
6. Suchocki, *God, Christ, Church*, 90.
7. William C. Placher and David Willis-Watkins, *Belonging to God* (Louisville, Ky.: Westminster/John Knox, 1992), 72.
8. Walter Lowe, "Christ and Salvation," in *Christian Theology*, ed. Peter C. Hodgson and Robert H. King (Minneapolis: Fortress Press, 1982), 221.
9. Presbyterian Church (U.S.A.), "Brief Statement," items 52–74.
10. A careful exploration of the character and interdependence of these three tasks for religious leadership is found in Jackson Carroll, *As One With Authority* (Louisville, Ky.: Westminster/John Knox Press, 1991), 97–118.
11. Placher and Willis-Watkins, *Belonging to God*, 150.
12. See Peter C. Hodgson, *Revisioning the Church* (Minneapolis: Fortress Press, 1988), 99–102, for a discussion of *nurture* as a metaphor for ministry.
13. Ibid., 56.
14. Ibid., 58.
15. Ibid., 62–63.
16. Suchocki, *God Christ, Church*, 190.
17. Joretta Marshall, "Toward the Development of a Pastoral Soul:

Reflections on Identity and Theological Education," *Pastoral Psychology* 43/1 (September 1994): 13.

18. Erik Erikson, *Identity and the Life Style* (New York: W.W. Norton, 1980), 120.

19. Joretta Marshall, "Toward the Development of a Pastoral Soul," 19.

20. Robert J. Schreiter, *Constructing Local Theologies* (Maryknoll, N.Y.: Orbis, 1985).

21. Judith Jordan et al., *Women's Growth in Connection* (New York: Guilford, 1991).

22. See, e.g., the insightful research of Robert Kegan, *The Evolving Self* (Cambridge, Mass.: Harvard University Press, 1982), and Jordan et al., *Women's Growth in Connection*.

23. Marshall, "Toward the Development of a Pastoral Soul," 11–38.

24. Janet L. Surrey, "The Self-in-Relation: A Theory of Women's Development," in Jordan et al., *Women's Growth in Connection*, 53.

25. Jean Baker Miller, "The Development of Women's Sense of Self," in Jordan et al., *Women's Growth in Connection*, 15–16.

26. Beverly Harrison, "The Power of Anger in the Work of Love," in Carol S. Robb, ed., *Making the Connections* (Boston: Beacon Press, 1985).

27. Ibid.; and Delores Williams, *Sisters in the Wilderness* (Maryknoll, N.Y.: Orbis, 1993), 200–201.

28. Froma Walsh, "Reconsidering Gender in the Marital Quid Pro Quo," in *Women in Families*, ed. Monica McGoldrick, Carol M. Anderson, and Froma Walsh (New York: W. W. Norton, 1989), 267–85.

29. See James B. Nelson, *Embodiment*, esp. chap. 3, for a careful discussion of the distortion effected by this dichotomy in Christian tradition concerning our understanding of the self and a value of embodiment. He also discusses its negative consequences when joined with the sexist dichotomy of patriarchy.

30. Harrison, "The Power of Anger," in *Making the Connections*, ed. Robb, 13.

31. Ibid., 14.

32. Ellyn Kaschak, *Engendered Lives* (New York: Basic Books, 1992), 43.

33. Ibid., 46–47.

34. Carter Heyward, "Notes on Historical Grounding: Beyond Sexual Essentialism," in *Sexuality and the Sacred*, ed. James B. Nelson and Sandra Longfellow (Louisville, Ky.: Westminster/John Knox

Press, 1994), 10–11. See also Mary McClintock Fulkerson, *Changing the Subject* (Minneapolis: Fortress Press, 1994).

35. See Nelson, *Embodiment*, chap. 3, for an extended discussion of the consequences of this double dualism.

36. Heyward, "Notes on Historical Grounding," 16.

37. See, e.g., Deborah Tannen, *You Just Don't Understand* (New York: Ballantine, 1990).

38. Rachel Hare-Mustin, "The Problem of Gender in Family Therapy Theory," in *Women in Families*, ed. McGoldrick et. al., 71.

39. See James B. Nelson, *Between Two Gardens* (New York: Pilgrim Press, 1983), 18, for a careful discussion of the relationship between embodiment and spirituality.

40. James B. Nelson, *The Intimate Connection* (Louisville, Ky.: Westminster/John Knox Press, 1988), 29–46.

41. Valerie Saiving, "The Human Situation: A Feminine View," in *Womanspirit Rising,* ed. Judith Plaskow and Carol Christ (San Francisco: Harper, 1979), 37.

42. Judith Plaskow, *Sex, Sin and Grace* (Lanham, Md.: University Press of America, 1980).

43. Nelson, *The Intimate Connection*, 92–96.

44. Mary Field Belenky et al., *Women's Ways of Knowing* (New York: Basic Books, 1986).

45. Ibid.

46. Ibid.

47. Ronald Levant and William S. Pollack, eds., *A New Psychology of Men* (New York: Basic Books, 1995).

48. Stephen J. Bergman, "Men's Psychological Development: A Relational Perspective," in *A New Psychology of Men*, ed. Ronald Levant and William Pollack (New York: Basic Books, 1995), 75.

49. Carol Gilligan, *In a Different Voice* (Cambridge, Mass.: Harvard University Press, 1982).

50. Hare-Mustin, "The Problem of Gender in Family Therapy Theory," 71.

51. Ibid.

52. Heyward, "Notes on Historical Grounding," 11.

53. Jacquelyn Grant, *White Women's Christ and Black Women's Jesus*, American Academy of Religion Academy Series 64 (Atlanta: Scholars Press, 1989), and Delores Williams, *Sisters in the Wilderness* (Maryknoll, N.Y.: Orbis Books, 1993), 162–64.

54. Williams, *Sisters in the Wilderness*, 162–64.

55. Judith Orr, "Ministry with Working-Class Women," *Journal of Pastoral Care* 45/4 (Winter 1991): 343–53.

56. Ibid., 344.

57. Ibid., 347.

58. Ibid., 349.

59. David W. Augsburger, *Pastoral Counseling Across Cultures* (Louisville, Ky.: Westminster/John Knox Press, 1986), 49.

60. Monica McGoldrick, John Pearce, and Joseph Giordano, eds., *Ethnicity and Family Therapy* (New York: Guilford, 1982), propose that the most significant factor for effective therapy across cultures is the therapists' awareness of their own cultural identity.

61. Derald Wing Sue and David Sue, *Counseling the Culturally Different*, 2d ed. (New York: John Wiley and Sons, 1990).

62. Ibid., 114–16.

63. Ibid., 140–47.

64. Vivienne Cass, "The Implications of Homosexual Identity Formation for the Kinsey Model and Scale of Sexual Preference," in *Homosexuality/Heterosexuality: Concepts of Sexual Orientation*, ed. David McWhirter, Stephanie A. Sanders, and June Machover Reinisch (New York: Oxford University Press, 1990), 251–56.

65. Kristine Falco, *Psychotherapy with Lesbian Clients: Theory in Practice* (New York: Brunner/Mazel, 1991).

66. Joretta Marshall, *Counseling Lesbian Partners* (Louisville, Ky.: Westminster/John Knox Press, 1997).

CHAPTER FOUR

❧

Pastoral Authority: Images of Strength in Behalf of Empowerment

We know that the way in which we conceive our ministry is of critical importance in determining whether there will be healing or failure. Wrong conceptions, distortions, repressed resentment of authority, can get in their destructive work where pastor and person meet. We have to ask how a right theology of authority enters into the practical task of pastoral care. [1]

DANIEL DAY WILLIAMS

Pastoral authority is a manifestation of the processes described earlier in the formation of an identity as pastor. Pastoral authority reflects the clarity of orientation and confidence of purpose that arise as the theological claims of one's faith community and one's religious experience are integrated into the core of one's identity and practice of ministry. [2]

The authority of a pastor is inherent in pastoral relationships and distinctive in character and effect. This chapter will explore what constructions of authentic power are legitimate and helpful for pastoral diagnosis.

Because diagnosis involves the power to name the reality of another through defining that person's predicament, authority is a significant dimension of any diagnostic process. Other dimensions—the anthropological assumptions and ethical framework—will be discussed in the following chapters.

Authority is a dynamic construction, not an entity. As Richard Sennett reminds us, it is an imaginative process,[3] involving images of relative strength and weakness operative among the parties involved. Authority is an emotional expression of power, the function of which is to convert power into images of strength that will offer a sense of trustworthiness.[4] This chapter offers reflections and theological analyses to suggest images of strength that are most appropriate.

A SITUATION IN MINISTRY

Margaret is the pastor of St. Mark's United Methodist Church (UMC). It is a five-hundred-member rather liberal congregation with a civic mission orientation. Its primary ministry is to the university that dominates the life and economy of the small East Coast city in which St. Mark's and the university are located. Margaret is fifty years old, has been the pastor of St. Mark's for four years, and is an effective administrator with good relational skills and is an excellent preacher. The District superintendent felt that her gifts would be helpful in this congregation in which administrative structures needed shoring up. Margaret has carefully nurtured congregational leadership in administrative and programmatic areas with encouraging results. Since coming to St. Mark's, she has enjoyed deepening her liturgical skills in a congregation that values creativity and music in worship. She is a good listener, but does not consider pastoral care and counseling a strong suit.

Last Sunday, for various reasons, the worship service included both sacraments—a unique situation for Margaret, who is attentive to time limits. However, since it was Lent, she decided to experiment and place the font at the front of the center aisle so that those who wished could renew their baptismal vows as they came to the altar rail for the Lord's Supper. Her sermon focused on themes of vocation and commitment. Many seemed to find the opportunity helpful and risked touching the water to themselves before or after communion.

Tom Fisher, a parishioner, called that evening to ask if he could meet with Margaret that week. He said that the service had had a profound effect on him, and he wanted to discuss an issue it had focused for him. Tom is a member of the Administrative Council at St. Mark's. Six months ago he reluctantly agreed to chair the University Ministry committee, and Margaret has been concerned that he seems overwhelmed by the task. She and Tom have a cordial relationship, although it is confined to congregational functions.

Tom is forty-five years old, an associate professor of biology at the university, and married to Lisa, forty, who teaches math in the private high school in town. His father-in-law is an eminent biologist (retired) formerly at the university. Lisa is a well organized, articulate woman. She does well in her work, and also oversees the educational program for children at the church. She has high expectations for herself and for others. Tom and Lisa have two children, a nine-year-old daughter and a son who is six. Margaret has observed them to be well-cared-for and loved children who are highly responsible and responsive in church school and other church situations.

When Tom arrives and the pleasantries are past, he confesses that he has had a rather perfunctory relationship to the church for some time. His membership on the council seemed something he should do. He was reared in the church, and he knows the language of faith, but it has had little power in his life for a long time. Even now he is not certain that Christian resources have much significance for his present dilemma, but last week's service moved him deeply. He was surprised by the power of making the sign of the cross with baptismal waters as he came to the altar for communion, and he found her sermon "close to home." Now he wants to explore how Christian faith may inform the mounting despair and anxiety in his life and career and his growing dis-ease regarding the direction of his daily life.

Tom describes an increasing sense of failure in most aspects of his life. Feeling "overloaded and inadequate" at work, he also experiences pressure at church with a committee assignment that is more than he bargained for. His department chair is pressuring him to increase his publications and research funding, but he considers her expectations to be unrealistic. The university's recent shift in vision toward becoming a premier institution has felt threatening—a "change of rules in the middle of the game." Tom is a good teacher, but those gifts are no longer as valued. His work is no longer gratifying, but a burden.

At home, his father-in-law's shadow looms bigger and bigger. Lisa's ambitions for Tom underscore the anxiety he feels at work; he can't measure up to her father. Her administrative skills and apparent ease in handling many things well leave him feeling less and less adequate.

It has been hard to share these fears because once again he finds himself confessing inadequacy to an obviously competent woman.

But it would also be hard to tell another man. Sunday's experience somehow created an opening in him to move past that barrier and ask for her help.

DEFINING POWER AND AUTHORITY

While there are many seams to mine in Tom's predicament, Margaret is aware that one of the most important and problematic themes has to do with the dynamics of authority in their relationship. Tom has acknowledged that the Christian faith they share has not had much experiential reality or authenticity for him for some time. While she doesn't yet know his history with previous pastors, it is likely that his authorization of her office is also weakened. Moreover, the transferential dimensions of his experience make her gender problematic for him. What seems to have caused him to seek her out is his experience with the sacraments, joined by the preached Word that was sufficiently close to his need to elicit a response. On what resources may Margaret draw to understand better the images of strength operative in Tom's authorization of her ministry to enhance the effectiveness of her care for him? What images of strength are most appropriate for her ministry with Tom? How can she deepen his trust that the faith she represents, and its symbols he recently found so powerful are reliable?

Tom's description of his dilemma discloses the tensive dynamic that Richard Sennett sees as underlying any process of authorization: connection and constraint.[5] We need images of strength—security to function in the contingencies of historical existence—but we also resist the dependency and subordination such trust creates. Thus our need exacerbates our resistance. And it is well to be careful both because of the difficulty of balancing our need and our resistance and because the ideal linkage between authority and trustworthiness is often precarious.

Freud, of course, called all conferrals of religious authority illusory with infantile roots.[6] Sennett underscores the imaginative quality of any construction of authority and warns against absolutizing what is better understood as a process.[7] He correctly reminds us that the search for that which may function authoritatively in our lives is neither illusory or infantile, but in fact vitally important.[8] The issues are to what we entrust authority, and how.

Jackson Carroll extends Sennett's theme well in relation to the church:

> What is true of human community generally is true also of the church. It is not possible for the church, in its various manifestations, to exist in faithfulness to its calling without the willingness of its members to submit themselves to the authority of its deepest convictions about God, God's purposes for the world, and the church's role in those purposes. But these core beliefs and values, which bind the church together, must be articulated and interpreted in ever-changing circumstances. Conflicts must be managed. Boundaries between the church and other communities must be maintained. Directions for the church's life and work must be envisioned. All of this implies leadership, and leadership implies authority.[9]

Ministry requires the exercise of power and authority. The issue is not whether but what kind of power and authority are exercised by pastors like Margaret or pastoral care specialists in the practice of ministry.

It is important to recognize that there are multiple ways to define power, and the implications of such differences are enormous. For example, does Margaret impose a definition of Tom's difficulty? Does she assume Tom has the answers to his struggle if she will help him hear his own wisdom? Does she presume that a collaborative effort is necessary with Tom, and if so, how does she assign accountability between the two of them?

These briefly described options are simply caricatures of much deeper cultural questions about power and authority. In fact, in faith communities many describe a crisis regarding the exercise of power and authority in ministry. There is some consensus about three interrelated factors: a crisis of belief, the disestablishment of religious institutions with a corresponding marginalization of clergy, and a cultural fascination with individualism and an egalitarian ethos that has significantly privatized what is intended to be a corporate faith. In such a context many are skeptical that any exercise of power and authority in religious leadership could be appropriate or even possible.

Yet, since the issue is not whether but what kind of power and authority are exercised in ministry, such a context as ours renders pastors and pastoral care specialists vulnerable, for power is most likely to be misused when it is denied. It is critical for the practice of ministry in general and pastoral diagnosis in particular to construct a theology of pastoral authority that will provide a corrective response to the current context for many Christian faith communities in the United States. Such a theology must include a normative vision for congregational life and ministry. Given this context, two passages from scripture offer guidance: Isaiah 61:1-3 and Ephesians 4:11-16. These passages have long been recognized in Christian tradition for envisioning ministry both within and beyond the bounds of congregations. It is a ministry to which we are all called by virtue of our baptisms. According to these verses from Isaiah, this ministry includes empowering those oppressed and in bondage, healing those broken in spirit, and comforting those who mourn. This passage understands God's Spirit at work in us to transform redemptively those structures, systems, and relationships that deform and destroy human life. The norm of such a vision is the joining of God's love and God's justice. Ministry guided by this mission witnesses to the hope that is in us. Ephesians 4 complements Isaiah's understanding of ministry as empowerment in behalf of others. In Ephesians, we also find that those who lead are authorized by the community in behalf of its ministry and witness. We are called to live in communities of mutuality and interdependence in which the love of Christ is the norm for our life together.

The normative vision that emerges from Isaiah and Ephesians suggests that power and authority in Christian communities are to be used in behalf of God's love and justice. They are guided by intentions to empower others, encourage mutuality, and enhance interdependence. This vision does help construct a theology of pastoral authority that dismantles both the patriarchal scaffolding of clericalism and the dangerous naiveté of an egalitarianism that denies the reality of power in every social construction.

The Ephesians passage suggests that the clue for responding to critical questions about the nature of power and authority in the church lies in the community itself. Here authority is conferred by the community on its members according to individuals' gifts and the community's needs. Authority emerges from a web of relationships and is entrusted to another for the well-being of the whole. This relational authority values the interdependence of life in community—the compassionate obligation to each other into which Christ invites us.

In our contemporary context relational authority is countercultural and clearly requires new thoughts about power. Part of our current dilemma in church and culture lies in the predominant exercise of unilateral forms of power as the effort to dominate or control. While some may seek to use it benevolently, unilateral power is not benign; it intends to dominate. It accompanies a worldview that is hierarchical, presumes inequality, and values autonomy of some at the expense of community. Unilateral power assumes a finite amount of power. For one to have it, another must have less, with the goal that one gets as much of it as one can. Such power exploits our expansive desire for autonomy and illusions of control. It divides power from justice and love, for it focuses power back on the self at the expense of the other.[10]

A corrective definition of power as relational lies in taking seriously both the dynamic relationality in which power is constructed and the normative goals scripture envisions for power—empowerment, mutuality, and interdependence. Theologian Kyle Pasewark, describing power as the "communication of efficacy,"[11] acknowledges that power is a pervasive dimension of human community. Power emerges between persons or institutions; it is not an entity one possesses or hoards, but is always given and received. By "efficacy" Pasewark refers to a normative or existential definition of power derived from God's creative power evidenced particularly in the life of Jesus of Nazareth. God gives life to us. We, as believers, in turn are called to love neighbors as ourselves.[12] Normatively, power is fulfilled in love and justice[13] more concretely experienced as empowerment, mutuality, and interdependence.

Pastoral authority emerges through the exercise of relational power in particular relationships and contexts. Pastors such as Margaret or pastoral care specialists know that these relational understandings of authority and power are difficult to put into practice. We live in relationships and serve in congregations in which such valuable resources as vision, energy, sensitivity, hope, and maturity are not equally divided. We have to cope with real and enduring differences and estrangement, as Tom's story suggests. Relational power and authority get messy and ambiguous because it is hard to sustain care when we are confronted with brokenness that seems not to yield. Relational power is concretely present. It is messy, ambiguous, and difficult. It is also far more like the power suggested in the passage in Ephesians.

If Margaret's responses to Tom are guided by a theology of relational pastoral authority, she can at least define the parameters for her exercise of power in the process of pastoral diagnosis. She will not unilaterally impose a definition of Tom's predicament, nor will she presume that her professional expertise and priestly role are of little value to Tom because his own wisdom is sufficient. Rather, she presumes to use her skillful presence in behalf of Tom's healing for which he, too, bears responsibility—that is, they will work collaboratively, sharing accountability for their different gifts. Her immediate concern is his empowerment; her long-term goal is their mutual empowerment for discipleship.

Margaret's clarity about a relational understanding of power and authority in her responses to Tom offers her a compass for her presence with him. The complexity of his predicament, however, and the multifaceted character of their relationship suggest that she will need other "markers" to help her be who she intends to be with Tom. Sennett contends that authority is an imaginative, emotional process of constructing images of strength that offer a sense of trustworthy care. He describes the dynamics of the process of authorization as a tensive balance between a longing for connection and a fearful constraint. In contrast to Pasewark's normative definition of relational power, Sennett describes at a concrete existential level how pastoral authority's goal of mutual empowerment often includes the proximate goal of safekeeping when persons are experiencing disempowering anxiety or fear.

Effective pastoral diagnosis relies on a pastor or clinician offering a sufficiently safe and authentic connection to allow persons like Tom to share their experience honestly. A theology of relational pastoral authority would further require that the connection's authenticity be proven by a goal of mutual empowerment. Just as diagnosis is itself processive and dynamic, it is clear that the therapeutic process involves an ongoing calibration of connection and constraint so that what offers strength and security to persons like Tom will vary.

IMAGES OF STRENGTH

What images of strength would serve Margaret's intention to chart a collaborative course in her care and counseling with Tom? This question is not unlike that posed by theological ethicists such as Karen Lebaqcz[14] and Eric Mount,[15] who urge pastors to reflect intentionally on those metaphors which articulate their values and ideals for pastoral practice. They argue that such metaphors act as the lenses that help us frame our present activity and anticipate the future. As Mount puts it, "seeing is behaving."[16]

Metaphors have disclosive, corrective, and constructive potential. The way we learn to see affects what we see—and what we miss altogether. Of course, we are each embedded in the stories and images of our families, cultures, and institutions. It becomes very important to know which metaphors or images are operative in our ministry. Some will be more adequate than others for assuring that our practice of ministry has integrity as well as congruence with the vision of Isaiah and Ephesians.

Moreover, as we noted earlier, ministry in general and pastoral diagnosis in particular are too complex for one metaphor to do. This is so not simply because of the variation in need within a particular care or counseling relationship but because pastoral relationships are so multifaceted and complex. In ministerial relationships dynamics of power, authority, responsibility, and identity vary dramatically. The vulnerability of persons in crisis situations such as abuse, grief, or illness colors our exercise of power and authority differently from sharing a committee assignment or playing softball together at a church picnic. The responsibility for preaching and leading liturgy colors our exercise of authority and our identity still differently from other occasions, so we find ourselves needing a cluster of metaphors or images of strength that together assure the accountability we desire for ministry.

Such a cluster of images is guided by our analysis of contextual ambivalence about the exercise of power and authority in ministry and our concern for constructing a theology and practice of relational pastoral authority. Different contexts and concerns could easily yield a different selection of images. Given Margaret's context and our concerns, we can explore a cluster that includes the images of midwifery, service, friendship, and shepherding.

Developing such a cluster requires criteria to help assure accountability and guidance in the selection of the images we want to shape our practice. The six criteria that follow reflect additions and adaptations to criteria proposed by Eric Mount in *Professional Ethics in Context*.[17]

First, it is important to determine that our images of strength or our metaphors ensure an understanding of the appropriate exercise of power for ministry and provide accountability for that power. For example, the metaphors of "friend" and "shepherd" imply quite different approaches to power. Subsequently I will propose that while ministry as friendship counters the hierarchy of clericalism, it may leave us vulnerable to this culture's conflation of authority with authoritarianism. Shepherd, on the other hand, clearly invokes power as safekeeping and need not include the paternalism some have assumed. Servant reminds those of us with power of the need to define it relationally.

Second, are our metaphors congruent with scriptural images of authority in ministry, and will they guide our exercise of authority? Authority is the legitimate exercise of power. The Ephesians passage includes the recognition of authority by virtue of the gifts one is given. Midwifery is a valuable metaphor because in its recognition of the expertise of the midwife, it does not diminish the one in labor as gifted and also responsible.

A third criterion for images of strength concerns whether they preserve the complexity and ambiguity of persons such as Tom. Do they project consequences for our actions toward others that are congruent with the justice and love envisioned by Isaiah and Ephesians? This criterion suggests the diversity of situations in ministry we noted earlier. For example, while friend, shepherd, and trustee all project somewhat different consequences for our actions, in each case we can anticipate love that is respectful, gracious, and just.

A fourth criterion has to do with whether our images accommodate the storied, dynamic context of congregational life. Do they together include the variety of situations and corresponding approaches required by ministry? Midwife, for example, is appropriate for those occasions in which we collaborate with persons who are discerning gifts and who need our support in bringing those to fruition. Shepherd, on the other hand, clearly anticipates situations of crisis in which vulnerability is honored and protection assured.

A fifth criterion has to do with the aptness of the image for one's own ministry. In order to guide one's practice, the image needs to connect with one's experience. Some may find coach more helpful than midwife, or gardener better than either one.

Finally, do our metaphors help us see what is truthful and important for ministry in this time and place? This is an important question to raise because our metaphors or images have the potential to disclose, correct, and construct our ways of seeing. Each alone also necessarily limits or even deflects our perspectives. A cluster of metaphors helps to assure that we recognize as many distortions in our seeing as possible. For example, friendship helps correct against dominating kinds of power, but it needs the corrective of shepherd and midwife in this cluster because of the occasions in ministry when protection and expertise are needed.

Isaiah's concern for justice toward those who are powerless and on the margins of culture, and Ephesians' concern for those who are tossed to and fro with every wind of doctrine, help to focus the value of this corrective function in our cluster of metaphors. Clearly, these criteria, however partial, suggest the importance of careful reflection on those metaphors that guide our exercise of power and authority. They also demonstrate the necessity for a cluster of metaphors that complement and correct the limits and distortions in each.

Midwife

In a culture anxious about both power and authority, this metaphor offers us a way to join caring, authentic presence and expertise while recovering the collaborative, differentiated authority envisioned in Ephesians. In this way it clarifies how a relational understanding of power and authority informs the practice of pastoral diagnosis.

Our first criterion in developing a cluster of images of strength to guide the exercise of power and authority in pastoral diagnosis has to do with assuring an appropriate exercise of power and accountability for our power. Midwifery does provide real help in our efforts to move from unilateral to relational power. This is a power that seeks to empower others while acknowledging one's own. Labor suggests the careful interdependence of persons who share a common goal— empowerment of the one in travail in behalf of new life and new possibilities that are uniquely his or hers to offer. The midwife finds real gratification in the success of the other.

Midwifery is helpful in terms of its congruence with scriptural images of authority—our second criterion. It contradicts hierarchical notions of authority without compromising the real expertise midwifery requires, and suggests a collaborative style of shared and differentiated authority in which the gifts and responsibilities of each are respected, much as we find in the vision of Ephesians. The authority of a caring and attentive presence also includes the expertise of the one who is present. Authenticity and authority are not mutually contradictory. The authority of expertise is used here to assist the other in a highly interdependent process—not to subordinate the other or elevate the midwife. Moreover, because midwifery defines the exercise of strength in behalf of the other, it not only corrects the excesses of unilateral power but also helps pastors like Margaret avoid any easy equation of authenticity and reciprocity in caring encouraged by her culture's egalitarian bias and suspicion of authority.

The image of midwife also helps us preserve the complexity and ambiguity of the other in the practice of diagnosis, for both processes require careful listening for another's particular needs, fears, and hopes. There is certainly ambiguity woven throughout the process of pregnancy and labor as there is with Christian life. Childbirth can be complicated. It is never painless. Babies are not always healthy or wanted. Infertility is painfully common. If life in community and Christian maturity were simple, the writer of Ephesians would not have gone on at such length. Diagnosis, like labor, is difficult, messy, and too often fraught with the ambiguities of life this side of the promised land, just as Tom's predicament illustrates. Midwifery keeps us honest about the day-to-day work of ministry in general and pastoral diagnosis in particular.

Servant

The appropriation of this metaphor to counter distortions of power and authority requires careful clarification. It represents an important countercultural dimension of the gospel regarding power and authority with deep roots in Hebrew Scripture—especially prophets such as Isaiah. This metaphor satisfies several criteria guiding our practice of ministry: the appropriate exercise of power and accountability for it, congruence with a biblical vision for relational authority, and help in discerning what is truthful and important in this time and place.

Despite the potential value of this metaphor, servant has a troubled history in the tradition. The authenticity of this metaphor lies in the freedom to choose to serve. Over time two distortions have arisen that complicate the usefulness of servant as a contemporary image of strength for religious leadership. Both of these distortions are relevant for pastoral diagnosis.

The first distortion arises from the fact that the call to service can be coopted easily by patriarchal values so that those with power and its corresponding autonomy impose service as an obligation on those whose power and freedom are subordinate to theirs. In other words, those in leadership retain their privilege while urging others in subordinate positions to embrace this image for ministry as their own. In such cases, service becomes subservience. The radical implications for sharing power and authority that are the context for this metaphor in scripture are rationalized away, if addressed at all. Too often, the purpose of service is to further not the ministry of church and and the love of God but the interests of those in power. Because diagnosis presumes a normative framework within which deviation may be noted, it is easy to see that pastors such as Margaret who are not alert to the dynamics of power in relationships could quickly be complicit in preserving inequities unquestioned in the status quo of a culture or her congregation. Tom's sense of inferiority in relation to an accomplished father-in-law and wife illustrate well the importance of Margaret's self-conscious accountability for her power.

The second distortion is related to the first and also arises from the importance of the freedom to choose service. Recent feminist theological and biblical reflection notes that this metaphor presumes that the one choosing to serve already has a sufficient sense of self to experience the choice to serve as freeing. As Elizabeth Schüssler Fiorenza has shown, the New Testament metaphor of service emerged in the early Palestine Jesus movement and subsequent Christian missionary movement.[18] It reflects their radical vision of a community of equals in which those with power chose to become like servants to others, and those who had been marginalized experienced the liberating wholeness of the new creation. In this context of mutual regard and freedom, the call to service and altruism could be authentically experienced by those once on the margins. But this radical vision of a community of equals gradually accommodated itself to its patriarchal, societal context.

Now the question is raised whether the metaphor of servant is freeing for those who continue to experience marginalization in church and culture, and who have internalized that subordinate status and worth. For these persons, this metaphor requires others to prevent its distortion into subservience rather than the empowering mutuality of care in which it originated.

As a woman in a patriarchal culture, Margaret has likely struggled with internalized subordinate notions of her status and worth. As a woman in a largely patriarchal tradition, she knows the story of women's marginalization. As a clergywoman in a relatively large church, she may know the more ambiguous reality of both marginalization and power. Certainly in relation to Tom she has power. Moreover, as a white, upper-middle-class woman in the United States she also knows some measure of privilege. This metaphor of servant can help pastors reflect on both the ambiguities of power and accountability for the power one has. In a culture reluctant to acknowledge the legitimacy of power while many experience subordination or marginalization, this metaphor helps clergy be honest about the power that diagnosis entails and the normative horizon of mutual regard and freedom by which that exercise of power is judged.

Friend

The metaphor of friendship functions as an image of strength for pastoral diagnosis because it easily brings to mind the experience of relational power and authority in which we enlarge each other through the reciprocity of care, encouragement, love, and support. The power operative in friendship relies on willing receptivity and trust. In fact, the only authority for the power of friendship is these bonds of trust and love.

This metaphor offers an important corrective to this culture's trivialization of love and its fear of power in the way friendship joins love and power. Ministry as friendship represents what ethicist Beverly Harrison describes as

> the most basic of all the works of love—the work of human communication, of caring and nurturance, of tending the personal bonds of community. . . . love's work *is* the deepening and extension of human relations. . . . Through acts of love—what Nelle Morton has called "hearing each other into speech"—we literally build up the power of personhood in one another. It is within the power of human love to build up dignity and self-respect in each other or to tear each other down. We are better at the latter than the former. However, literally through acts of love directed to us, we become self-respecting and other regarding persons, and we cannot be one without the other. If we lack self-respect, we also become the sorts of people who can neither see nor hear each other.
>
> We may wish, like children, that we did not have such awesome power for good or evil. But the fact is that we do. The power to give and receive love, or to withhold it—that is, to withhold the gift of life—is less dramatic, but every bit as awesome, as our technological power. It is a tender power.[19]

Ministry as friendship, it turns out, is not some benign and senti-mental image. Rather, it helps us recover an appreciation for the con-structive power of love.

Clearly the metaphor of friendship is an important contribution to pastoral diagnosis in our contemporary context. It offers a way to confound unilateral power with love's tender power. What may be problematic with this metaphor, requiring the corrective of another, is the difficulty friendship has in accommodating the lack of symme-try in power between religious leaders and those for whom we offer care. Friendship relies on interpersonal power. The reciprocity of vul-nerability serves as a safeguard in the relationship. But ordained min-istry is also characterized by symbolic and representative power, which creates an asymmetrical power arrangement. In much of the daily work of ministry this imbalance can be minimized, but it is never absent. While Margaret works collaboratively with Tom on a com-mittee assignment and flips burgers with parishioners at a picnic the next day she knows she may be with one of them in the emergency room or coronary care as a priest on whom they rely, sharing utter vul-nerability. This is a functional difference, not a hierarchical distance.

This enduring asymmetry poses a helpful caution in our reading of Ephesians 4. It reminds us that while this passage describes a dif-ferentiated authority according to gifts and functions, some of these functions carry a different psychological weight or quality that is more apparent at particular times. Yet, such asymmetry does not diminish the interdependence of us all.

Friendship is a helpful image of strength for pastoral diagnosis because of the way it broadens and enhances our understanding of the quality of love we join with power in the practice of ministry. Like midwifery it points to the empowering intention of care, but it deep-ens our understanding of care with love that is at once tender and powerful. We will come back to this image in discussing Margaret's symbolic authority, but here this image reminds Margaret that Tom authorizes her care now in the context of an enduring relationship more often characterized by reciprocity. Most likely the quality of that relationship makes possible the trust required to overcome his resis-tance and share his vulnerability as he has. Pastoral diagnosis is prac-ticed most often when an experience of crisis leads parishioners to heighten the asymmetry of a pastoral relationship, but they do so rely-ing on a more foundational experience of interdependence that friendship envisions. The authenticity of that enduring relationship authorizes Margaret now.

Shepherd

Though timely and useful, the metaphor of friendship does not help us to be accountable for the asymmetry of power that predictably characterizes occasions calling for diagnosis in ministry. The image of shepherd offers strength because it envisions the trustworthy exercise of power as care that is protective. Ezekiel 34 is a powerful illustration of this metaphor in which responsible care and justice are joined by God as the good shepherd. The vulnerable are those for whom God has particular concern.

Ethicist Karen Lebacqz uses the more contemporary term *trustee*[20] to underscore the covenantal trust of ministry as shepherding described in Ezekiel. This metaphor insists that power is a primary issue for ministry, and it makes clear that such power is a fiduciary power. The metaphor of shepherd joins justice and love as the central norms for ministry. It requires attention to the equitable distribution of power in behalf of enlarging the power of others.

The image of shepherd is indeed helpful in regard to our criteria about power and authority. It is also capable of helping us preserve and honor the real differences among us if we hold on to the relational definition of power suggested by scripture. Otherwise, this image is easily compromised by the paternalism of unilateral power which seeks to help but not in ways that would empower the other or challenge existing systems and structures. Crisis experiences, in which people share their vulnerability more readily, are times when we are asked to exercise more power and control for their safekeeping. Shepherding is not benign paternalism but a temporary protection that intends to enlarge the power and well-being of all. This image of strength is well suited to Sennett's insight about the tensive balance of bond and constraint, for shepherding offers safekeeping in the context of care. It requires attentive listening to discern how we can participate in the empowerment of another.

The metaphor of shepherd does help us see what is truthful and important for ministry in this time and place. It requires us to acknowledge the reality of power that accompanies pastoral diagnosis, and also poses the centrality of justice and empowerment in defining the trustworthy exercise of power. It is important for shaping the practice of diagnosis in our context because it discloses the dishonesty of a naive denial of power, the presumption of a condescending exercise of power, and the pretense of defining power as exercised individually, apart from a web of relationships and responsibilities.

CONCLUSION

In reflecting on these metaphors of midwife, servant, friend, and shepherd, we have recognized that congregational dynamics are a complex tapestry of the various needs and possibilities of believers. Congregations interact with a cultural context that significantly influences both their understanding of the gospel and strategies for ministry. We focused particularly on the complex and dynamic character of power and authority in ministry in general and pastoral diagnosis in particular. The vision of Ephesians 4 and Isaiah 61 has helped us see a strong biblical tradition that places the exercise of power and authority in the covenantal context of trust and joins love and justice as the norms for power. We have found that these metaphors help us talk about issues of power, authority, honesty, and trust. They help us understand diagnosis differently because these images of strength have forced us to revise some definitions and to recover the proper context of others.

We have attempted to construct a theology of relational pastoral authority that provides a corrective response to current confusion about the exercise of power and authority in ministry. We have rejected both the extremes of clericalism and egalitarianism, choosing instead a biblically informed understanding of relational power and authority. We have proposed metaphors that together offer images of strength that project the careful exercise of this vision of relational power and authority. With these images we have described pastoral authority as a dynamic, interactive construction rather than a static entity.

NOTES

1.   Daniel Day Williams, *The Minister and the Care of Souls* (San Francisco: Harper & Row, 1961), 30.

2 .   For a full and incisive discussion of the internal processes that contribute to the development of pastoral authority and its relation to pastoral identity, see Joretta Marshall, "Internal Pastoral Authority in an Ecclesial Tradition: Psychological and Theological Dynamics," Ph.D. diss., Vanderbilt University, 1992.

3.   Richard Sennett, *Authority* (New York: Random House, 1980), 4, 197.

4.   Ibid., 165, 197.

5.   Ibid., 15.

6.   Sigmund Freud, *Civilization and Its Discontents*, trans. and ed. James Strachey (New York: W. W. Norton, 1962).

7.   Sennett, *Authority*, 19.

8.   Ibid., 197.

9.   Jackson Carroll, *As One With Authority* (Louisville, Ky.: Westminster/John Knox, 1991), 35.

10.   Bernard Loomer, "Two Kinds of Power," *Criterion* 15/1 (Winter 1975): 15–18.

11.   Kyle Pasewark, *A Theology of Power: Being Beyond Domination* (Minneapolis: Fortress Press, 1993), 213.

12.   Ibid., 198, 325.

13.   Ibid., 331.

14.   Karen Lebaqcz, *Professional Ethics* (Nashville: Abingdon, 1985).

15.   Eric Mount, *Professional Ethics in Context* (Louisville, Ky.: Westminster/John Knox Press, 1990).

16.   Ibid.

17.   Ibid.

18.   Elizabeth Schüssler Fiorenza, *In Memory of Her* (New York: Crossroad, 1983).

19.   Beverly Harrison, "The Power of Anger in the Work of Love," in Carol S. Robb, ed., *Making the Connections* (Boston: Beacon Press, 1985), 12.

20.   Lebacqz, *Professional Ethics*.

CHAPTER FIVE

§

Pastoral Authority:
Structural and Symbolic Dimensions

Our exploration of pastoral authority as a dynamic construction and an imaginative, affective process is helpful for the practice of diagnosis; yet, it does not exhaust the nature and complexity of pastoral authority. Pastoral authority also has distinctive structural and symbolic dimensions that exist in a dynamic and complex interdependence. We turn now to discern the significance of these two dimensions for pastoral diagnosis.

STRUCTURAL AUTHORITY

Structural categories—sociological and descriptive features, historical and representative factors, and functional expectations for areas of expertise—are relevant for the dynamic construction of authority in the process of pastoral diagnosis. Together these suggest the complexity of pastoral authority in relation to other paradigms.

Sociological and Descriptive Features
Six sociological/descriptive features are significant for pastoral diagnosis. *First, ministry is a highly public endeavor in which one's fundamental convictions are a matter of public record.* As the United Methodist Church's *Book of Discipline* declares, "Ordination is a public act of the Church."[1] In Margaret's sermons, prayers, liturgy, administration, teaching, and social interactions, Tom and others have ample oppor-

tunity to know her beyond some more limited professional persona familiar in therapeutic and medical paradigms. Margaret's ordination vows also include references to matters of lifestyle, health, trustworthiness, and accountability.[2] When Tom comes to Margaret's study it is possible that he knows as much or more about her through their varied experiences and her highly public role than she knows about him. Surely this affects his experience of bond and constraint as described by Sennett. It complicates Margaret's task because she does not know how Tom has interpreted his experience of her, and how it affects his presentation of himself. Of course, it also means they may have some common ground on which to build their relationship.

A second feature of pastoral authority relevant for our purposes is its communal context in which a shared confession of sin and a shared baptism help to "level" undue distances between clergy and parishioner in some traditions. In the UMC, for example, a description of the relation of ordained ministers to the ministry of all begins with the assertion that "All Christians are called to ministry, and theirs is a ministry of the people of God within the community of faith and in the world."[3] The community of believers then authorizes the ministry of those whose gifts suggest their ability to offer leadership in Word, Sacrament, and Order. "In ordination, the Church affirms and continues the apostolic ministry which it authorizes and authenticates through persons empowered by the Holy Spirit."[4] General ministry and ordained ministry are described as distinct but complementary. The hierarchical structure of ministry in the United Methodist Church does assure Margaret functional authority at St. Mark's, but she is also accountable to the discipline of the denomination. For our purposes the important issue is that her authority vis-à-vis Tom is qualified.

A third feature of ministry relevant here is that it is enduring—a point noted earlier in our discussion of friendship as a metaphor of pastoral authority. Margaret and Tom knew each other before this time of crisis, and they will continue to relate after some resolution to the present difficulty. The longevity of their relationship is foundational for briefer periods of imbalance such as this one. The dynamics of authority may be altered many times over the years of Margaret's ministry with Tom. Once again, we find Margaret's authority qualified by a larger intent to retain a relative balance in her authority in relation to Tom.

Closely related to this longevity is a fourth feature, multidimensionality. Not only does Margaret know Tom over a period of years, but they know each other in a variety of situations. The minister whose counsel he now seeks, Tom also knows from church picnics and potluck suppers, discussions around the table at Administrative Council, as well as the more heavily symbolic contexts of pulpit, chancel rail, and font. She too knows Tom in several roles. Their relationship is multifaceted, suggesting the dynamic and complex character of pastoral authority especially in congregational contexts.

A fifth feature is that of the larger social context. The construction of authority in their relationship does not occur in a vacuum. Margaret is called to embrace her authority within a historical/cultural context deeply ambivalent about the exercise of authority. Questions about the authority of faith claims, the marginalization of the church in culture more generally, dependence upon voluntarism in the congregation, and uncritical avowals of shared ministry that neglect necessary complementarity of tasks have all contributed to a pervasive ambivalence among clergy and parishioners regarding the exercise of authority in ministry.[5] Tom's comment about his reluctance to be vulnerable with a woman also bespeaks significant ambiguities about gender rules and roles that Margaret and he have no doubt internalized to some extent. Moreover, this is a rather liberal, mostly white, middle- and upper-middle-class UMC congregation with a significant proportion of highly educated persons who experience considerable influence in their lives and community. In other words, the larger political dynamics of their place and time affect the way Tom and Margaret will construct an image of strength sufficient for Tom's experience of care.

Finally, the particularities of Tom's and Margaret's experience as persons must be attended to. Margaret is a UMC clergywoman. Her authority is a blend of both the office of ministry and her person, with the importance of her sacramental functions heightened relative to that of the Baptist and UCC pastors in nearby congregations. As a woman, her authority is somewhat ambiguous since she is in a role for centuries denied to women and in a tradition that is complicit in the oppression and marginalization of women in the institution of the church. This, in addition to the culture's confusion about gender rules and roles, underscores the significance of gender as a category in reflection on the exercise of pastoral authority, whether in same- or other-gender relationships. Tom's particular history with women makes this even more the case. His perceived inadequacy vis-à-vis personal, relational, class, and gender role expectations also enter into any consideration of the dynamics of authority. These particular issues in the lives of Margaret and Tom illustrate the importance of transference and countertransference for our consideration of the dynamics of pastoral authority.

These six features of ministry color the imaginative construction of pastoral authority differently, of course, in every situation. Yet, their significance must be accounted for in any exercise of pastoral diagnosis.

Historical and Representative Factors

Another important and complex dimension of the structure of pastoral authority has to do with the tensive balance between the authority inherent in the office of pastor and that derived from the charismatic gifts of the person of the minister, that is, her or his personal credibility. Three authors from the fields of management theory and psychiatry have recorded their observations of the physician's authority in ways that prove suggestive for the reciprocity of these structural features of authority in ministry.

In *Models of Madness, Models of Medicine*,[6] Miriam Siegler and Humphrey Osmond expand on the research of T. T. Patterson to examine carefully the authority of physicians, which Patterson labeled Aesculapian or healing authority.[7] This authority exists in the particular context of illness, and it is derived from the fear of death and the drive to survive. Out of the vulnerability of human frailty, patients and their culture grant to physicians the right to confer the sick role—without blame—and to require submission to treatment with a corresponding release from responsibilities.

Patterson observed three dynamically interdependent, multivalent dimensions of Aesculapian authority, apparently adapting these from Max Weber's legal, traditional, and charismatic forms of authority.[8] He described these as sapiential, moral, and personal authority. Sapiential authority entitles one to be heard "by reason of knowledge or expertness." Moral authority entitles one "to control and direct by reason of 'rightness' and 'goodness'" according to the ethos of the culture. Personal authority entitles one to "control and/or direct by reason of the fittingness of the personality with the purpose of the enterprise."[9]

Siegler and Osmond use these three dimensions in their elaboration of Patterson's work, nuancing his category of "personal authority" by the title "charismatic authority." Their description of this authority is particularly intriguing:

The third ingredient of Aesculapian authority is charismatic authority, the right to control and direct by reason of God-given grace. This element in Aesculapian authority reflects the original unity of medicine and religion which still exists in many parts of the world. In Western culture, the charismatic element in medicine has to do with the possibility of fully assessing the doctor's knowledge. There are too many unknown and unknowable factors in illness for medicine to rest entirely on sapiential authority. For this reason, the doctor still retains some of his [*sic*] original priestly role.[10]

It is interesting to pursue the similarities in the structural dynamics of authority between physicians and pastors. Medicine and ministry have shared a long-standing unity at the common horizon of death. While it is important not to confuse the experience of vulnerability to disease and death with vulnerability to sin and death, both point to the limits of creaturely existence. The vulnerability of human frailty underlies the trust patients and parishioners place in doctors and pastors respectively. The structural dynamics of Aesculapian authority are suggestive for the experience of pastors. Pastors are expected to know the *wisdom* of the tradition. They are *representatives* of the values and symbols of that tradition and of its manifestation in particular institutions by virtue of their ordination to office. They also rely on the trust that originates through their own *charismatic* ability to convey their personal credibility. In pastoral authority these three dimensions are also dynamically interdependent and may be weighted in importance differently.

The process of authentication for Aesculapian and pastoral authority is also similar. Siegler and Osmond have noted that Aesculapian authority is granted formally at that point in time when boards are passed and a license is given. But they have also pointed out that this authority is conferred over time as patients respond to the doctor's increasingly mature judgment and wisdom. Ordination certainly represents a similar official occasion when authority is granted for ministry. Yet, congregations also confer this authority over time.

We noted in chapter one some of the dissimilarities in the nature of authority exercised by physicians and pastors, such as the physician's hierarchical status and relative anonymity with patients. It is clear, however, that the dimensions and dynamics of Aesculapian authority seem strikingly applicable to pastoral authority.

The sapiential, representative, and charismatic dimensions of Aesculapian authority disclose the dynamic complexity of Margaret's pastoral authority and the importance of her self-awareness of these dimensions so as to use them in behalf of Tom's well-being. They offer Margaret resources to guide her process of pastoral diagnosis.

Sapiential authority refers explicitly to the wisdom of the tradition—the biblical and theological resources that United Methodist pastors (and other Christian clergy) are to know and share. In Tom's case this dimension of Margaret's authority does not seem to be foremost in his authorization of her since he acknowledged ambivalence about the faith claims of the tradition. He was more aware of the symbolic power of the sacraments and the efficacy of Margaret's sermon in relation to these sacraments. Further reflection on his response is suggestive for a broadened understanding of the "wisdom" funding Margaret's authority. Sapiential authority does not refer to some static knowledge stored away to be interjected through occasional references as needed or imposed with finality when all else fails. Rather, it is a praxis-oriented knowledge that is necessarily accompanied by relational and communicational skills.[11] In fact, this authority involves precisely the skills described in our earlier definition of practical theological reflection. It is shared, disciplined reflection on experience informed by critical correlation of theological/biblical resources and those of the behavioral sciences or other relevant disciplines. Its intent is to mediate the transformative, redemptive love of God in behalf of empowering persons for discipleship. It is likely that Margaret's effectiveness in interpreting scripture and as a preacher, the creativity of the worship she planned and led, and the hospitality of her leadership style all contributed to Tom's decision to confer authority on her. All these activities demonstrate informed pastoral praxis extending the reconciling love of God in Christ.[12]

As Margaret assesses Tom's situation, she listens for areas in which Tom's identity as a Christian and the development of his faith requires their constructive effort. In Tom's case issues such as the nature of vocation, the possibility of hope, the relation of freedom and accountability, and the providence of God are all relevant. She will need to draw on her knowledge of psychology and therapy, gender rules and roles, theories of change in institutions, family systems theory, and so forth, to discern effectively the dynamics of Tom's predicament and possibilities for healing and more empowering experience of Christian faith. Her knowledge in these areas of behavioral science is a feature of her sapiential authority.

Representative authority—the authority of the office of ministry—includes a rich albeit troubled legacy of ordained ministry and the institutional church and associated values and ethical assumptions. The particularities of this dimension of Aesculapian authority vary among different communions of the Christian tradition. For Margaret and Tom, the evangelical piety and social conscience of Wesley as well as the sacramental theology and hierarchical polity of Anglicanism, from which the Methodist movement began, shape their self-understanding. Margaret's representative authority is funded by her accountability to scripture and to the order and discipline of the United Methodist Church.[13]

Functional Expectations
Representative authority functions in a dynamic, reciprocal relation to sapiential and charismatic authority. That is, Margaret may be due Tom's respect as minister of Word, Sacrament, and Order in the UMC, but his conferral of trust in her as his pastor is also influenced by the gifts she brings in her person and evidences of professional competence.

As she attempts to assess Tom's needs, Margaret's diagnosis will need to account for the way her "office" functions symbolically for Tom. What rules and roles does Tom assign to the office of ministry? Surely this particular congregation's expectations and those of Methodism also affect his expectations. Very likely, such expectations are peopled by earlier pastors who shaped Tom's definition of "minister." His experience with them and those of persons important to him will now affect his availability with Margaret. He has expressed skepticism regarding the faith claims of Christian tradition; yet, he was deeply moved by Margaret's sermon and its convergence with the sacraments. Margaret needs to discern whether and how the office of ministry functions for Tom as an image of strength. Is it a resource for hope? Does it convey trustworthiness? How does Tom deal with the fact that now this office is filled by a woman only slightly older than he? Certainly, the interdependence of structural and symbolic authority is evident here; however, the office of ministry is sufficiently distinctive to warrant our attention to its particular significance for pastoral diagnosis.

Finally, we also need to inquire about Margaret's charismatic authority. Certainly her personality and relational gifts deeply color the other facets of her authority. While her tradition values the priestly office and its apostolic authority, United Methodist itinerancy and North American religious expression put considerable emphasis on the authenticity of the person of the pastor. Margaret has the challenge of knowing that in spite of Tom's negative associations with her gender and status, he has entrusted to her his painful vulnerability. It is at least the case that their relationship through Tom's work on the Council and various congregational events seems to have helped mitigate the negative transference her gender created for Tom. To the extent that her own personality is infused throughout her preaching and sacramental ministry, Tom's positive response to those experiences likely includes some positive transference as well. Margaret will need to determine how she herself may contribute to Tom's trust in her and perhaps enhance the possibilities for deepening Tom's experience of God's presence and care.

Our reflection on this case discloses that the structure of pastoral authority, like that of Aesculapian authority, is multidimensional. Pastoral authority also reflects the reciprocal dynamics of Aesculapian authority. It is at once earned or warranted by virtue of knowledge, ordination, and integrity; yet, it is also conferred by the faith community in general and particularly by Tom. The authenticity of Margaret's administration of the sacraments is enhanced by the centrality of sacraments in her tradition. The complexity of pastoral authority is also suggested by this pastoral situation, for it is clear that at some points Tom will weigh more heavily Margaret's representative and sapiential authority, but later in the conversation her personal authenticity will be more persuasive.

The contextual and Aesculapian dimensions that structure pastoral authority are, in themselves, convincing regarding the distinctive complexity of pastoral authority. Such complexity, however, is not exhausted by these structural factors. As Tom's response to the sacraments suggests, the symbolic dimensions of pastoral authority are also quite significant for the exercise of pastoral diagnosis. In fact, the structural and symbolic dimensions of pastoral authority are closely intertwined and dynamically interactive. The office of ministry with its long history helps create the expectation of one whose presence validates the Spirit's "call." The qualities of person described earlier as charismatic authority are intimately related to the authentic mediation of God's presence in the signs, symbols, and rituals of religious faith.

SYMBOLIC AUTHORITY

Tom has indicated that it was the convergence of Margaret's sermon on vocation and commitment alongside the opportunity to renew his baptismal vows as he approached the Lord's Table on that Lenten Sunday which precipitated his decision to call her for an appointment. For Margaret, this convergence was a serendipitous experiment. Now skillful diagnosis requires some depth in understanding the powerful experience of symbolic authority that brought Tom to her office.

For our purposes, symbolic authority refers to the authorization of persons whose practice of ministry includes those signs, symbols, and behaviors mutually understood as mediating the nearness or presence of God. Its primary locus is the context of worship. Elaine Ramshaw correctly asserts that liturgical leadership is the paradigmatic act of pastoral care that focuses and seems to authorize pastoral practice in other settings such as Margaret's and Tom's appointment.[14] Our recognition of the dynamic reciprocity of the several dimensions of pastoral authority allows us also to claim that Margaret's sensitivity to her symbolic authority in this individual pastoral care setting could deepen Tom's experience of God's presence in worship. In fact, this seems to be the opportunity with which he presents her here, for his recent experience in worship begs for exploration and elaboration.

He has expressed skepticism regarding the faith claims of Christian tradition and also a deep longing for a renewed experience of God's presence. In what ways might Margaret's representation of Christ be useful to Tom, and in what ways might Tom's fears or concerns about God require her skills in mitigating possible negative transference? Tom has expressed ambivalence regarding her gender because of his personal experience. Surely such ambivalence extends to areas of spirituality. Since Tom feels inadequate in his work and his marriage and has resentment about both contexts which include "competent" women, how does he experience a woman as a representative of God's presence and love? What is God like for Tom? In response to his experience of God, how may Margaret best communicate her status as a representative of God and the church?

Even this brief reflection on Margaret's ministry with Tom is suggestive for the relevance of symbolic authority to the practice of pastoral diagnosis. Margaret's sensitivity to her symbolic authority in pastoral care and counseling contexts will prove a constructive resource for helping many persons like Tom whose diminished faith is disclosed in the context of facing personal and relational crises. The efficacy of her mediation of God's care and presence may well help Tom and others rediscover the authenticity of God's presence in their lives and world. This reauthorizing function of symbolic authority discloses the constructive possibilities for pastoral diagnosis among those whose theological commitments are no longer experientially available.

In the next few pages we will explore several other ways in which symbolic authority and ritual action often associated with it are relevant for pastoral diagnosis. Our explorations will include the nature of power associated with symbolic authority and accountability for it. We will also discuss the transformative possibilities associated with religious ritual and the ethical vision that nourishes ritual action.

"Rituals are repeated, normative, symbolic, and functional behaviors."[15] They establish the order necessary for human interaction. They help restore our sense of belonging, mark transitions, interpret meaning—especially when it is ambiguous—open us to experiences of transformation, and help manage ambivalent feelings[16] in behalf of those feelings more valued. In Christianity religious ritual action is intended to mediate the nearness or presence of God through symbols of God's saving love. God is the host of religious ritual action.

Religious ritual action is quite significant for pastoral diagnosis in part because it involves such complex communication. As Gilbert Ostdiek notes, the meaning of liturgical action can never be exhausted[17] because it is dynamically and interactively constructed by the gathered assembly with multiple levels of significance. While rituals necessarily must provide continuity, they also have to be responsive to the evolving dynamics of the context. Moreover, while ritual leaders may know what they intend in a ritual action, it is especially important to attend to the experience and meaning that participants give to ritual action.[18] For Margaret this means she may know the traditional theological interpretations for baptism and communion, but it remains for Tom to interpret to her his experience, and even then their understanding will be partial.

The complexity of ritual communication lies especially in the fact that ritual language is performative. That is, its meaning is not abstract, but located in the activity itself. An embodied knowledge emerges from ritual action which lends to such action an integrative power at the intrapsychic, relational, and spiritual levels of experience.[19] Moreover, this performative character of ritual language is the key for understanding the transformative role of ritual practice in religion.[20] As Tom came forward that Lenten Sunday after the sermon to receive communion from Margaret and also paused to renew his baptismal vows, touching the water from the font to his forehead, he was actively constructing an alternative social world. He embodied in that moment the freedom intended by these sacraments to live as if the vision of Margaret's sermon and these sacraments were available to him personally and as a disciple in the world.[21] Of course, that transformative power lay not only in its constructive possibilities, but also in its capacity to critique or disclose as problematic Tom's current sense of self and vocation.[22]

The complexity of ritual communication only serves to magnify the importance of Margaret's self-conscious exercise of her symbolic authority in providing liturgical leadership. As the doctrine of the priesthood of believers reminds us, all believers embody Christ's presence in the world, but clergy have a distinctive sacral authority[23] as institutionalized symbols of God's presence—"bearers of the sacred."[24] The power inherent in ritual action requires of religious leaders both skill in the practice of ministry and a keen appreciation for the trust such ministry entails. Our earlier attention to pastoral authority as the collaborative construction of images of strength between a pastor and parishioner(s) is certainly applicable here, for we find that the power associated with ritual leadership operates at both apparent and latent levels[25] in a dynamic and interactive fashion. Apparent are all the symbolic elements that point to the sacred quality of space, language, and action, such as Margaret's vestments, the pulpit in which she stands, the act of preaching, the communion table and font, the bread and wine with their fragrance, the resonance of liturgical language, and the sanctuary itself. All these elements add significance to her words and actions. They assist her in constructing images of strength that will enhance Tom's experience of God's presence and care.

At the latent level of ritual power we find Tom's projections and transference operative.[26] The needs, hopes, and fears at work in Tom as he participated in that Sunday service and came forward for communion contributed to his ability to entrust more of himself to the possibilities of that ritual action. Similarly, they encourage him to pursue the significance of his experience now in Margaret's office. His needs and longings interact with the strength Margaret seeks to convey as she mediates God's caring presence, allowing him to risk the relative vulnerability a construction of symbolic authority requires.

Surely at this latent level we also need to be mindful of the needs, hopes, and fears related to Margaret's embodiment of her ritual leadership. Our earlier reflections on pastoral identity serve us here. Pastoral leadership does not arise in a vacuum. Margaret's willingness to embrace the "functional hierarchy"[27] of ritual leadership and to be a "bearer of the sacred" for her congregation will require her careful negotiation of cultural distortions, gender constraints, and her own spiritual development. It is not simply Tom who brings vulnerability to the construction of symbolic authority.

Obviously, diagnostic skill in recognizing and responding to these latent and apparent levels of ritual power in the construction and exercise of symbolic authority is crucial for effective pastoral practice. We have already addressed the importance of Margaret's self-conscious construction of the images of strength that convey how she intends to exercise her power in ministry. Such reflections will surely help her consider how she draws upon the apparent level of ritual power. Her skillful response to the latent level of ritual power requires our attention to the human needs that invite ritual as a means of care.

In *Ritual and Pastoral Care*, Elaine Ramshaw suggests five such needs:[28] establish order, reaffirm meaning, bond community, handle ambivalence, and encounter mystery. Within our attention to the first we will also address what Tom Driver names as ritual's importance in facilitating transformation.[29] We will consider these needs in relation to our situation in ministry with Tom and Margaret.

We have already noted the way in which ritual action is in fact a dynamic and interactive process; thus the order to which Ramshaw refers needs to be flexible, although, as she notes, corporate, formal, religious ritual is less changeable than other daily habits because of the levels of meaning it must carry. In Tom's experience we see the principle of balance between some spontaneity and the continuity that ritual provides, for Margaret experiments in placing the font before the altar rail and in this new possibility the predictable nature of the two sacraments allows for a valuable new experience.

As we noted in our previous attention to the transformative possibilities of ritual, the performative nature of ritual communication and the integrative effect of change through ritual action point to the way in which ritual helps us negotiate significant transitions and sometimes real transformations in our self-understanding and agency. Confirmation and weddings suggest such developmental transitions that may have transforming possibilities. In Tom's case, Margaret may well determine that beyond the developmental transitions of midlife, Tom is describing a nascent experience of transformation begun in the convergence of the needs arising from his sense of personal and relational crisis and his ritual practice in worship. She would do well to be attentive to the liberative themes grounding the eucharist and baptism. How did the sermon's themes of vocation and commitment correspond to the internal needs informing his participation?

Human beings are meaning makers. One of the significant resources ritual action offers us is the opportunity to reaffirm those core values that guide our lives as people of faith. In this way ritual action has a normative force, for it is tied to those symbols which summon up the central values of the tradition such as bread shared and water that cleanses and claims us or scripture read and proclaimed. Especially in times of crisis the power of ritual action to reaffirm our symbolic worldview provides a steadying presence. Tom has described a sense of personal, relational, and spiritual crisis that led him to participate in Sunday's worship with a more acute sense of need. Through the ritual action he found himself more able to imagine a different future and to recover resources available through his faith tradition. Margaret now must discern what Tom experienced that was helpful and how to extend his renewed experience of faith.

Theorists have long identified that rituals help bond us with others and can intensify our sense of community and belonging. Religious ritual, especially corporately shared ritual action, strengthens our sense of place within the community of faith and helps weave more securely our personal narrative within the larger story of Christian faith. It is not surprising that the two ritual actions apparently most powerful for Tom—eucharist and baptism—symbolize communal life, its sustenance and initiation into it. Diagnostically, it is well for Margaret to be curious about the level of alienation in Tom's life. How helpful was the bonding power of ritual action? What would deepen his renewed sense of belonging?

Precisely because we are inherently relational, the power of ritual to help us deal constructively with our predictably conflicting feelings is an important feature for our reflection on pastoral diagnosis. As Ramshaw points out, feelings of love and caring are often "shadowed" by envy and resentment which evoke anxiety and guilt.[30] Ritual action can help us contain the negative feelings safely and reinforce the feelings we want to shape our experience and behavior. Consider, for example, the liturgy of memorial services that acknowledge anger and deep loss within the larger horizon of affirming God's promises of care and hope, or the Psalms of lament which express anger with God quite directly but within a framework that affirms God's overarching provision. Margaret has heard a bit of the ambivalent feelings Tom has regarding his father-in-law, wife, and department chair. She has also heard his guilt and diminished sense of adequacy. Diagnostically, she may well wonder how she can better discern the depth and nature of Tom's ambivalent feelings and to what extent her symbolic authority may provide ritualized avenues for the safe expression of Tom's anger and pain.

Finally, we do well to remember that ritual action helps us meet our need for encountering the mystery and awe of God's presence. Keenly aware of the contingencies of historical existence and the fragility of human life, our experience of awe and mystery allows us to trust that dependency to an ultimate image of strength. It is not clear from Tom's opening remarks whether the alienation he has experienced relationally and spiritually has included the absence of this sense of mystery or an imbalance of it to the detriment of a sense of belonging in the faith community. It is especially relevant for Margaret's symbolic authority to discern Tom's history in experiencing the mystery or otherness of God. Discerning the character of this otherness—benevolent, indifferent, judgmental, and so forth—will be useful for anticipating more helpful ways to be present to him.

The ritual needs we have explored here are central to our experience of being human, which may help clarify both the power of ritual action and the significance of symbolic authority for the practice of ministry. The authority to symbolize the presence of God and handle symbols that carry the core values of Christian tradition must be used responsibly. Because ritual action is a dynamically interactive, constructive, and contextual process, the ethical import of the ritual is highly dependent on the participants rather than inherent in the ritual itself. It is well to articulate norms to guide the exercise of symbolic authority.

Once again it is important to describe a normative vision for the exercise of power that is sufficient to disclose its abuse in ritual leadership as well as guide its use. In the previous chapter we drew from Isaiah and Ephesians to articulate a rationale for relational power that seeks mutual empowerment, the liberation of the oppressed, and the protection of the vulnerable. Justice and love are joined in this understanding of power.

From Ephesians we also voiced an understanding of authority as derived from the community in order to enhance its ministry of justice and love. This means that the authority to symbolize the presence of God is guided by a relational norm.

Honesty also emerges as an important norm for the exercise of symbolic authority. Elaine Ramshaw correctly insists on our attention to honesty in ritual leadership.[31] She describes several ways in which this power may be used manipulatively to impose ritual action that does not reflect the intentions of the participants. For the purposes of pastoral diagnosis it is important to distinguish between what one may hope is the experience of a parishioner and their own articulation of their experience.

Thus far our guidelines have helped frame our exercise of symbolic authority within the biblical vision of love and justice, and we have defined such authority as derived from the community of faith so that it is to be exercised relationally in the service of that community's life and mission. But our earlier description of the contextual factors shaping the exercise of pastoral authority suggests the need for additional guidance to ensure that pastors such as Margaret exercise symbolic authority with intentionality. That is, we need to be accountable not only to prevent the abuse of such power but also to assure its use as the healing and transformative resource it is for ministry. Daniel Day Williams suggested that when pastors fail to embrace such authority fully it reflects a crisis in their faith.[32] How can one convincingly convey an image of strength for which one has learned to feel ambivalent or that one does not experience? How can one convey an image of strength readily if strength is suspect? The two observations of course inform each other and reflect a deeper contemporary crisis with authority. As our exploration of the complexity, transformative possibilities, and power of ritual leadership has suggested, effective pastoral diagnosis relies on skillful intentionality in the exercise of symbolic authority. At issue is both a sufficiently formed pastoral identity to accept one's symbolic role and the courage to embrace its possibilities in one's pastoral practice.

NOTES

1. United Methodist Church (UMC), *Book of Discipline* (Nashville: United Methodist Publishing House, 1992), par. 432.
2. Ibid., par. 431.
3. Ibid., par. 401.
4. Ibid., par. 429, 430.
5. Jackson Carroll, *As One with Authority* (Louisville, Ky.: Westminster/John Knox, 1991), 19.
6. Miriam Siegler and Humphrey Osmond, *Models of Madness, Models of Medicine* (New York: Macmillan, 1974).
7. Miriam Siegler and Humphrey Osmond, "Aesculapian Authority," *The Hastings Center Studies* 1 (1973): 41–52.
8. Max Weber, *On Charisma and Institution Building*, ed. S. N. Eisenstadt (Chicago: University of Chicago Press, 1968).
9. T. T. Patterson, *Management Theory* (London: Business Publications, 1967), 114, 196, 181.
10. Siegler and Osmond, *Models of Madness,* 94.
11. UMC, *Book of Discipline*, par. 431.8.
12. Ibid., par. 429.2.
13. Ibid., par. 431.8,9.
14. Elaine Ramshaw, *Ritual and Pastoral Care* (Philadelphia: Fortress Press, 1987), 13–14.
15. Pam Couture, "Ritual and Pastoral Care," in *Dictionary of Pastoral Care and Counseling*, ed. Rodney Hunter (Nashville: Abingdon Press, 1990), 1088.
16. Ramshaw, *Ritual and Pastoral Care*, 30–31.
17. Gilbert Ostdiek, "Ritual and Transformation," *Liturgical Ministry* 2 (Spring 1993): 36–50.
18. Ibid., 46.
19. Ibid.

20. Tom Driver, *The Magic of Ritual* (San Francisco: Harper, 1991), 167.

21. Ibid., 190–204.

22. Ibid., 190.

23. I am indebted to Clifton Guthrie for this apt phrase, received in correspondence August 29, 1995.

24. Carroll, *As One with Authority*, 186–87.

25. Ibid.

26. Ibid., 192–93.

27. Ramshaw, *Ritual and Pastoral Care*, 59–60.

28. Ibid., 23–35.

29. Driver, *The Magic of Ritual*.

30. Ibid., 30–33.

31. Ibid., 25–27.

32. Daniel Day Williams, *The Minister and the Care of Souls* (San Francisco: Harper & Row, 1961), 34–63.

CHAPTER SIX

§

A Story of Freedom's Corruption: Sin as a Response to the Human Condition

In chapter one I demonstrated that diagnosis depends on three dynamically interdependent criteria: mutually understood dynamics of authority in the helping relationship, guiding ethical values, and anthropological assumptions. In the past two chapters we have explored the implications for pastoral diagnosis posed by careful consideration of the dynamics of authority for pastoral practice. Now we turn to anthropological assumptions operative in contemporary pastoral diagnosis. Pastors and pastoral care specialists are confronted daily with persons' painful predicaments that represent a confusing blur of both sin and psychopathology. Often in our culture persons conflate sin into psychopathology assuming there is little difference between these two sources of bondage. In this chapter we will explore what those differences are and why they are important. At stake is a richer and more informed understanding of the limits and possibilities of human freedom and our accountability for it.

In our earlier comparative analysis of several psychological paradigms and an ecclesial one, we disclosed that psychopathology and sin refer to different experiences of vulnerability. Psychopathology arises from a kind of original vulnerability that exists simply because we are historical embodied creatures. The intrapsychic structures on which we depend for our experience of identity and exercise of relative autonomy are vulnerable to distortions. Sin presumes a theocentric frame of meaning. It arises as a fearful response to the existential vulnerability that experiences the fragility of human life and the contingencies of historical experience. Sin presumes sufficient freedom to construct the pretense of a less precarious world either through our own supposed self-sufficiency or some other ordinary or mundane good. Theologically, of course, we call this idolatry.

In this chapter we will explore how sin and psychopathology arise differently in human experience, but once under way, they intertwine and reciprocally deepen the constraining effect of each other on human freedom. We will consider how classical theology of sin does help us distinguish sin from psychopathology and retrieve ethical accountability for the exercise of freedom. We will also consider difficulties in classical theology for acknowledging the vulnerability of human agency to the sorts of precritical distortions represented by psychopathology.

As in previous chapters, we will explore these issues through a process of pastoral theological reflection on a situation in ministry. I will use a particular theological tradition illustratively. We will return to this case throughout the chapter, allowing human experience to inform and challenge our correlation of theological and behavioral resources in behalf of the redemptive transformation the practice of ministry intends.

A CASE

Dick, sixty years old, is divorced from his wife because of his admitted molestation of their daughter over a period of several years, when the daughter was aged between ten and thirteen, which she reported to her mother when a young adult. He had lost his job earlier when charged with indecent public exposure. Dick was reared by his mother after his parents divorced. Prior to his marriage to Pat, Dick had a son with Joan, when she was thirteen and he was sixteen, but they did not marry. Dick himself is a survivor of sexual abuse. Dick is voluntarily participating in an intensive therapeutic program of recovery related to his sexually abusive behavior and is also in individual therapy with a licensed clinical social worker. He accepts responsibility for his actions and is learning to identify the feelings and experiences that precipitated his acts of molestation and exposure. He is not currently in contact with his daughter or son, but he hopes for that. He is employed again.

Dick is now worshiping in a Presbyterian church in his new community. Members of the congregation know he is divorced and not in touch with his family. Dick has sought the supportive counsel of his pastor, Steve, as Dick comes to terms with the devastating effects of his behavior on his victims, his guilt and shame, and efforts to find hope for the future. More details of Dick's experience will unfold in this chapter as they would in a pastoral relationship.

Dick's situation presents Steve with a problem. It is clear that psychopathology is present. We have several different therapeutic resources for assessing Dick's situation that may explore his own history of trauma, the family's dynamics—including his wife's—his lack of impulse control, and the convergence of such dysfunctional preconditions that together may account for Dick's deviant behavior.[1] No one of these resources, or theories of psychopathology, has won universal acceptance; at best they describe for us relevant psychological and relational factors to guide assessment and intervention, and they help disclose the tragic vulnerability of human existence and the factors that may combine to yield extraordinarily destructive behavior.

RESOURCES FROM TRADITION

These theories of psychopathology are less helpful in allowing us to explore the moral and ethical dimensions of Dick's behavior. In fact, the language of psychopathology avoids moral or ethical references. This is an important fact, for it signals a danger in conflating the language worlds of psychopathology and sin as is sometimes done in contemporary culture. If they are not the same, how do they differ?

Psychopathology, in varying degrees, diminishes at preconscious levels the relative autonomy of the person it affects. That is, it alters those intrapsychic structures by which we perceive and respond to the world so that persons may be less able to respond unselfconsciously and constructively to various situations in their environment. Sin describes the abuse or corruption of freedom. Traditionally sin assumes the formal capacities of freedom as ordinary autonomy. Its concern is rather with freedom as a symbol of life's goal to make life-enhancing, faithful choices—to be the self one is created by God to be. The concept of sin presumes that freedom is God's gift, and it projects the ethical language of responsibility and accountability.

We must assess the extent to which victimization has reduced Dick's ability to act freely as well as his agency in corrupting his freedom to "choose life" in the abundance God intends. At stake in pastoral diagnosis is more clarity about how psychopathology and sin limit our freedom differently and how these two phenomena coinhere. This is especially true in a culture whose language often suggests that psychopathology is sufficient to explain problematic behavior. Sin rarely appears as a useful or relevant category. Two concerns guide this chapter: first, if the bondage that sin and psychopathology impose on our freedom is not the same, it is important to discern how that bondage differs; second, is the language of sin truthful and helpful for responding to Dick?

Our classical Augustinian paradigm for the doctrine of sin affords Dick's pastor, Steve, crucial guidance in three important ways. First, it asserts that our true fulfillment lies in relationship to our Creator in whose love and justice our freedom finds its compass. Sin is not simply about the violence we do to others and ourselves; it is first a turning away from faithfulness to the One who calls us into life and whose love is the horizon defining our vision for life in communities of mutual respect and care. Awareness of sin casts life in a theocentric light. This theocentric vision is the normative context in which pastoral assessment takes place. Second, awareness of sin reminds us that what is at stake for Dick and for us is ethical accountability in the exercise of freedom. Classical Christian tradition has asserted that human evil arises as rebellion. It is a refusal to entrust our lives to God's care. As such, sin is an absolutization of our own desire for a sense of control or power achieved through idolatrous trust in some mundane good. Once our freedom is so alienated, the self is no longer able to "right its own course." The bondage of sin is thus self-imposed, radical, and progressive. That is, once our trust is shifted away from God, the fear that led to sin can only deepen because no mundane good can secure us. Third, human evil is not the same as our finitude. Evil is not a necessary response to our creatureliness but a corruption of the ideal of faithfulness to God and to love that is just, for ourselves and others.

These three claims have immediate implications for Steve's assessment of Dick's predicament. First, to say that awareness of sin casts life in a theocentric light points to the distinctively theological affirmation sin bespeaks of a vision of faithfulness, prophetic transformation, and love that functions normatively in pastoral practice. The violence and violation woven throughout Dick's story are a tragic distortion of who Dick is called to be and how he is called to live. Nevertheless, these distortions do not exhaust God's love for Dick or the possibilities for Dick to experience a renewed freedom.

Second, sin implies the possibility of redemption. Moreover, this redemption is not simply restorative; just as sin underscores accountability for the abuse of freedom, it also points to the transformative goal implicit in Steve's care for Dick. Steve intends not simply to ease sin's bondage in Dick's life but to nurture freedom properly directed. The freedom for love is a correlate of Dick's abuse of freedom and subsequent bondage to sin. But the term *bondage* signifies the radical, progressive character of sin's effect so that Steve anticipates the way sin's distortions have metastasized throughout the web of relationships and experiences that shape Dick's identity. To lose sight of sin's radical and progressive bondage would have Steve vulnerable to Pelagius's error which presumes our undiminished freedom to choose rightly.

Third, in separating finitude and human evil, this doctrine helps Steve avoid confusing the vulnerabilities of Dick's experience of familial and psychological dysfunction with sin's bondage. Many are those who hear stories like Dick's and find sociological and psychological explanations sufficient. Theirs is the contemporary version of the Gnostics, who presumed that sin was the consequence of finitude.[2] But Steve realizes that while the vulnerability that these behavioral sciences disclose no doubt interacts with sin's fearful self-securing, Dick's freedom as a human being is not exhausted by dysfunctional family structures and psychopathology; nor does the freedom for love he envisions for Dick exist somehow apart from or above the contingencies of historical existence. Rather, it has to do with living ethically in the midst of such vulnerability. Psychopathology and sin coexist interactively. Even these brief reflections on the guidance available in traditional concepts of sin suggest that Christian pastors like Steve have important, distinctive, and truthful contributions to offer to persons like Dick and to broader societal conversations about the roots of our violence against ourselves and others.

A CRITICAL REASSESSMENT OF TRADITION

There are difficulties, however, in this classical understanding of sin that require careful, constructive response if it is to prove adequate for guiding Steve's efforts in Dick's behalf. Our problem begins with Augustine's reliance on a literal interpretation of Genesis and thus on a historical schema for understanding the emergence of human evil. This schema obscures the reciprocal influence of various forms of vulnerability and the emergence of sin. Making his way between the Scylla of the Manicheans and the Charybdis of the Pelagians, Augustine asserted the origin of human evil as the self-imposed, radical bondage of the will. It arose as a refusal of finitude, which meant turning away from a fulfilling experience of God's presence in Eden's paradisiacal setting.

In asserting a period of original righteousness for Adam and Eve in an idyllic setting, Augustine differentiates creation and human evil, but he clouds the reality of suffering and temptation as a context for sin's rebellion. In fact he writes: "All evil is the result of sin and punishment."[3] This focus on voluntarism that helped rebut the fated perspective of his day with its conflation of finitude and sin meant that his more nuanced passages received less attention. In the *City of God*, for example, he imagines that the first couple, like the angels, were vulnerable to sin in that they could not be certain of the "eternity of their happiness."[4] Later, perhaps in reference to the snake's role, he suggests that all sin began with the lies of the Devil.[5] Calvin also refers to the "serpent's deceit" of Eve.[6] But, with Augustine, he put the stress on a corruption of the will. A consequence for the Augustinian/Calvinist tradition has been inadequate attention to the tragic context in which sin's corruption of freedom arises.

Related to the problems posed by the concept of original righteousness are the difficulties posed by Augustine's doctrines of original sin and guilt. Augustine's historicism and assertion of a biological transmission of the propensity to sin[7] have made many fail to appreciate this doctrine's continuing relevance. The doctrine of original sin helps us deal with the tensive relation between the self-imposed character of sin's bondage and the weight of the tragic context for the experience of sin. A story like Dick's helps to illustrate what is at stake in rescuing this doctrine from Augustine's bio-historical schema, for surely Dick's experiences of early, severe trauma and violence suggest the influence of tragic vulnerability in shaping sin's corruption of freedom and the progressive radicality of that sin as bondage which is not merely occasional. But his experience also discloses the existence of at least a wedge of freedom[8] rather than fate. Augustine's references to "the law of sin as the strong force of habit"[9] echo in Dick's description of his molestation of his daughter.

Contemporary insights from the social sciences and developmental psychology render thoughts of biological transmission of sin and guilt very problematic. We need to adapt Augustine's insights about the radicality of sin's self-imposed bondage so as to include the complexities that external forces and developmental and intrapsychic vulnerability introduce. The need for such a constructive response is illustrated well in Steve's Presbyterian tradition. The Presbyterian Church (U.S.A.)'s "A Brief Statement of Faith" describes sin thus:

> But we rebel against God; we hide from our Creator.
> Ignoring God's commandments,
> we violate the image of God in others and ourselves,
> accept lies as truth,
> exploit neighbor and nature,
> and threaten death to the planet entrusted to our care.
> We deserve God's condemnation.[10]

As expected, these lines are deeply rooted in Augustine's classical emphasis on sin as the self-imposed corruption of freedom—a disobedient turn from God. Previous items stress the radicality of such sin by noting the necessity of redemption. These sentences avoid Augustine's historical schema, but they do not reflect contemporary insights and resources regarding the tragically structured context in which sin arises. Rebellion here suggests a sheer, inexplicable turn away from God's good creation. This statement is a helpful description of the destructive consequences of sin, spiritually and relationally. While such a brief confession is necessarily limited in the development of any theological theme, Steve's pastoral care with Dick requires a better accounting of the dynamic interaction between the tragic vulnerability of the human condition and sin's anxious response. Certainly Dick's experience of sin is accurately characterized by rebellion, hiding, violation, deceit, and exploitation. But the corruption of freedom such actions disclose is more complex than the sheer voluntarism suggested by these lines.

To summarize, we need to develop a constructive, contemporary response to Augustine's earlier profound insights into the origin and enduring bondage of sin. We must find a way to hold on to the central reality of sin as a self-imposed, radical, progressive corruption of freedom while also recovering and developing further Augustine's recognition that sin's unfaithful turn from God arises in the context of a tragically structured human condition. That is, we must explore sin not only as a cause of suffering but as a response to the tragic structures of the human condition and psychopathology in particular. We do so realizing that the influence of context and historical experience does not exhaust responsibility for the exercise of freedom but does affect the degree of freedom available to us. As Whitehead observed, our historical and relational particularity includes both constraints and possibilities for our freedom. Steve's hopes for Dick lie not simply in healing sin's distortions, that is, in freedom from sin, but in a larger freedom for love that arises through Dick's response to God's grace in his life. Clearly, a more adequate construct for analyzing the dynamics of sin in human experience requires our appreciation for the tragic structures of the human condition itself.

HUMAN REALITY AND ITS CONDITION

To the extent that we understand sin as a response to a tragically structured human condition, it is important to address three questions: (1.) What is it about human reality that makes it subject to violation? (2.) What leads us to violate ourselves and others? (3.) How is it that we may receive redemption? When we describe human reality as tragically structured, we are referring to the inescapable ambiguities of our context. Such ambiguities are especially apparent when we focus on our inherent relationality. From birth we know ourselves relationally. When young we are utterly dependent on such relationships and especially vulnerable to their fragility, even as we require the strengths and meaning they may also afford us. At best our needs are met well enough rather than fully satisfied. Experiences of redemption and evil alike are mediated by the structures of relationality.[11] Certainly overcoming evil in such a context can only be partial.

One way to characterize human reality that helps disclose its structural vulnerability lies in focusing on its three constitutive, interdependent spheres: the interhuman, the social, and individual agency recently carefully described by theologian Edward Farley.[12] We will give priority to the interhuman sphere because it is in relationships that we recognize a deep summons to transcend preoccupation with ourselves and move toward a sense of compassionate obligation for one another in recognition of our fragility.[13] Very briefly we will sketch the outlines of these three spheres and the vulnerability they disclose in order then to focus on Dick's experience as illustrative of sin as a response to these tragic structures.

Interhuman Sphere

The interhuman sphere refers to the intrinsic relationality of human experience. We use relationality here both in the descriptive sense of lived experience and normatively to refer to the intentionality required to sustain relationships. According to Farley, our relationality has three formal dimensions: the radical otherness of our particular experience, the fabric of relationships necessary for individual identity, and the sometimes profound experiences of emotional intimacy.[14] Through our relationality we are confronted with both tragic and ethical dimensions of the human condition. Such experiences may give rise to compassion and a sense of obligation, the experiential fruit of relationality.

Philosophers such as Emmanuel Levinas suggest that the normative aspect of the interhuman sphere is created when we recognize "the face" of the other. The face summons us beyond self-preoccupation into responsibility, for we see in the other their physical and emotional fragility that mirrors our own vulnerability. Theologically, the face symbolizes an incarnational God disclosing the sanctity of life. In response to the face we realize that compassion and obligation are required of us. As Levinas put it, "the face orders and ordains me."[15] Farley notes, along with philosopher Nel Noddings, that the interpersonal claim of care is a "primordial summons" foundational for life together.[16]

I describe the interhuman sphere as tragically structured because of the vulnerability to suffering that is intrinsic to being in relationships. Two kinds of such suffering are apparent in Dick's experience: interpersonal and a benign alienation.[17]

Interpersonal suffering is intrinsic to our deepest relationships such as family, marriage, and friendship. These relationships shape us in significant ways. They are the context of joy as well as suffering.

However significant, no relationship is secure from the contingencies of historical existence. For example, Dick's parents found their love undermined and replaced by antagonism. Even in less extreme examples, it is clear that suffering inevitably occurs in daily relationships. Often interpersonal suffering is sharpened by the empathic connection with another's pain.

Benign alienation may be closely related to interpersonal suffering, but it describes more indirect suffering. It refers to the inevitability of suffering in light of the competing needs even of those who love each other. Divorcing parents feel this acutely as they seek to buffer their children's experiences of loss. While benign alienation refers to pain arising indirectly, rarely do we experience such pain dispassionately. Certainly Dick did not as his parents divorced and his father remarried so that a half-brother received the attention Dick ached to have. These two types of suffering disclose well the tragic ambiguity of our relationality in which the very structures that provide opportunities for love, care, and joy also include possibilities for deep suffering.

Social Sphere

This sphere refers to the complex environment of language, customs, institutions, and norms that shape us individually and interpersonally.[18] It expands the dynamics of relationships in the interhuman by virtue of the scope and interplay of institutions. For example, through this sphere arise the norms for care and family life, the assumptions carried in language, and the ethos surrounding gender, race, and class that frame and are in turn modified by our relationships. Farley suggests that this sphere includes two kinds of vulnerability: social incompatibility and social suffering. They represent a societal version of the vulnerabilities of relationality.[19]

Social suffering, for example, refers to a variety of ways in which the structures and systems of society may expand the possibilities for suffering that individuals encounter. When Dick's parents divorced, his mother's income dropped precipitously. The sexism that formed the context of the financial gulf between his parents reflects a structural or systemic consequence of patriarchy. The absence of adequate structures to assure help for children and affordable shelter for Dick and his mother illustrate social incompatibility—the societal form of benign alienation. Given the competing demands for limited social funding, legitimate needs are met inadequately, if at all. Of course, political priorities illustrate the interaction of these two forms of social vulnerability.

Sphere of Individual Agency
This sphere has three interrelated dimensions that we will find painfully present in Dick's experience: subjectivity, embodiment, and what Farley describes as our elemental passions.[20]

Subjectivity is the experience of being ourselves. It includes a tensive interdependence between our particular, finite possibilities and our infinite aspirations witnessed in our capacity for imagination and interpretation. Dick, for example, is a white man from the U.S.A. with a particular family history; yet, he is never reducible to these several categories because he experiences himself as able to imagine and create alternative possibilities. This capacity for transcending particularity is the foundation for both our agency or freedom and our moral accountability. The specificity of our particular social location joined with this capacity for transcendence yields our autonomy[21] and discloses the tragic structure of personal being. There are real limits to our autonomy, but such limits do not exhaust the possibilities available to our imaginations.

Embodiment affords profound pleasure. It also foreshadows the tragic condition of human reality because all creatures, by virtue of bodily requirements, experience limitations. Striving for the necessities of life and opposing whatever thwarts these needs occurs in an environment that, while abundant, may also be indifferent and sometimes dangerous. Benign aggression describes a genetically necessary capacity to resist and defend ourselves from harm.

Bodily requirements for human life include the developmental character of human reality. While these developmental structures provide rich possibilities for human striving and relationships, they also render human beings especially vulnerable since we are dependent on others' care for an extended period. This makes us susceptible to enduring distortions conveyed through the social, relational, and physical spheres here described. Dick's experiences of sexual abuse between the ages of seven and ten illustrate the developmental vulnerability of sexuality—a core dimension of identity and relationality—and the enduring, often tragic, consequences.

"Elemental passions" is Farley's intriguing phrase meant to describe both the vitality fueling our agency and the guiding center of our reasoned actions such as love and justice.[22] As hope far exceeds a wish, these passions anticipate broader states of affairs than a single event. They also seek to negate what might obstruct fulfillment and therefore reflect a natural egocentrism. Two such passions especially inform Dick's experience. The first we might call a passion for one's survival and well-being. It draws on the capacity for transcendence to resist any challenge to autonomy, diminished determinacy, and threat of death. Dick's response to his loss of place in his father's attentions to a half-brother suggests the strength of this first passion. The second is a passion for mutually sustaining relationships in which we are valued and able to give care—that is, relationships in which "the face" of one another is viewed. This is a passion for relationships in which we experience compassion and obligation. Dick's hopes for his marriage and life with Pat illustrate this passion. Of course, his story also illustrates the vulnerability of these passions to distortion—an issue to which we will return.

In sum, it is apparent that the tragic vulnerability attending our personal, embodied, and impassioned experience of individual agency is well illustrated in poignant ways in Dick's early life, for sexual abuse violates every dimension of the sphere of individual agency. In this tensive relation between determinacy and transcendence, we are vulnerable to others' refusal or distortion of our determinacy. Certainly the older boys and later the stranger who molested Dick denied the determinacy and boundary of his body. Similarly, we are vulnerable to actions that humiliate, reduce, control, or objectify our embodied transcendence, which sexual abuse dramatically illustrates. Abuse also illustrates well the vulnerability of the passions for survival and the reciprocity of care. Dick's passion for the survival and validation of his selfhood were utterly denied by his experiences of molestation. His hopes for reciprocity of care—especially with the older boys—were cruelly exploited.

Exploring these three spheres of human reality has disclosed our tragically structured existence and helped us to recognize the remarkable vulnerability to violation of our psychic center or that self-initiating center of our identity.[23] Human suffering may accumulate as the daily humiliations of political tyranny or the debilitating effects of physical illness. In Dick's case, reviewing the vulnerability of his spheres of reality reveals the archaeology of psychopathology's onset with its corresponding limitations. The interpersonal suffering of a six-year-old boy feeling the security of his familial world disintegrate suggests the "cracks in the foundation" of his sense of safety. The sexism and classism mediated through the social sphere are especially important as the former established the context of Dick's sexual abuse and the latter contributed to his sense of poor self-esteem. In the sphere of individual agency the actual experiences of abuse exploit Dick's heightened longing to be valued and his normal developmental vulnerability as a sexual being. It is easy to imagine how these several particular events and enduring losses set in motion psychopathological patterns of response that progressively limited Dick's freedom to trust others and himself. Dick's vulnerability to suffering is the result of the cumulative effects of the violations he has experienced, for these violations have led him to develop habitual styles of defense and other symptoms of dis-ease.

These defenses alter freedom in precritical ways. That is, they originate in particular events and processes of violation, but then they endure through altering the very structures of being such as our experience of safety or our ability to love ourselves and others. When these structures are altered, our capacity for self-determination is diminished, often with little if any conscious awareness, for we are simply responding to the world as we are able to perceive it.

We have seen the violability of human reality and the insidious consequences of that violation for human freedom. Now we turn to sin as violation, drawing once more on Dick's experience as a victim and perpetrator of sexual violence.

THE EMERGENCE OF SIN

Original Sin

Our review of the tragic structures of the human condition, and Dick's reality in particular, helps us to distinguish between evil or sin and human suffering. It is also apparent from Dick's experience that at the concrete level of human behavior such suffering and human evil are closely intertwined. In his care of Dick, Steve will likely find it difficult to distinguish suffering and sin. Having explored a schema that discloses the tragic structure of human reality and the particular ways psychopathology arises and endures in that reality, we need to identify the ways in which sin arises and endures as a response to such suffering. We will also explore how sin and psychopathology limit human freedom differently and interactively. Such analysis may help Steve discern the interplay of sin and suffering in ways that support his care for Dick and his empowerment of Dick's freedom for love. There are a number of perspectives from which to observe this relationship between sin and suffering.

Original sin reminds us of the impersonal and historical dimension of sin. It is true that sin's alienation has a cumulative force carried transculturally and transgenerationally, as sexism, racism, and various forms of abuse attest.[24] Dick's story suggests the way in which what begins as an objective reality insinuates itself into one's subjective experience. He was born into a nuclear family in which his parents experienced such conflict that they chose divorce, a situation in which Dick was an innocent party, although the stress of a third child likely was an issue. Nonetheless, Dick is not at fault here, nor is he responsible for the serious economic differences that meant his half-brother's stock of toys and access to his father's care were superior to his. Dick did have a choice, a wedge of freedom, in developing intense envy and malice toward his half-brother. Given this complicity, however, we would still need to acknowledge the weight of those forces at work in his childhood and youth that together served to diminish his freedom to choose life-enhancing possibilities. As Dick assented to postures of malice, envy, and self-doubt, moreover, he contributed to the cumulative historical force of sin for others as well. As Paul reminded us in Romans, ironically, Dick chose sin's bondage. Original sin helps us recognize that he did so in a context tragically structured.

In addition to the massive historical force described by original sin, fear of the future and the death(s) it brings is a critical factor in sin's origin and dynamics in our lives. Fear itself is death-dealing.[25] Sin lies not in our anxiety about real or symbolic limits to our lives but in the ways we then choose to narrow our possibilities for experiences and relationships. We choose to foreclose the risking of ourselves that being fully alive entails.

In Dick's life story one can easily imagine how poor self-esteem functioned to limit his hopes and possibilities as well as his willingness to risk new relationships. But his story also indicates how these origins of sin interweave, for his decision to begin acts of sexual violence occurs in response to a marriage in which he describes the emotional withdrawal of both partners. Each seemed to hide more of themselves, closing off the future of their marriage.

Clearest in Dick's story is the reality of sin as violation—the absolutization of one's own satisfaction or the absolutization of others' needs in such a way that relationality and interdependence are negated.[26] On the one hand, we see Dick's response to Joan's pregnancy and her subsequent disregard for him as a good description of false dependency. He absolutized her and their son's needs at the expense of his own, despite her refusal of mutuality and interdependency. Later, when Pat rejected possibilities for emotional and physical intimacy and relationality, Dick began a pattern of violation earlier perpetrated against him. This time he absolutized his own needs, violating those to whom he exposed himself and later his daughter. His victims are valued only according to the egotism of his own needs and thus are dehumanized through this process of objectification. In a rather paradoxical way his earlier response of false dependency was similarly controlling in that his construal of the situation provided some sense of control and also effectively cut off possibilities for genuine relationality as he sought to live through others by providing for their needs.

Pretense is the common denominator in these various perspectives on sin's emergence. Pretense describes sin's distortion of the tragic structure of reality into some more tolerable version. Sin as "the lie" is Suchocki's way of describing the assent to sin in its various forms.[27] We lie to ourselves that we were or are not free to act differently than we do. Farley describes this lie as the refusal to accept the tragic structures of our human condition and the insistence on interpreting such vulnerability as contingent on others' or our own control.[28]

In the Christian paradigm these postures of refusal and resistance are the idolatrous turn, for our anxiety requires some relief from our fearful recognition of these tragic structures. We attempt to make some mundane good fulfill our passion for being and our longing for reciprocity in intimate, caring relationships.

Once we make this self-securing turn required by the lie, then, the destabilizing dynamics of sin compound our dis-ease because no penultimate good can satisfy our needs. Resentment, greed, fear, malice, and so forth arise in place of a more secure and authentic posture of openness and reciprocity. Sin's bondage, which begins as fearful self-securing (pretense), diminishes our freedom to actualize capacities for love of God, self, and neighbor.

Sin is not the only way human beings deal with their tragic vulnerability and their discontent. Sometimes—perhaps because of biochemical reasons or other developmental disabilities—persons may find themselves relatively incapable of discriminating between life-enhancing and destructive actions or relatively unable to control such choices. Alzheimer's disease and forms of schizophrenia are examples.

Psychopathology, however, which is more experiential in origin—as Dick's history of trauma suggests—illustrates the way evil's corruption of human experience alters another's possibility for historical freedom. Sin involves a corruption of freedom's normative vision for life-enhancing behavior for one's self, others, and creation. It presumes sufficient autonomy for accountability. Psychopathology describes the precritical erosion of one's relative autonomy. It diminishes those intrapsychic structures by which one perceives and responds to the world rendering one less free or able to be unselfconscious and constructive.

Shame

The destructive consequences of psychopathology that arise as shame from experiences of victimization particularly illustrate the ways in which sin and tragic vulnerability intertwine. By coloring our perceptual capacities with fear, shame diminishes our freedom to be unselfconsciously present and at ease with ourselves, others, and our environment. Shame organizes the psychological reality of adults molested as children through its effects on the individual's sense of self and consequent diminished capacities for relationality that are shaped by love and trust.

> Identity is that sense of individuality that has continuity over time. It is that "vital sense of who we are as individuals, embracing our worth, our adequacy, and our very dignity as human beings." . . . Ordinarily, identity emerges as a child's natural needs are met in mutually significant caring relationships. An inner sense of wholeness, belonging, and connection develops through a reciprocal process of identification and differentiation. Shame ensues when a devastating experience of rupture breaks that interpersonal bridge . . . [with trusted or valued persons] and brings a consequent sense of betrayal and the unexpected exposure of unmet internal need. . . . When such experiences in relationships are not repaired or are chronic, they leave the individual's sense of [self] diminished, painfully small or belittled, filled with self-doubt, and overwhelmed by self-consciousness.[29]

Dick's experience of shame, not met by any repair, does reflect this internalized experience of shame; that is, he now feels toward himself the contempt he experienced from others whose acceptance he valued. The interdependence of our spheres of reality means that, once internalized, such self-contempt renders Dick vulnerable to diminishment in every aspect of his experience. Thus, unrepaired, shame has progressively destructive consequences for Dick's experience of agency, relationships, and the social sphere as well. Moreover, sexual abuse arises around the violent experience of bodily invasion that includes the experience of powerlessness to protect one's self. Thus one's sense of safety in the world is reduced. Dick's sexual abuse experiences, especially unmet by efforts to repair broken trust, mean that his freedom to be at ease with himself and others or to feel secure in his environment is significantly diminished. The primacy of relationality is apparent in the fragile, developmental processes of our emerging personality structures as children, so that the familial deprivation and sexual abuse Dick experienced did constrict his possibilities for life-enhancing freedom. Remembering that sin arises from fearful insecurity, it is obvious that Dick's experiences of victimization reflect the significance of the context to which sin is a response.

Yet, not all victims of sexual abuse become perpetrators. As Dick acknowledges, he chose to violate his victims. He describes such occasions, though, in the language of compulsive behavior, referring to sin as "the lie" even as it also bespeaks the constricting legacy of his victimization.

Sin is a refusal—an active resistance—to our tragically structured finitude. Its origin is distinct from the victimization of psychopathology. But, precisely because the structures of existence are so closely intertwined, the *corruptions* of sin and the *constrictions* of psychopathology, while limiting our freedom differently, do inform one another as Dick's experience of victimization and perpetration illustrate. The shape and effects of sin vary in the several spheres of human reality as does its interrelation with psychopathology. We turn now to explore how sin arises and corrupts Dick's experience of human reality in its several spheres: individual agency, the interhuman, and the social.

SIN AND THE SPHERES OF HUMAN REALITY

Individual Agency

Our earlier exploration disclosed several dimensions operative in this sphere: subjectivity, the passions, and embodiment. Drawing on Dick's experience, it is striking to see how sin corrupts these dimensions of his agency.

Subjectivity. Subjectivity is our experience of ourselves—self-transcending in our aspirations and imaginations and finite in our actual possibilities. Distortions in the tensive relationship between transcendence and finitude lead to patterns of sinful behavior. For example, when Dick perpetrates sexual abuse, he is singularly concerned with the immediate gratification of his need for control. He absolutizes his present finite needs, and they begin to define him. In such a moment he cannot bear the self-transcending functions of criticism or vulnerability in relationships, so they are reduced. This reduction in transcendence is a corruption of Dick's autonomy because now he has absolutized his needs and objectified other persons so that he no longer is drawn past himself toward authentic relationships but is motivated by a narrow priority for himself.[30]

The Elemental Passions. Elemental passions are the vital energy that fuel our agency. They reflect a natural egocentrism that seeks both the survival of our particular identity and mutual expressions of care necessary for the well-being of our intrinsic relationality. This passion for reciprocity of care is distinct from but supports the interhuman sphere. While sin's corruption cannot be isolated to one of these passions, it will subvert their interdependence.[31] Dick's situation painfully illustrates the desire to be valued relationally and to reciprocate that caring. The intensity of Dick's relational needs likely reflect the losses of early shaming experiences he had surrounding his parents' divorce and his two experiences of sexual abuse. This passion for the reciprocity of care corresponds with developmental needs for trustworthy relationality, especially in the early years of life.

Dick's early shaming experiences, especially with his father, the abusive older boys, and the stranger, significantly distorted his sense of self-esteem and confidence in his value to others. These experiences of victimization then intertwine with the vulnerability of his normal developmental needs for experiences of acknowledgment and the possibility that his care would be valued. Not surprisingly, several years later, we find Dick seeking to secure himself through relational dependence with Joan, the young adolescent with whom he fathered a child when himself a teen. Dick's false optimism regarding this relationship and later his relationship with Pat, his wife, bespeaks the corruption of pretending he could secure himself through absolutizing the good of their love. It may be that his sexual misconduct was precipitated by the recognition that Pat had rejected his care. It does seem clear that shame and the corruption of Dick's passion for an intimate, caring relationship destructively coincide to lend a primacy to this dimension of his experience in our assessment.

Embodiment. Embodiment refers to the biological possibilities and realities of human life. The natural egocentrism of our needs for satisfaction and competition begin as biological urges and are soon extended by the values and symbols of culture such as achievement in school and work.[32] Any dimension of human reality—agency, relationality, and the social—interacts with our physical being. Corruptions of human reality or contrasting experiences of being founded (secure in God's love) in any sphere will affect us biologically. Because our agency is embodied, our benign, biologically rooted capacity to resist whatever frustrates our fulfillment may be corrupted into enmity when the dynamics of idolatry lead us to absolutize whatever resists us.[33]

Because we remember the past, resentments and old assaults—both personal and cultural—accumulate and structure our personality. Malice and control are two resulting forms of enmity.[34] Malice is a personalized form of resistance to those identified as enemies because they have in some way threatened what we have absolutized for a sense of security. Control represents a less personalized response to persons or institutions that seem to threaten the conditions deemed necessary to assure the continuation of our absolutized satisfaction.[35] Of course, malice and control may also be combined.

Dick's experience after his parents' divorce illustrates the cumulative resentments that resulted in a posture of malice toward his half-brother because of his apparent favored status and privileges due in fact to the divorce rather than any action by this child. But how does our threefold schema of the vulnerability of human reality to violation offer us insight into Dick's sexual violence, first through his exposure of himself to young girls he did not know and then through the molestation of his daughter?

To answer this fully we will need to include how idolatry or "the lie" corrupts the sphere of the interhuman or relationality. But it is important to discern the possible significance of the ways Dick's experience of sexual abuse may have altered the freedom of his bodily life. Remember that corruptions in any of the several spheres of human reality have access to our biologically rooted striving for satisfaction or resistance and may corrupt those benign forms of our resistance.[36] When he was eight years old, Dick's passion for the interhuman—the longing to have his being and need for belonging confirmed—was exploited and cruelly violated by much older adolescent boys who required him to submit to oral sex as an initiation into their group and rejected him even after such humiliation.

Vast are the destructive consequences of such an experience of violation. This abuse was an utterly dehumanizing, insulting disregard for the irreducible uniqueness and value that characterizes the way Dick or any of us experience the unity of our embodied selves. We attribute meaning and value to our biological and physical givenness. Though not yet sexually aware, Dick realized he had experienced evil or violation and the humiliation otherwise described as shame from those whose affirmation he had absolutized. Shame's destruction is now intertwined with the vulnerability of physical sexuality. What Levinas describes as face—that fragility of being which ideally elicits reciprocities of compassion and obligation—was utterly violated. Later, when Dick was eleven, a stranger also sexually violated him, an experience that he describes as a source of great shame. To some extent the consequences of such violations are subject to a victim's idiosyncratic psychical structures and history. We can, however, discern that these violations set in motion severe deprivations that would metastasize from this sphere of individual agency to the spheres of the interhuman (relationality) and the social.

The medium of sexuality is highly symbolic for gender identity and communication. If one's sexuality is the locus of extremely shameful and violent experiences of evil and powerlessness, it is not difficult to imagine how one's freedom to be at ease with one's self or others of the same or different gender would be significantly diminished. That Dick's perpetrators were male is also complicating because of this culture's pervasive homophobia. His sense of self-contempt originates in his sexuality. Such violations, moreover, no doubt accumulate resentment that may contribute to subsequent attitudes of malice and control. It is no accident that Dick began to perpetrate sexual violence when his wife abruptly ended all physical and emotional intimacy. He experienced this rejection through the frame of one whose security in the world lay in this relationship and whose poor sense of self-esteem and powerlessness made direct confrontation seem impossible. The psychopathology of shame and the lies sin requires weave tightly together in this story.

The Sphere of the Interhuman
This sphere draws our attention to a phenomenon easily missed because we focus on individuals or social structures rather than on the more elusive relation between persons. Violation in this sphere causes two reciprocally related sinful postures: resentment and guilt.[37] The posture of resentment is an "enduring wound" created by another's violation of the wounded one's personhood; that is, the vulnerability we bring to relationships (the summons of the face) is disregarded or abused. When violation happens in relationships, the summons of this fragility or vulnerability changes to accusation. Similarly guilt arises when one violates the implicit relational obligation to care for the other. These two responses affect the relationship itself and are not simply internalizations of individual participants. These wounds also are internalized and thus have widespread effects.

Dick's life story includes several significantly alienated intimate relationships characterized by resentment and guilt as well as his personal history of victimization and his reported postures of resentment. Imagine the toxic effect of the feelings Dick and his daughter experience in their relationship. We do not know her feelings directly, but judging by her decision not to see him, it is fair to presume resentment. We do know that Dick describes enormous guilt. The gulf between them is currently unbridgeable. His guilt has sometimes created suicidal feelings, and his sense of value and worth have been minimal. Dick's guilt and his daughter's resentment are enduring factors in any future relationship between the two. In Dick's marriage certainly his perception of Pat's rejection left him feeling deep resentment. If his assessment be accurate, she, too, acted out of resentment, not only with him but with earlier husbands who violated her. Those old wounds, internalized earlier, festered and poisoned this later relationship.

Dick's relationship with Joan, the thirteen-year-old with whom he fathered a child, was certainly colored by his sense of violation and eventual resentment. At the time he reports his first acts of public sexual exposure, Dick describes a seriously alienated marriage in which he felt utterly and unfairly rejected by his wife, Pat. At the time he only knew that she had emotionally and sexually withdrawn from their relationship. Now he believes she was reacting to her own history of sexual and physical abuse. He felt that once again what had been promised (as with his father and the abusive boys) was withheld.

It is not difficult to imagine how responses of malice, control, resentment, and guilt could arise from Dick's personal and relational history. He brought to this marriage deep relational needs, hoping that they would be honored and that his need to offer care would be welcomed. The respective relational and sexual humiliation he felt with his half-brother and with the older abusive boys created a significantly heightened vulnerability to further emotional losses with a far less resilient sense of self. The relationship he describes with Joan is characterized by what Farley terms "false dependence" and current therapeutic language names as codependency—an emotional dependence in which one's own needs are met derivatively. This emotional vulnerability is certainly predictable given Dick's history. It is tragically predictable that having known first-hand the humiliating objectification and dehumanization of sexual abuse, Dick would choose this same medium in which to reclaim his sense of power and agency, although he found he needed to increase the frequency of his exposures to satisfy his need for a sense of control.

Once again we find the inextricable relation of shame-based postures of release and control and the idolatrous corruption of the spheres of individual agency and relationality or the interhuman.[38] The shame seems to add a paradoxical counterpoint of self-loathing that exacerbates the fearful threat feeding Dick's cycle of sexual violence. Indeed, he describes that self-loathing as deepening with each act of exposure, increasing his need for the power and confidence such acts brought, albeit briefly.

Placing a theological analysis alongside the therapeutic lens of shame-based compulsive behavior illumines further the tragedy of Dick's sexual violence. Now we can see more clearly the consequences of freedom diminished by victimization and corrupted by fear. Our analysis is incomplete, however, without attention to the larger social sphere also formative and interactive with Dick's behavior.

The Social Sphere
Individual agency and relationality do not exist in isolation but come together in the public or social sphere that is more than the sum of its parts. The social sphere is that historical cultural context in which powerfully formative forces, such as language, symbols, and values, are at work. In this sphere, of course, come the sedimentation of sin's effects in individual and relational experience. But sin is not limited to these. Infection is an apt metaphor to describe the way sin insinuates itself in such social structures. Of course, it may only remain to do its corrupting work through a cooperative process of collusion to systemically extend and absolutize enmity into subjugation.[39] For example, the idolatry of racial purity pervades a school system and maintains itself in the angry defense of segregation. Sin as subjugation presupposes the infection of social structures. Idolatrous self-absolutization in the sphere of individual agency here expands to infect the particular identity of an institution, ethnic group, or nation. Such entities then fearfully abuse their power to deny to other groups all elements of compassion that would summon obligation to them.[40] Now these other groups and individuals may be used or violently opposed, as racism illustrates painfully well.

In Christian tradition, original sin and the demonic describe this process of corruption in the social sphere. Suchocki describes the tragic structure of the social sphere as demonic—the cumulative result of sin in the personal and relational spheres. This demonic element surrounds individuals with overwhelming powers of destruction and inevitably involves all in the alienation of sin.[41] Unfortunately, those who experience subjugation likely internalize the alienation and violence projected toward them so that they participate in further limiting their own freedom and well-being. Those who subjugate others assent to evil, thus deepening their own bondage and increasing the force of the demonic.[42] However forceful this power of the demonic may be, one engages in "the lie" of sin if one denies the possibilities present for life-giving choices that are also available when "choosing" the demonic.[43]

In Dick's story we see evidence of the tremendous force of patriarchy in which the interests and goals of white men are granted pri-

ority with the corresponding right to use power unilaterally to subjugate women, people of color, and others whose status is deemed infe-
rior. The predominance of sexual abuse by older boys and men against
children suggests the interpenetration of corruption in the three
spheres but certainly the emergence in the social sphere of the tolerance of violence and the objectification of those "of no use" or "in the
way." The abusive older boys assented to the demonic character of
patriarchy in trivializing the no doubt irritating pleas of a lonely little boy whose mama had just brought him along when she moved in
with a man whose trailer was in their rural area. They had learned that
power was joined with their sexuality, and they abused Dick's vulnerability. Even as a young boy Dick had learned the constraints of
sexism that inhibited his freedom to seek comfort or help after his
experiences of abuse. He bore it "like a man" and certainly didn't want
to encourage homophobic suspicions.[44] As a man, Dick carried his history of such humiliation alongside the second rejection by a woman
in whom he had absolutized his worth and hopes. He, too, had learned
that in this culture he could objectify and control young girls who,
even with his diminished self-esteem, could be objectified for his use.
They, along with his daughter, were the anonymous girls to whom he
exposed himself. He assented to the demonic force of this ideology as
it interacted destructively with the corresponding vulnerabilities in
his individual and relational life. And he assented to "the lie" that he
was not free to act otherwise.

A NORMATIVE VISION OF HISTORICAL FREEDOM

Having ventured into the destructive consequences of human evil, it
is important to explore a normative, Christian vision of historical
freedom and faithfulness against which the language of sin's bondage
and idolatry are so starkly drawn. Suchocki's "lie" and Farley's theme
of refusal and resistance depict persons unable to tolerate the precarious ambiguities of historical existence who give way to the pretense
of some more immediate sense of security, meaning, and love. But evil
originates in this active refusal or lie because it leads us away from
God's power to found or secure and initiates destructive distortions of
worldly goods now forced to satisfy ultimate longings.[45]

Rather than a stoic bravado, the Christian paradigm asserts that
only God's sacred presence as Creator can assume or found our long-

ing for meaning and care. Such redemptive experience is mediated historically through the milieu of a community of faith, and faith is witnessed through acts of love. In faith communities, of course, we are not immune to the dynamics of evil, but these are mediated in conjunction with God's saving presence through disciplines of worship, service, and prayer.[46]

This experience of "being-founded" is the moment in which the bondage of sin yields to true freedom, a posture from which we can relativize the value of worldly goods and restore to them a penultimate status, consent to our historical existence with appreciation for what is beautiful and good, and, trusting God's care, risk venturing amidst the ambiguities of historical existence with courage and hope.

In this Judeo-Christian paradigm the evil we have described is a refusal or lie about God's power to found or save. Hence, this communally mediated experience of God's gracious presence is one of reconciliation. Acts of relativization, consent, and risk are dimensions of faithful obedience. In fact, Dick recognizes that his process of recovery includes very different transformative experiences of God's presence. He describes the sense that as a perpetrator "I was turning my back on God," but as he has acknowledged his violation of others and faced his accountability as well as his own history of abuse, Dick now says, "I am receiving unconditional love I couldn't get from anywhere else." Dick is describing the historical freedom made possible as he rejects the lies of his earlier perpetration of abuse and the distortions of the psychopathology that contributed to his diminished freedom. It is important to recognize that just as the corruptions and constrictions of evil and psychopathology destructively intertwine, the liberation of faithfulness and healing are similarly expansive. Of course, this normative vision of historical freedom or redemption is not simply the absence of idolatrous distortion. Rather it arises through the experience of being founded in a tragically structured world by God's reconciling presence. It is not simply a freedom from sin; it is a freedom for love.

One description of this normative vision for love that guides Dick and his pastor is briefly articulated in "A Brief Statement of Faith" mentioned earlier. Here Steve has a communally shared resource for encouraging Dick to deepen his experience of being founded by God's reconciling love. The themes of reconciliation, the relativization of mundane goods, consent to the limits and possibilities of historical existence, trust of God's care, and the risks of discipleship are accessible for their reflection together and their shared experience of worship.

> We trust in God the Holy Spirit,
>> everywhere the giver and renewer of life.
> The Spirit justifies us by grace through faith,
>> sets us free to accept ourselves and
>>> to love God and neighbor,
>> and binds us together with all believers
>> in the one body of Christ, the Church. . . .
>
> In a broken and fearful world
> the Spirit gives us courage
>> to pray without ceasing,
>> to witness among all peoples to Christ
>>> as Lord and Savior,
>> to unmask idolatries in Church and culture,
>> to hear the voices of peoples long silenced,
>> and to work with others for justice, freedom,
>>> and peace.
> In gratitude to God, empowered by the Spirit,
>> we strive to serve Christ in our daily tasks
>> and to live holy and joyful lives. . . .[47]

This description of life in the Spirit, or being founded, suggests a life of faith that relies on the possibilities inherent in the several spheres of reality. But these lines also disclose an awareness of a constant tension with the possible corruptions of these same spheres of individual agency, relationships, and social structures. The bondage of evil and suffering are the backdrop of this vision as it describes in previous lines sin's corruption in the human community and among people of faith. The struggle is contemporary, for this world is described as broken and fearful. Who could repeat these lines thinking faith's trust or the life of faith is easy? Such vulnerability requires courage. The life of faith is a commitment to justice shaped by reverence and joy. Gratitude to God is the "habit of being" for those who experience God's founding love.

CONCLUSION

We began this exploration with the troubling realization that our classical theology of sin was not adequate for helping us discern how

Dick could choose to perpetrate sexual violence. We have carefully explored the proposal that sin arises as a response to the tragic structures of our human condition rather than as sheer, inexplicable volition in rebellion against God and a violation of neighbor and self. On the other hand, we have been able to confirm with the tradition that sin is not equated with the suffering of the human condition, however oppressive its destructive force may be. In taking this context of tragic vulnerability seriously, we have recognized the centrality of the theme of freedom in exploring the different ways in which sin and psychopathology arise and endure in human experience.

Through the tragedy of Dick's experience, we have also observed how closely sin and the victimization of psychopathology interpenetrate, shaping each other interactively. The victimization of shame metasticized like cancer throughout the three spheres of Dick's reality. Deepened by his alienating and fearful behavior, it created the particular vulnerabilities his controlling, angry resentment and his guilt would exploit in futile efforts to secure himself in a relational environment that was ambiguous at best and often hostile. Those structures of Dick's life most affected by victimization—self-esteem, sexuality, and relationality—were precisely the points of fearful vulnerability at which the corruption of sin occurred. Dick's angry control, resentment, and guilt erupted in the repeated subjugation of young girls through sexual molestation, both anonymous and incestuous. It is a tragic illustration of the way sin and psychopathology interact, deepening their destructive consequences.

This exploration of the different ways in which sin and psychopathology impose bondage on our freedom reinforces the importance of refuting any conflation of these two categories in pastoral diagnosis. Sin is a distinctive, truthful, and important lens for interpreting the roots and dynamics of the violence and suffering that tear the fabric of the human community. There is much room for fruitful dialogue between therapeutic approaches and theological analysis around such themes as freedom, shame, power, and fear. While our focus has been sin, the lens of shame offers promise of further insight as a common psychological and theological resource for understanding the bondage of sin and psychopathology as they interact.[48]

Beyond assessment, the experience of being founded and the freedom emerging in faithfulness are also suggestive for the helpfulness our theological resources offer toward healing and the profound free-

dom for love. What is encouraging about this attention to the significance of sin as a response to our tragic context is that the interpenetration of these spheres of human reality that contributed to sin's
power to corrupt also extends the life-giving experience of being
founded by God's grace. The interdependence of sin and psychopathology also suggests how healing the wounds of victimization and
reconciling the alienating corruption of sin inform one another
positively. Attention to sin's reality and power will enhance our
resources for mediating the enlivening power of God's gift—the freedom for love.

NOTES

1.   For particularly helpful discussions of current therapeutic theo-
ries, see David Finkelhor, *Child Sexual Abuse* (New York: The Free
Press, 1984), and Terry S. Trepper and Mary Jo Barrett, *Systemic
Treatment of Incest* (New York: Brunner/Mazel, 1989).

2.   For a further exploration of the correspondence between the
ancient debate about sin and freedom and our contemporary context
see Robert R. Williams, "Sin and Evil," 168–95, in *Christian Theology*,
ed. Peter Hodgson and Robert King (Minneapolis: Fortress Press,
1982).

3.   Augustine, *On Free Choice of Will*, trans. Anna S. Benjamin and
L. H. Hackstoff (Indianapolis: Bobbs-Merrill, 1964), III–xvii.

4.   Augustine, *City of God*, trans. Gerald Walsh, Demetrius Zema,
Grace Monahan, and David Honan (New York: Image Books, 1958),
XI.12.221.

5.   Ibid., XIV.3.330.

6.   John Calvin, *Institutes of the Christian Religion*, 2 vols., trans. Ford
Lewis Battles (Philadelphia: Westminster Press, 1960), vol. 1,
2.1.4245.

7.   Augustine, *City of God*, XIV.1295.

8.   Marjorie Suchocki, *God, Christ, Church*, new rev. ed. (New York:
Crossroad, 1993),17.

9.   Augustine, *Confessions*, trans. Rex Warner (New York: New
American Library, 1963), 8.6.169.

10.   Presbyterian Church (U.S.A.), "A Brief Statement of Faith," in
The Book of Confessions (Louisville, Ky.: Office of the General Assembly,
1991), 10:3.

11. Cf. Marjorie Hewitt Suchocki, *The End of Evil* (Albany: State University of New York Press, 1988), 81, for a fuller discussion of this ambiguity.

12. I am indebted to Edward Farley's careful philosophical reflections on the nature of human reality and the tragic structures of the human condition that are a significant context for the origins and dynamic process of human evil. Farley's discussion of three spheres of human reality provides the structure for the following reflections on the human condition. Edward Farley, *Good and Evil* (Minneapolis: Fortress Press, 1990), 124–30.

13. Farley makes an essential move here to establish the interhuman as a key to understanding tragic and ethical elements of human reality. Noting the shortcomings of cognitive and utilitarian foci on relationality, he relies especially on Martin Buber and Emmanuel Levinas, philosophers of dialogue. They attend to the irreducible of mystery of face, codiscerned fragility, and summons to compassionate obligation that may be honored in the sphere of relationality. Cf. Ibid., 37–44.

14. Ibid., 33–40.

15. Emmanuel Levinas, *Ethics and Infinity*, trans. R. A. Cohen (Pittsburgh: Duquesne University Press, 1985), 97.

16. Farley, *Good and Evil*, 41, and Nel Noddings, *Caring* (Berkeley: University of California Press, 1984).

17. Farley, *Good and Evil*, 43.

18. Ibid., 47.

19. Ibid., 57ff.

20. Ibid., 63–113.

21. Ibid., 72.

22. Ibid., 98.

23. See Edward Farley, "Psychopathology and Human Evil: Toward a Theory of Differentiation," in *Crosscurrents in Phenomenology*, ed. Ronald Bruzina and Bruce Wilshire (Boston: Martinus Nijhoff, 1978), 211–30, for an extended discussion of the different ways psychopathology and sin arise and endure in human experience and the ways they limit freedom differently.

24. Cf. Suchocki, *God, Christ, Church*, 14–17.

25. Ibid., 22.

26. Ibid., 24.

27. Ibid., 18, 26–27.

28. Farley, *Good and Evil*, 132–33.

29. Gershen Kaufman, *Shame: The Power of Caring,* 2d ed. rev. (Cambridge, Mass.: Schenkman Books, 1985), 7, 11, 29–30; cited by Nancy J. Ramsay, "Sexual Abuse and Shame: The Travail of Recovery," 112–23, in *Women in Travail and Transition,* Maxine Glaz and Jeanne Stevenson-Moessner, eds. (Minneapolis: Fortress Press, 1991).

30. Farley, *Good and Evil,* 160–64.

31. Ibid., 209.

32. Ibid., 214.

33. Ibid., 222–25.

34. Ibid., 224.

35. Ibid., 225.

36. Ibid., 222.

37. Ibid., 238–42.

38. For a helpful discussion of shame-based patterns of compulsive cycles of behavior, see Merle A. Fossum and Marilyn Mason, *Facing Shame* (New York: W. W. Norton and Co., 1986).

39. Farley, *Good and Evil,* 256–60.

40. Ibid., 260.

41. Suchocki, *God, Christ, Church,* 15.

42. Ibid., 17–18.

43. Ibid., 18.

44. For an insightful exploration of the consequences of patriarchy on men's sexuality and spirituality, see James B. Nelson, *The Intimate Connection* (Louisville, Ky.: Westminster/John Knox, 1988).

45. Farley, *Good and Evil,* 144–50.

46. Cf. Craig Dykstra, "The Formative Power of Congregations," *Religious Education* 82/4 (Fall 1987): 530–46.

47. Presbyterian Church, "Brief Statement of Faith," 10.4.

48. For additional reflection on the relation between shame and experiences of freedom and sin, see Donald Capps, *The Depleted Self* (Minneapolis: Fortress Press, 1993); Nancy Ramsay, "Sexual Abuse and Shame"; and Susan L. Nelson, "Soul-Loss and Sin," in *Losing the Soul: Essays in the Social Psychology of Religion,* ed. Richard Fenn and John McDargh (Buffalo: State University of New York Press, 1995).

CHAPTER SEVEN

§

Freedom for Love:
A Relational Ethic

For freedom Christ has set us free. Stand firm,
therefore, and do not submit again to a yoke of slavery.

Gal. 5.1 (NRSV)

Freedom for love served as the horizon against which we explored sin's
bondage in the previous chapter. Freedom for love suggests more than
simply a freedom from sin—a restoration to some status quo; rather,
it refers to an intentional response to God's grace founded on a trust
that life is loved in God's care. Both freedom and love are subject to
various distortions in our culture, though each is inveighed as if universally understood and valued. Christian tradition envisions love as
the goal of human freedom—love for God, self, and neighbor; love
that intends encouragement of each other and the strengthening of the
whole community. Christian love has a historical concreteness that
begins with God's creation for life in community and continues
through the incarnation's invitation to love as Jesus of Nazareth loved
us. Nearly every Christian would quickly agree that love is the guiding ethic of this faith. Sometimes it seems we can be just as equally
divided in discerning what love requires when faced with particular
situations. In this chapter we will explore sources of confusion about
love that plague the contemporary practice of pastoral diagnosis.

Of course, diagnosis presumes shared values or normative images
of human fulfillment by which the level or severity of brokenness is

175

measured and recovery assessed. As we discovered, such images may vary dramatically depending on the paradigm or lens by which one views dis-ease.

In the several psychological paradigms with which many pastors work, we find a remarkable diversity of normative images. In the medical model Freud and the subsequent psychoanalytic tradition propose a rational, self-aware individual who is competent in work and love, that is, who is able to sustain loving relationships and be productive in her or his career. Larger expectations of commitments beyond self-interest are explicitly rejected.[1] Normative images in the humanistic psychology model also presume a fundamental individualism and define freedom as autonomy, but the sense of constraints on human possibilities evident in the medical model are replaced with a goal of unrestrained self-potentiation. The image of harmony with others is a harmony of individuals each engaged in self-development. Bowen's systemic image of a "solid self" is one who is differentiated in relationships, relies on logic for decision making, defines freedom as autonomy, and is accountable to her- or himself for self-defined principles and commitments.

Christian tradition projects a quite different normative image that presumes theocentric and communal reference points. Human beings are created in the image of a loving and just God for life in community. Rather than an autonomy motivated by self-potentiation, persons are called to exercise a freedom disciplined by God's loving justice disclosed most fully in Jesus of Nazareth. Clearly, the normative images in these several psychological paradigms and in Christian tradition vary so much as to compete with each other around such issues as the relation of the individual to the community, the notion of accountability beyond one's self, and universally or culturally rather than individually defined norms for behavior.

However, having identified such differences at this level of generality does not advance the task of pastoral diagnosis very far. Simply asserting the priority of love and relationality does not give Christians sufficient guidance for the complexities of life in community. Daniel Day Williams defines love as "that expression of spirit that has communion in freedom as its goal"[2] and reminds us that, having named love as our guiding ethic, we must still sort through often competing interests to discern what action will best serve growth in our communion with God and one another.[3]

Effective pastoral diagnosis requires more clarity at two junctures: (1.) What does critical reflection on long-standing differences within Christian tradition's interpretation of love and freedom suggest for pastoral practice? (2.) How do we engage in the public theological task of claiming a priority for Christian norms of relationality in which freedom is constrained by love that is ordered by justice and guided by the vision of a mutuality of care? Consideration of these two concerns will guide this chapter. We will focus first on finding our way through differing Christian responses to the norms of love and freedom and then move to the implications of such perspectives for engaging differing therapeutic normative images.

CHRISTIAN INTERPRETATIONS
OF LOVE AND FREEDOM

In Christian scriptures the primary definition of faithfulness is love for God and for our neighbors as we love ourselves.[4]

> You shall love the Lord your God with all your heart, and with all your soul, and with all your strength, and with all your mind; and your neighbor as yourself.[5]

In this chapter we will pursue how this normative image in Christian tradition offers guidance for the practice of pastoral care and counseling. Accepting the complex ties of neighbor-love is always a challenge. In contemporary North American Christianity this is so at two particularly striking ways: recovering the threefold command to love and incorporating into pastoral practice an intrinsically relational concept of the self and of human freedom. These two concerns are closely related.

The threefold command to love God, neighbor, and self has long been reduced to a twofold command to love God and a domesticated version of neighbor. In congregations any positive interpretation of love of self has been undermined by a singular focus on pride as the definition of sin. One consequence of this was inadequate attention to the sin of refusing to be a self and to develop one's gifts. Love as a guiding ethic was further diminished by a limited definition of neighbor that trivialized the radicality of scripture's vision of love into care for those like one's self. This division of love and justice reduced love to sentimentality and justice to charity. We will explore interpretations of neighbor-love that recover a balance between sacrificial love and love of self so that mutuality rather than self-sacrifice is the ideal we seek to create. Moreover, such mutuality is radical—a solidarity with all whom God loves.

The second and related difficulty for interpreting the love command lies in the strikingly separative concept of the self that prevails in North American culture. Maturity has become defined by the ideal of highly individuated persons who exercise freedom as autonomy. These values for differentiation and autonomy are pervasive in personality theory and therapeutic practice. We will explore alternative developmental and personality theories that allow us to incorporate models of maturity that reflect the complexity of living with love and exercising freedom disciplined by commitments to love.

A SITUATION IN MINISTRY

These issues of love and freedom arise daily in pastoral practice. The following situation in ministry discloses their significance for shaping those norms that guide our diagnoses and interventions.

Pat is a thirty-five-year-old Caucasian woman who divorced her husband, Jeff, after years of emotional and then physical abuse that had begun to include their oldest child as well. Despite several law enforcement interventions, Jeff was able to avoid a trial and remains in town as a prominent realtor. Pat has primary custody of the two children, Mary, age eight, and Jeffrey, age ten. She receives minimal child support from Jeff and is employed as an administrative assistant in a bank. She has chosen to move her church membership to Good Shepherd Lutheran (ELCA) since Jeff is an officer in First Lutheran where they were married eleven years ago.

Good Shepherd, a small parish of two hundred persons, was founded eight years ago as a new development project by the synod in what was then the growing suburban area of the city. George, forty-five, is the second pastor. He has been at Good Shepherd for two years. The congregation supports a nearby community ministry, but its public witness is largely limited to the practices of individual members. The church includes many principally Caucasian young and middle-aged, professional and managerial middle-class families. Mary and Jeffrey are finding friends, and Pat hopes she will feel at home.

Pat sought counseling at the Spouse Abuse Center while she was making her decision to reject Jeff's battering, and she continues to see a therapist there on a biweekly basis. As religious issues arose in her therapy, Pat decided to seek out George for pastoral care.

Over several conversations, Pat describes her struggle to cope with her choice to divorce Jeff. She decided to leave Jeff and the marriage only when Jeff hit Jeffrey when he sought to restrain his father during an argument with Pat. Jeff continued to refuse treatment for battering, citing Pat's incompetence as a wife and mother as just cause for his temper. She spent eleven years of her life trying to please her husband and give their children the love they needed. Jeff was under a lot of pressure as he built up his business. Pat tried to accommodate his needs so that gradually she gave up the activities she enjoyed to be more available to meet his demands, but she could never get things just right. She had failed to be the wife he needed, but he had crossed the line when he hit Jeffrey. She needed to protect the children so she left. But it is so hard to see them suffer from the divorce. Financially, things are much harder. Jeff remarried quickly, and the children spend weekends there twice a month, where they enjoy their earlier standard of living and report that their father is fun to be with now. She knows Jeff has a problem with his temper and had no right to hit her or the children, but can she be sure she did everything she could? She had promised to love him in sickness and in health. Did she love him enough? Good Christians are willing to suffer in behalf of love. Did Jesus expect her to stay and be beaten?

DISCERNING AMONG THEOLOGICAL RESOURCES

Pat's situation poses a number of concerns George could pursue that theological ethicists such as Marie Fortune and theoretical material on domestic violence have taught us to address.[6] However, the absence of any understanding of the place of love for self alongside the norm of sacrificial love Pat has learned so well is surely a central theological theme in her poignant conversations with George.

George faces particular challenges as a Lutheran pastor in the constructive retrieval of resources for a liberative and transformative response to Pat's need for a new understanding of love for God, self, and neighbor. Martin Luther was a strong voice in behalf of the priority of love for neighbor based on the freedom that God's grace in Jesus' life and death provides for us.[7]

Luther turned to the second chapter in Philippians in which Paul writes:

> Do nothing from selfish ambition or conceit, but in humility regard others as better than yourselves. Let each of you look not to your own interests, but to the interests of others. Let the same mind be in you that was in Christ Jesus. . . .[8]

Of course Luther came to this concern for recovering the freedom to love from the abuses of grace reigning in the Roman church in the sixteenth century.

More important for our purposes, Luther presumed a dualistic notion of the self in which all persons were engaging in a "battle" to subdue a strong, autonomous, self-absorbed, carnal self whose obedience to such a call for humility would be the appropriate corrective discipline for the desires of the flesh. Luther presumed that pride, the assertion of too much self, was everyone's dilemma. In fact he could not imagine anyone unable adequately to love themselves. This assumption on his part is especially clear in his *Lectures on Romans* in which he comments on the command to love our neighbors as ourselves, noting it can be understood in two ways and commending only one:

> First, one can take it to mean that both are commanded: we shall love our neighbor and ourselves as well. But another way to understand it is that it commands us to love only our neighbor and this according to the example of our love for ourselves. This is the better interpretation, for because of the defect of his nature, man [*sic*] loves himself above everything else, he seeks himself in everything, and loves everything for his own sake, even when he loves his neighbor or his friend, for he seeks only his own therein. . . . For who is so useless that he hates himself? However, nobody is such a nonentity that he does not love himself, and the love he has for others is not like the love he has for himself.[9]

Luther's emphasis on this interpretation of neighbor-love that idealizes self-sacrifice at the expense of mutual love of self and neighbor was extended in this century by the Lutheran theologian Anders Nygren. Nygren also presumed the dualism Luther described and contrasted self-serving desire (eros) with sacrificial love for others (agape).

> Agape . . . excludes all self-love. Christianity does not recognise self-love as a legitimate form of love. Christian love moves in two

directions, towards God and towards its neighbour; and in self-love
it finds its chief adversary, which must be fought and conquered. It
is self-love that alienates man [*sic*] from God, preventing him from
sincerely giving himself up to God, and it is self-love that shuts up
a man's heart against his neighbour. . . . Agape recognises no kind of
self-love as legitimate.[10]

Martin Luther and Anders Nygren are representative voices for an
interpretation of neighbor love that idealizes sacrificial love and warns
against the danger of love of self. The influence of their interpretation
extends far beyond Lutheran tradition. Certainly it is not difficult to
understand how a woman like Pat, despite her history of being bat-
tered and seeing her son hit, still wonders if her love was sufficiently
long-suffering. Her situation helps disclose problems intrinsic to this
interpretation of the love command. It is quickly apparent to George,
her pastor, that the traditional interpretation in which he has been
schooled is not adequate at all for responding to a woman whose primary experiences include inadequate self-regard and victimization by
another. As pastoral theologian Marie McCarthy suggests, when agape
or, more popularly, neighbor-love is reduced to self-sacrifice, there is
"no basis for distinguishing between attention to other's needs and
submission to their exploitation. Nor . . . [is there] any warrant for
resisting the latter."[11]

The traditional interpretation of the threefold command as a
twofold one and the exclusive elevation of neighbor-love to defend
against presumed inordinate self-love reflect a patriarchal bias. This
interpretive bias left both Luther and Nygren unable to imagine Pat's
experience of too little sense of self. The clause "as yourself," which
assures mutuality as the ethical criterion for human love, was viewed
as dangerous.

The reduction of mutuality to self-sacrifice created several significant problems that continue to haunt any of us who engage in the
practice of pastoral care:

(1.) It contributes to a naiveté about power in relationships by
making invisible those who experience the other side of the dominance of too much self so worrying to Luther and Nygren.

(2.) It reduces the complexity of the human experience of alienation from God and one another by collapsing descriptions of sin
exclusively into pride.

(3.) It narrows our understanding of God's love to a singular focus on the crucifixion that ironically has encouraged a privatization of love and human freedom and a division of love and justice.

(4.) It has supported a very inadequate concept of the self not amenable to subsequent theological and psychological insights.

CREATED IN GOD'S IMAGE:
THE NORM OF MUTUALITY

If we shift the hermeneutical key for interpreting the love command from the lens of the crucifixion to that of God's creation of us in God's image, we find a way to restore attention to all three foci of this command, restore mutuality as the ethical criterion for human love, and respond to the four concerns listed above. Gene Outka, a Lutheran theological ethicist, describes such a shift as placing the love command within a "theocentric frame."[12] To do so is to recover the priority of the first command to love God with all our being. Our value and identity are rooted in God's creative love for each of us equally. This affirmation orders our love for one another properly, for it clarifies that the value and worth of each person is unique in God's eyes. When we make this universal love of God our hermeneutical key for the love command, we recover mutuality as our ethical criterion for love in the human community. We are called to love whom God loves.[13] Through the lens of God's universal love it is also clear that each of us is equally dependent on God's redeeming grace and given gifts to serve. We are born into a relational web of interdependence, as the Genesis stories affirm.

The criterion of mutuality affirmed in the ethic of God's universal love substantiates the importance of adequate self-regard and verifies the importance of attention to power and empowerment in every relational sphere. The imbalance of power is especially clear in abusive relationships such as Pat's. As Daniel Day Williams points out, "Love is that expression of spirit that has communion in freedom as its goal."[14] When mutuality replaces self-sacrifice as the norm of love, it becomes clear that in his work with Pat, it is not a matter of George giving her power as if it were his to give; however, he can choose to work alongside her and in the congregation and public to transform structures, systems, and attitudes (including her own about herself) that deflect, distort, or seek to destroy her own sense of empowerment worn away by her abuse. Williams's phrase "communion in freedom" makes mutuality more concrete, for it clarifies a goal of empowerment for those whose agency is undermined. It also bespeaks a proactive tone in that it rejects what we earlier described as sin's "lie"[15] of assenting to self- and other-destructive behavior as if it could not have been otherwise. Love's goal of communion in freedom calls for choosing to see and hear and act in behalf of the empowerment of all whom God loves as well as ourselves.

Mutuality as the ethical norm for life in community also helps George respond to the obvious problem with the traditional interpretation of neighbor-love that presumes pride is the singular form of sin. Mutuality as our norm does not refute the importance of pride as a form of sin, but because mutuality asserts the worth and value of each person in God's eyes and the value of the gifts of each of us for the community, the refusal to be a self or sloth emerges as equally problematic. It is this sin of too little value for herself and the long refusal to act in her own behalf that Pat's predicament illustrates painfully well. When Pat wonders with her pastor whether she loved her abusive husband enough, he may engage her around the absence of love for herself as an even more pressing question in her situation. Why would she so disregard herself as one whom God treasures? It is especially important to realize that mutuality asserts the value and service of each life within the context of the whole community. This means that encouraging Pat to practice self-regard is not at all like the larger culture's preoccupation with self-gratification because one "deserves it" or is "worth it." Behind the wisdom of recovering the sin of sloth is the awareness that Pat's life is of value because God created and loves her. Self-love is directly referenced to God rather than an arbitrary assertion of value.[16] We want Pat to realize that her life is as valuable as the lives of those for whom she has cared so solicitously. We also want her to realize that her life is not interchangeable with their lives; rather, she has particular gifts to offer that the community needs.[17]

Our third concern with traditional interpretations of the command for neighbor-love lies in the distortion it requires of our understanding of the crucifixion and the atonement of Christ. Luther and Nygren both assert the crucifixion as the defining hermeneutical key that establishes sacrificial love as the exclusive ideal for Christian life. Pat's situation, however, dramatically illustrates the difficulties with such a valorization of suffering.

This exclusive focus on the crucifixion obscures its context in the life and ministry of Jesus where the Gospels suggest that mutuality was the predominant form of love he modeled. To focus only on the crucifixion makes it appear as if the sole purpose for Jesus' life was to die so as to resolve the alienation between God and humankind. Lost is the connection between his death and the radical way he embodied love that made him too dangerous for civil and religious leaders alike. Jesus' life and ministry is the story of God's involvement in the concrete, liberative, transforming work of building communities in which each is valued and respected. As Daniel Day Williams suggested, "justice is the order which love requires,"[18] and Jesus' ministry showed the inextricable linkage of God's love and justice. But when the crucifixion is pulled from this context and idealized in an inevitably abstract way, its meaning is distorted and the linkage of justice and love is lost. Love apart from justice is subject to sentimentalization and trivialization. But that does not necessarily imply benign consequences, as we know from the number of women like Pat who have been counseled by clergy to go home to abusive spouses and love them more. No questions were raised about the right of a spouse to emotionally abuse and hit her or his partner. Similarly, as Beverly Harrison has noted, this trivialization of love has resulted in a discounting of the labor involved in the concrete acts of love not surprisingly classed as "women's work."[19] Ironically, denying the correlation between the importance of nurture and care that strengthen self-esteem and other-regarding behavior contributes to the frighteningly naive notions about self-love as dangerous in traditional interpretations of neighbor-love.

Decontextualizing the crucifixion also obscures who it was that Jesus loved. He did not define "neighbor" as those like oneself; rather, we find him modeling mutual regard with those marginalized in culture and religion by the shame of their circumstances, their gender, past actions, physical condition, and so forth. Jesus' death was linked with love that sought to empower and enfranchise. It was transformative and liberative in intent.

Outka's use of a theocentric frame helps us here, for its ethic of God's universal love embraces and undergirds Jesus' linkage of love and justice. It suggests an alternative interpretation of the crucifixion that retains its place in the broader context of God's love and Jesus' ministry in particular while not idealizing suffering. Through what

Calvin describes as the "whole course of his [Jesus'] obedience,"[20] we see a commitment to a radically mutual love, and in his death we see Jesus' refusal to renege on this way of loving one another. In this perspective, sacrificial love is offered as a means toward the realization of mutual love rather than love's ideal kept pure from other forms of love. Borrowing from the work of Josiah Royce on loyalty, Daniel Day Williams describes our understanding of atonement through this theocentric frame. He refers to the "double vision" we need for love, since its ideal as communion (full mutuality) also requires sustained loyalty to a humanity whose love for one another is not yet fully realized and is still marked by brokenness.[21] Jesus' choice to accept the cross was an act of commitment to a community of love still waiting a fuller realization.

It is important to emphasize that Jesus chose the cross as an active commitment to the love he embodied. In modern life the witness of Mahatma Gandhi and Martin Luther King, Jr. testify to the transforming power of the freedom to choose temporary suffering in behalf of love's possibilities. This choice of self-sacrifice is far different from some traditional interpretations of neighbor-love in which passive endurance of suffering seems to be a virtue. Certainly such an interpretation is painfully close to Pat's words to her pastor. If she had been willing to suffer longer would the marriage have healed? Her poignant self-abnegation is a logical consequence of a depiction of suffering as itself a value. Theologian Elizabeth Johnson describes the oppressive consequence of such an interpretation of the atonement for women, though similar consequences could be drawn from examples of antebellum preaching to enslaved African Americans:

> Structurally subordinated within patriarchy, women are maintained in this position, not liberated, by the image of a God who suffers in utter powerlessness because of love. The ideal of the helpless divine victim serves only to strengthen women's dependency and potential for victimization, and to subvert initiatives for freedom, when what is needed is growth in relational autonomy and self-affirmation. The image of a powerless, suffering God is dangerous to women's genuine humanity, and must be resisted.[22]

Johnson's prediction is chillingly verified in Pat's story.

Through his study of René Girard's research on the pervasive theme of the scapegoat in cultural and religious myth, William Placher reminds us that in the context of the whole of Jesus' ministry the atonement reverses this scapegoating of the troublemaker whose removal resolves the problem.[23] Rather, we see here that it is not Jesus but those who persecute him who are the problem. As Placher puts it,

> The story of Jesus tells us that love in its vulnerability risks suffering, that in a world of violence those who tackle injustice will sometimes suffer, and that, for those who have power, to renounce violence is the only way to move toward a world of equality. It is therefore a story that teaches its readers how to work to struggle against suffering, not how to glorify it.[24]

In identifying this ideal of mutuality, William Placher returns us again to the value of Gene Outka's theocentric ethical frame that locates the atonement within the sweep of God's universal love rather than abstracting it from the whole of Jesus' ministry, as Luther and Nygren's traditional interpretations do.

For us engaged in pastoral diagnosis and pastoral practice, recovering love's connection with justice and the radicality of mutuality demonstrated in Jesus' life and crucifixion is crucial. It returns the suffering of persons like Pat to a larger systemic context that revises and corrects temptations in contemporary pastoral practice to privatize suffering and obscure the transformative and liberative systemic possibilities of care. Not only is George encouraged to facilitate Pat's empowerment and more adequate self-regard, he is also reminded to view her abuse in the context of a society far too tolerant of violence against women and children. In responding to Pat, her pastor, George, joins her in struggling against violence by naming violence as the problem rather than allowing her to wonder if her love was inadequate. Diagnosis is the practice of "powerful knowledge."[25] George has the opportunity to challenge Pat's definition of the problem as her inadequate love for others[26] and to reframe her experience as an abuse of power and her husband's betrayal of covenantal promises. By responding in this way George refutes an enduring if often unintended collusion between clergy and the systemic, patriarchal violence by which Pat is victimized. He can challenge her meager self-regard by revisiting those same passages she has learned to read through the sacrificial lens of traditional interpretation. This case is a striking example of the ethical importance of clarity regarding interpretations of the love command for contemporary pastoral care.

A PUBLIC THEOLOGICAL CONVERSATION: CLAIMING A PRIORITY FOR CHRISTIAN NORMS OF MATURITY

Our concern here is not only to revise current understandings of love and freedom in the Christian community related to pastoral practice. We also need to offer a response to alternative images of self-fulfillment and relationality in therapeutic paradigms often used by pastors. Rather than responding to the several perspectives of the paradigms noted at the outset of the chapter, we will raise the common concern of the nature and possibilities for the self and offer a theologically informed proposal. Through the critical correlation of process-theological thought and an emerging developmental theory, we will demonstrate the remarkable interpretive power of a particular Christian theological view of the nature of the self and possibilities for love and freedom in relationships. In this way we are engaging in the process of practical theological reflection required by pastoral diagnosis.

We will continue to rely on Gene Outka's theocentric ethical frame and its roots in our creation in God's image to explore consequences for concepts of the self implicit in traditional and theocentric theological interpretations of the love command. But we will also turn to psychological research particularly identified with the Stone Center at Wellesley College that proposes a developmental theory of a self-in-relation and suggests related therapeutic concerns.[27] While the authors developed their theory focused particularly on women's experience, its implications clearly extend to human development more broadly, and subsequent research has noted its heuristic implications for men's experience.[28] This theory proposes that each person is intrinsically relational so that human development occurs in a dynamic, continuous, relational pathway across the lifespan. Clearly there is a remarkable convergence between such a developmental theory and Outka's description of a highly systemic, interdependent human community created for love of God and each other. While we will explore this convergence in depth, it is important to recognize difficulties in how the traditional interpretation of neighbor-love, when it conceptualizes the self, idealizes self-sacrifice as the exclusive norm of love.

Overcoming Dualism

Most striking is the dualism that pervades the self in Luther's and Nygren's interpretations. Luther describes the self as having a spiritual and bodily or carnal nature.[29] Nygren presumed this dualism and went on to propose a corresponding dualism in human capacities for love. He defined eros as self-love and emphatically stated that it could not be a legitimate form of Christian love.[30] While this dualism has its roots in Hellenism, its influence in Christian tradition is pervasive. Of course, such dualism is contradicted by an appreciation for the importance of God's affirmation of our created physical being and the incarnation of God's love in human form. Moreover, scripture does not adhere to a strict compartmentalization of *agape, eros,* or *philia.* Rather, if we repudiate this dualism, we can affirm that every human love participates in the goodness of God's creation.

Agape or self-giving does not displace all other forms of human love; rather, as Williams reminds us,

[a]gape offers the reconstituting of life so that every human love participates in a love greater than itself.

We now see human loves in a new light. *Agape* is not another love which is added to the others. Neither is it their contradiction. It is the love which underlies all others, leads them toward the discovery of their limits, and releases a new possibility in the self which is created for communion.[31]

We cannot love in isolation nor with disinterest because our very identity is intertwined in relationships. Pastoral care for Pat will require a relational, dynamic, interdependent concept of the self that can accommodate the development and nurture of her premoral needs for identity, relationality, and sociality as well as the historical and political realities of life in community. Moreover, such a concept also needs to accommodate the asymmetry that exists in our agency with regard to ourselves and toward others.

We have more control over our own behavior than that of others. This is true both in our relationship with God and with one another. As Outka suggests, we can direct our own actions (imperfectly), but we can only encourage another to act or feel in some particular way.[32] Correspondingly, we are most accountable for our own behavior. Pat can choose to love her husband, but she cannot force him to love her, nor is she responsible for his failure to do so. She is accountable for her choices and commitments. She needs a concept of the self that helps her identify not only her responsibility for her neighbor but also the boundaries or limits of her agency in behalf of her neighbor.

Love as a Relational Ethic

Pastoral diagnosis needs to be rooted in a theocentric ethical framework that is anchored in our creation in the image of God. This frame allows us to construct an alternative to the dualistic, separate self. Pastoral diagnosis is better served by a concept of the self that is dynamic, relational, and interdependent as well as cognizant of historical and political realities of personal and relational development. We find a promising and creative synthesis for such a concept of self in Daniel Day Williams's phenomenology of love through the lens of process theology and the emerging theories of the self-in-relationship.[33]

Both these resources share a profound appreciation for relationality as the ecology of human experience. Williams grounds this assertion in his description of the image of God as love—a dynamic relatedness for which we are created with our neighbor.[34] We are created for love or communion normatively defined in the life and ministry of Jesus of Nazareth. Recovering an appreciation for the ontological status of relationality helps us appreciate the power of the need for mutual, relational expressions of care. Williams rightly asserts that at the core of our selfhood is the will to belong which is more central than the will to power.[35] Of course, belonging is a dynamic that involves both the giving of self and receiving the influence of other(s). Williams described a dipolar self with both a drive for the integrity of its own identity and a drive for relatedness.[36] Abuses of power arise whenever the tensive balance of reciprocity in mutual respect and care is undone. One can see here how the value for an ethic of mutual respect and care is well grounded in such a theocentric, dynamic view of a relational self for whom giving and receiving are essential.

Just as our search for a more constructive theological ethic required retrieval of alternative resources to challenge traditional interpretations, so we also need to consider carefully the theoretical resources available to us in our construction of a more relational ethic. Many contemporary theories of development presume a linear process of individuation and separation toward a relatively self-defined exercise of freedom or agency.[37] In doing so they certainly reflect and extend this culture's value for the individual. It is apparent that such theories are problematic for a theological worldview that asserts relationality as an ontological reality. Janet Surrey,[38] a leading self-in-relation theorist, defines the self as intrinsically relational, arguing that relationships are the developmental context throughout our lives. Surrey describes development as a synchrony of progressive differentiation in both relationship and identity.[39] Of course, her definition of relationship lacks the christological content of Williams's "communion," but she shares his sense of a highly dynamic, evolving reciprocity with the expectation of mutuality. She defines relationship as "an experience of emotional and cognitive *intersubjectivity*: the ongoing, intrinsic inner awareness and responsiveness to the continuous existence of the other or others and the expectation of mutuality in this regard." She uses the apt metaphor of "conversation" to convey the sense of emotional and cognitive dialogue over time.[40] Her phrase "relationship authenticity" suggests the normative character of this dialogue that requires a commitment to risk, honesty, sharing the full range of emotions, working through conflict, and change.[41] Surrey does not use the word *love*, but the reciprocity of care woven throughout this description of authenticity in relationships suggests important continuities with Williams.

In asserting the value of Christian norms for the exercise of love and freedom in community, it is important to demonstrate the usefulness of such norms in relation to current psychological theory. It is also important to indicate the public value of these norms; that is, they are useful for human community, not simply Christian relationships. A question that poses both these issues well is, what is it about human beings that when nurtured in us allows love to flourish?

The Capacity for Love

Williams identified five interdependent features[42] that we will explore in dialogue with Surrey and her colleagues. These five features are: individuality, freedom, agency, openness to the causality of love, and a capacity for rational judgment within loving concern for others.

Individuality. The feature of individuality is important to both authors, as we find in their dipolar self whose concrete particularity is not lost despite its intrinsic relationality. The reciprocity of care does not require the negation of either party. Obviously, this feature implies a value for negotiation and a capacity for change without discounting the value of each person's experience. Relationship authenticity presumes two such individuals in ongoing conversation. The absence of respect for Pat's individuality is a striking characteristic of her husband's abuse of her. The particularity of her hopes and needs was negated.

Freedom. Apart from freedom our commitments to one another are meaningless because love presumes the absence of coercion. To enter into a relationship is to risk freely the dangers and possibilities of such a commitment. But once we exercise this freedom to enter a relationship, it is then characterized by historical, political, and emotional realities that become a part of our history and of the relationship. Freedom is shaped by its context. As Williams put it, "One of the marks of authentic love is growth in freedom to acknowledge the realities, and to keep the integrity of the self within those realities." The importance of this caution is poignantly apparent in the context of Pat's life where she felt less and less free to acknowledge the diminished possibilities for herself or to act to recover her own integrity.

Agency. Love or authentic relationality presumes the power to act. Because power is both the ability to influence and to receive the influence of another, obviously this will entail mutual accommodation to the needs of each other. As Williams points out, love inevitably entails suffering both because one chooses to limit one's self and because one experiences empathically the losses of the other. But while Williams discussion of the inevitability of suffering notes that it may be destructive, he does not help us discriminate when such suffering ought to be rejected, as would be the case in the context of domestic violence. Here Surrey offers a helpful corrective through her observation that authentic relationality is characterized by mutual empowerment in which a synergy is created that enlarges the energies, resources, and creativity of each.[43] Such empowerment requires the shared intentionality to nurture each other. This insight regarding mutual empowerment helps us to discern when suffering on the part of one or both of the parties in a relationship is destructive rather than painful but sustaining in a creative or life-enhancing way. It is important to acknowledge the presence of power in relationality and its reciprocal character, but it is also necessary to provide criteria for identifying mutual empowerment as a primary norm for love or relational authenticity.

Surrey's research also identifies empathy as a key resource for enhancing authentic relationality and the mutual empowerment that characterizes it. When relationality is identified as the ecology in which identity flourishes, then empathy emerges as a foundational skill. Judith Jordan, a colleague of Surrey, defines empathy as a complex threefold process that begins with (1.) the capacity and motivation to relate to the other; (2.) the affective surrender and cognitive structuring that allows one to experience the needs of the other as one's own; and (3.) the resumption of one's own reality now enlarged by the temporary identification with the other.[44] Obviously this is a skill that must be learned and practiced. It is dependent in part on the natural evolution of ego boundaries, but it also alerts us to the importance of the development of adequate, resilient, and flexible ego boundaries so that one may identify and differentiate one's own experience as well as relax and then recover one's own boundaries. As Jordan points out, in this culture many men may have such firm ego boundaries that it proves difficult for them adequately to imagine the affective experience of the other, so that they either intellectualize or project their own experience in place of the other's. Many women in this culture may experience such permeable boundaries that they lose the "as if" quality of empathy and either merge with the other or use the other as an extension of their own needs.[45] In the case of Pat it does appear that Jordan's analysis helps us identify inadequate ego boundaries. These permeable boundaries leave her vulnerable to merger with her husband's needs at the expense of her own; in fact, her needs or value seem unavailable to her awareness. Developing accurate empathy is an important skill that a relational concept of the self discloses.[46]

Causality of Love. The future-oriented, processive character of human experience is the fourth dimension to which Williams attended in his reflections on love. He rightly observed that this unfolding character of human being allows us to experience the causality of love.[47] By this he meant that love is a force that may alter human motivations and practices. In this he is reinforcing what Surrey has observed about empowerment in relationships. As Williams put it, "Being loved creates a new person."[48] Both Williams and Surrey pose an important ethical point for pastoral practice because they are observing that actions that intend the well-being and enhancement of another may well have enduring transformative effects at personal, interpersonal, and structural levels. Self-regard has other-regarding consequences. Pat's meager self-regard makes this point poignantly well. The absence or perversion of love in our relations is not benign— it is sin; it is destructive. On the other hand, the power of love to heal

Pat's experience of abuse is hopeful. This is one reason it is so problematic to sentimentalize and privatize love by a dualistic division of love and justice. Justice is the transforming order love intends.

Rationality. Williams' fifth observation about our capacity for love follows easily from the above discussion, for he asserts that love includes our rationality.[49] Here he means not only to refute once more the dualistic linkage of love with emotionality, but also to assert the appropriateness of our calculation of the needs of another.[50] He and Surrey presume our ability and responsibility to assess the needs of another and to act intentionally to advance the cause of love. Surrey refers to this as respons/ability that corresponds with our mutual empowerment to act through relationships.[51] Accurate empathy intends to refine our respons/ability. Since both authors have claimed the importance of mutuality in any interpretation of neighbor-love or relational authenticity, the norm of equity guides such calculation of need. Yet, the norm of equity never precludes our choice to set it aside temporarily in response to the need of another. "Choice" and "temporarily" are the operative words, for they signal that in a theocentric ethical frame sacrificial love is valued as a means toward the fullness of mutuality.

This dialogue between Williams and Surrey and her colleagues suggests the richness of this image of a relational self for pastoral practice and for healing responses more generally. Through their insights about the dynamics of our individuality, freedom, agency, responsiveness, and rationality, we see more clearly the possibilities for enlarging human freedom for love that is mutually life-giving and transformative. To be created in the image of God is to be created for love in community with all whom God loves. Such love serves God and neighbor. It is not some abstract possibility but concretely participatory. Because we are intrinsically relational, love that intends our mutual empowerment is vitally important. In fact, it would be fair to speak of sin as the failure to effect love in life—for others as well as for oneself.[52]

CONCLUSION

This more active and systemic understanding of love and of sin contributes to the public theological task in which pastoral diagnosis participates. Earlier in this chapter we noted how Pat's pastor, George, could draw on an understanding of love shaped through a theocentric rather than sacrificial lens to help Pat reframe her experience of suffering from a sign of her inadequacy in her marriage to an experience of an abuse of power. To do so he would break an enduring if unintended collusion between clergy and the norms of a culture that tolerates violence against women and children. George's action in this regard is not only a recovery of more adequate Christian resources for pastoral care; it also contributes to the public theological task of claiming a priority for Christian norms of relationality.

For example, George, pastors like him, and the congregations they serve can inform public conversations about the priority given to responding to domestic violence. As our reflection in this chapter suggests, they can do so with a theologically and psychologically sound understanding of the healing power of authentic relationality that is more helpful than contemporary more autonomous conceptions of the self.

Pastoral diagnosis is a praxis theological method. It begins in response to the concrete moments of pain that arise from the refusal to effect love in life or the distortions of such love in human relationships. Of course it is a valuable resource for articulating love that is life-giving and transformative in those particular situations. But the task of involvement in those concrete, painful situations offers valuable theological insight to empower religious leadership in both congregational and public contexts in which informed advocacy may shape opinion and action.

We began this chapter seeking a Christian ethic of love that could recover the mutuality of scripture's threefold command to love and offer us an alternative model of maturity to that of the linear, separate self so prominent in this culture and in the therapeutic models so influential for pastoral practice. Gene Outka's theocentric frame allowed us to broaden our focus on love from Luther's and Nygren's singular attention to the sacrificial death of Christ. Rather, we began with the affirmation of our creation in the image of God to love all whom God loves. We used this context of universal love to understand the atonement as an indication of God's commitment to a loving relationship with us and an invitation for us to love one another with the radical mutuality disclosed in the ministry of Jesus. The relationality explicitly valued in accounts of creation in God's image also led us to the theology of Daniel Day Williams and contemporary psychological theorists such as Janet Surrey who each describe an intrinsically relational self. Here maturity is found not in autonomous self-sufficiency but in relational authenticity and accurate empathy that promote mutual empowerment

Through these two shifts of focus, we have found a more adequate ethic to guide both our pastoral practice with those like Pat who struggle to embrace the freedom for love into which God invites us and our public advocacy for systemic change in behalf of love and justice.

NOTES

1.   Sigmund Freud, *The Future of an Illusion*, ed. James Strachey (New York: W. W. Norton, 1989).

2.   Daniel Day Williams, *The Spirit and the Forms of Love* (New York: Harper & Row, 1968), 3.

3.   Ibid., 272.

4.   See esp. Leviticus 19:17-18,34; Matthew 22:36-40; Mark 12:29-31; and Luke 10:25-28.

5.   Luke 10:27-28.

6.   See esp. Marie Fortune, *Violence in the Family* (Cleveland, Oh.: Pilgrim Press, 1991); Mary D. Pellauer, Barbara Chester, and Jane Boyajian, eds., *Sexual Assault and Abuse* (San Francisco: Harper & Row, 1987); and Pamela Cooper-White, *The Cry of Tamar* (Minneapolis: Fortress Press, 1995).

7.   Martin Luther, *Christian Liberty*, ed. Harold J. Grimm, trans. W.A. Lambert (Philadelphia: Fortress Press, 1957).

8.   Philippians 2:3-5 (NRSV).

9.   Martin Luther, *Lectures on Romans*, trans. and ed. Wilhelm Pauck (Philadelphia: Westminster Press, 1961), 366–67.

10.   Anders Nygren, *Agape and Eros,* trans. Philip Watson (Philadelphia: Westminster Press, 1953), 217.

11.   Marie McCarthy, "The Role of Mutuality in Family Structures and Relationships: A Critical Examination of Select Systems of Family Therapy from the Perspective of Selected Options in Contemporary Theological Ethics," Ph.D. diss., University of Chicago, 1985, 230.

12.   Gene Outka, "Universal Love and Impartiality," in *The Love Commandments*, ed. Edmund N. Santurri and William Werpehowski (Washington, D.C.: Georgetown University Press, 1992), 2.

13. Ibid.

14. Williams, *Spirit and the Forms of Love*, 3.

15. See here Marjorie Suchocki, *God, Christ, Church*, new rev. ed. (New York: Crossroad, 1993), 14–27.

16. Outka, "Universal Love," 84.

17. Ibid., 84–85.

18. Williams, *Spirit and the Forms of Love*, 250.

19. Beverly Harrison, "The Power of Anger in the Work of Love," in Carol S. Robb, ed., *Making the Connections* (Boston: Beacon Press, 1985), 12.

20. John Calvin, *Institutes of the Christian Religion,* 2 vols., trans. Ford Lewis Battles (Philadelphia: Westminster Press, 1960), 2.16.5.

21. Williams, *Spirit and the Forms of Love*, 14–15.

22. Elizabeth Johnson, *She Who Is* (New York: Crossroad, 1993), 253–54.

23. William C. Placher, *Narratives of a Vulnerable God* (Louisville, Ky.: Westminster/John Knox, 1994), 119.

24. Ibid., 119–20.

25. Karen Lebacqz, *Professional Ethics* (Nashville: Abingdon, 1985), 119–21.

26. Mitzi Eilts, "Saving the Family: When is Covenant Broken?" in *Violence in the Family*, ed. Marie M. Fortune (Cleveland, Oh.: Pilgrim Press, 1991), 235–42.

27. For a very helpful summary of this research see Judith Jordan, Alexandra Kaplan, Jean Baker Miller, Irene Stiver, and Janet Surrey, *Women's Growth in Connection* (New York: Guilford, 1991).

28. Stephen J. Bergman, "Men's Psychological Development: A Relational Perspective," in *A New Psychology of Men,* ed. Ronald Levant and William Pollack (New York: Basic Books, 1995), 68–90.

29. Luther, *The Freedom of a Christian*, 7.

30. Nygren, *Agape and Eros*, 216–17.

31. Williams, *Spirit and the Forms of Love,* 210.

32. Outka, "Universal Love and Impartiality," 64.

33. See Williams, *Spirit and the Forms of Love*; Jordan et al., *Women's Growth in Connection*; and Bergman, "Men's Psychological Development."

34. Williams, *Spirit and the Forms of Love*, 134–35.

35. Ibid., 205.

36. Ibid., 206.

37. Eric Erikson, *Childhood and Society*, 2d ed. (New York: W. W. Norton, 1963); Daniel J. Levinson, *Seasons of a Man's Life* (New York: Knopf, 1978); Lawrence Kohlberg, *The Philosophy of Moral Development* (San Francisco: Harper & Row, 1981).

38. Surrey is an editor of *Women's Growth in Connection* and has several chapters in this volume that offer key insights regarding the self-in-relation theory.

39. Surrey, "The Self-In-Relation," 61–62.

40. Ibid.

41. Ibid.

42. Williams, *Spirit and the Forms of* Love, 114–22.

43. Surrey, "Relationship and Empowerment," 164–67.

44. Judith Jordan, "Women and Empathy," in *Women's Growth in Connection*, 29.

45. Ibid.

46. Surrey, "The Self-In-Relation," 54.

47. Williams, *Spirit and the Forms of Love*, 19.

48. Ibid, 120.

49. Ibid, 121–22.

50. Ibid.

51. Surrey, "Relationship and Empowerment," in Jordan et al., *Women's Growth in Connection,* 167.

52. Williams, *Spirit and the Forms of Love*, 192–213.

CHAPTER EIGHT
§

Pastoral Diagnosis: Powerful Knowledge

As a way of summarizing what I have proposed in the previous chapters about pastoral diagnosis, I want to reflect on several of the richly multifaceted kinds of knowing represented by pastoral diagnosis and the ways in which they offer resources for ministry. Diagnosis is powerful knowledge. At the personal level it challenges practitioners to honest and increasingly adequate forms of faith and life. In helping relationships it is pregnant with transformative possibilities that also require humility on the part of practitioners who must not forget or misrepresent the source of the empowerment they offer. In an increasingly pluralistic context in which many voices compete for authority it asserts that the usefulness and truthfulness of Christian tradition remain compelling. This powerful knowledge relies on personal, trustworthy, and truthful knowing.

PERSONAL KNOWING

Throughout this book I have referred to diagnosis as a hermeneutical process and have noted how that gives particular importance to the self-understanding of the practitioner because she or he becomes the "lens" through which diagnosis proceeds. In chapter three I described such self-understanding as pastoral identity. It is a dynamically evolving integration of one's faith tradition and relational identity that is always embodied and socially located in particular ways.

199

By personal knowing I am referring to the kind of knowledge pastoral identity offers.[1] It is at once cognitive, affective, and moral, and inseparable from the fabric of who one is. It cannot pretend to provide objective distance on the topic at hand. This does not mean pastoral diagnosis is lacking rigorous attention to complex theories of personality and therapy or difficult theological concepts. Rather, somewhat like Jordan's concept of accurate empathy also discussed in chapter three, personal knowing must move such concepts from abstraction to skillful clinical judgment that also requires one's own affective and moral responses.

Personal knowing is most valuable when we appreciate the fact that it is also partial. That is, we may trust our insights as truthful while we also know they can be enhanced and will need to be refined or corrected by the insights of others. This is more obvious when there are explicit differences of social location in the helping relationship, such as race, class, gender, or sexual orientation. But it is also true when we are with those whose experience is familiar. This is one reason why I have described diagnosis as collaborative with those seeking help. It is important to share our theological and clinical insights with those who seek our help not only because it is empowering for them, but because it helps assure the accuracy of our assessment. I also encourage collegial consultation or supervision for this reason.

Having affirmed the partial character of our knowing, it is also important to value the unique insights of our particular, embodied social location. Recognizing the hermeneutical character of pastoral diagnosis underscores the importance of heightened self-consciousness, for who we are shapes what we "know." Imagine, in the case of Pat who shared her struggle with domestic violence with her Lutheran pastor, George, how important it was for him to be aware of the personal, professional, and theological issues informing his presence and responses to her. Had he any personal experience with familial violence? To what extent had he reflected on what he had internalized in this culture regarding masculinity and the treatment of women? Had he thought much about how being a man informs his ways of knowing and communicating with women? Was he aware of the socioeconomic class implications affecting Pat and her children in the context of the middle-class congregation he served? Was he comfortable critically reflecting on those points in his own theological tradition that Pat's dilemma disclosed as problematic? Such questions suggest how important it is for George to be aware of the sources that shape what he knows and how he knows.

Because identity develops through a relational pathway, we may also acknowledge that personal knowing is intrinsically relational. Our knowing not only develops through historical and contextual variables, it also arises in dynamic reciprocity with others. Pastoral diagnosis does not involve the simple application of preconceived ideas catalogued by certain sets of variables. Rather, it is a process like accurate empathy in which we bring informed self-awareness to a conversation. How the other engages us will itself shape the unfolding process of conversation. What George now knows about the nature of Christian love is deepened by the constructive theological task required by diagnosis in response to her questions and pain.

Christian faith is socially mediated. The personal knowing of a pastoral diagnostician is inevitably shaped by contextual forces, and it is important to be aware of how such factors shape one's responses. For example, George's response to Pat reflects an assimilation of increasing public awareness of domestic violence and the critical challenge such awareness has posed to Christianity's long-standing complicity in violence against women. Similarly, it will be important for George to be aware of the countercultural dimensions of the way he encourages Pat to think theologically about herself and her freedom.

The value of theological formation, personal therapy, supervision, and consultation become apparent as we explore the role of personal knowing in pastoral diagnosis. These processes encourage self-critical intentionality in pastoral practice so necessary for the work of diagnosis.

TRUSTWORTHY KNOWING

I have described power as an imaginative, dynamic construction involving images of relative strength and dependency. It is pervasive in relationships. Power exists within a web of relationships. In this culture, unfortunately, power is often confused with domination—a distortion of its relationality that intends the subordination of the other. This has led many to an ambivalence about exercising power. Ironically, since power is pervasive in relationships this denial of power makes even responsible persons more likely to abuse it.

A normative Christian vision for the exercise of power is shaped by God's love and justice. It intends to empower, encourage mutuality, and enhance interdependence. Relational power is conferred according to a person's gifts in order to meet the community's needs. It presumes trustworthy care. The criterion for the authentic exercise of power in ministry is empowerment of the other for mutual ministry.

Given contemporary cultural misapprehensions about power, there is a certain paradox about power and pastoral diagnosis. The more attentive we are to the dynamics of power in pastoral relationships, the more likely we are to use that power in a trustworthy way. Pastoral diagnosis is powerful knowledge because it involves naming the predicament of another according to values inherent in Christian normative images of life in relation to God and one another. Exercising such interpretive power involves a tensive awareness of the privilege entrusted to us as an incentive to use such power for good and an abiding appreciation for how precarious the mutuality envisioned by relational power is in a culture accustomed to power as domination.

I have described the process of pastoral diagnosis as collaborative. We join with those we seek to help in order to mitigate against imposing the powerful knowledge of theological and clinical expertise that is buttressed by structural and symbolic authority. I do not want to imply that such collaboration is simple or easy to practice. The powerful knowledge of pastoral diagnosis is concretely present. It is often messy and ambiguous; thus it is likely that what we offer will be at least partly resisted. It may be threatening because of the level of change it suggests from more familiar albeit problematic patterns. It may even require courage if naming a predicament justly, such as abuse, threatens the stability of the web of relationships on which we too depend, as might be the case in a congregation. We will also be tempted to use such power to enhance our position perhaps by creating dependency rather than empowering the other.

It is important to remember that pastoral diagnosis is exercised in the context of trust—the trust of another and of a faith community. They rightly expect our commitment and competence to draw on the resources of Christian tradition, and they expect us to share this powerful knowledge intending to heal and to empower for mutual ministry.

TRUTHFUL KNOWING

To affirm the distinctive value of pastoral diagnosis is to assert that Christian tradition is a useful and truthful resource amidst various competing paradigms. Pastoral diagnosis relies on biblical and theological resources that proclaim the redemptive love of God. It is fundamentally a witness to God's presence and power to save. It is powerful knowledge by virtue of the effect it envisions for those with whom it is shared.

It is at this point that we see how truthful and personal knowing are joined in pastoral diagnosis. The practice of pastoral diagnosis requires more than commitment to a particular theory of personality and therapy. It is an act of faith. According to Daniel Day Williams:

> To enter with any person into the search for the healing which the Gospel brings means to risk having one's understanding and one's faith challenged. We never know where a new human problem may lead us. . . . when the question of authority to speak the words of forgiveness, of hope, and of judgment is decisively raised, we will discover that the crisis of authority is the crisis of faith itself. Without risking our very being in the service of Christ, we have no authority to speak in his name.[2]

Williams was not endorsing any form of theological and biblical reductionism that disregarded the usefulness and truthfulness of therapeutic paradigms for healing. Rather, his challenge is to recognize that ambivalence about the value of theological resources or denial of their place in conversation with therapeutic paradigms is, at heart, a crisis of faith. To some extent it is also less than honest if persons come to a representative of faith seeking the resources of the tradition.

The process of pastoral diagnosis I have described in previous chapters presumes a confidence in the usefulness and truthfulness of Christian tradition. It must be a confidence strong enough to engage therapeutic paradigms in critical conversation, recognizing that authentic conversation requires an openness to be changed by the insights of the other. In chapter six, for example, such a conversation yielded a renewed appreciation for the distinctiveness of sin and psychopathology in understanding how it is that human freedom is limited yet real. In chapter seven a conversation between a theological perspective and emerging developmental theory yielded a more adequate understanding of the self and the freedom for love that suggests an ethic at least as compelling as those now reigning in the public sphere.

At the outset of this book I described pastoral diagnosis as a hermeneutical process that offered constructive possibilities for contemporary pastoral practice. Those constructive possibilities lie precisely in its truthful knowing. This is so not only for us who practice pastoral diagnosis and find that it challenges our own faith; it is also true for those to whom we offer care at individual and congregational levels and in the public sphere. There is widespread consensus on a declining theological and biblical literacy among many believers in this country as well as a decreasing sphere of influence for the public voice of Christianity apart from conservative evangelical and fundamentalist pronouncements. Pastoral diagnosis represents an opportunity to offer the interpretive power of Christian tradition in personal, congregational, and public contexts in which challenges create a possibility for redemptive change. Pastoral diagnosis is practical theological reflection. At the individual level this involves the possibility to help shape, revise, or construct more adequate theological and spiritual resources. Through the careful reflection diagnosis entails, practitioners also gain resources for pastoral practice in congregational and public contexts. For example, diagnosis offers resources at the congregational level as it informs the use of symbolic and liturgical resources that contribute to a deepened critical authorization of the tradition in the community's life and witness. Diagnosis has implications for the public sphere because it helps disclose foundational philosophical and ethical issues at the heart of public debates, such as the nature of human freedom and the character of accountability or normative images for fulfillment and maturity.

Pastoral diagnosis is powerful knowledge because it bears witness to the redemptively transforming power of God's love. It is knowledge that lays claim to the hearts of those who practice it and humbles those who are privileged to share it.

NOTES

1.   For an extended discussion of personal knowledge see Michael Polanyi, *Personal Knowledge,* corr. ed. (Chicago: University of Chicago Press, 1962).

2.   Daniel Day Williams, *The Minister and the Care of Souls* (San Francisco: Harper & Row, 1961), 44–45.

BIBLIOGRAPHY

Auden, W. H. *Collected Longer Poems*. New York: Random House, 1969.

Augsberger, David W. *Pastoral Counseling Across Cultures*. Louisville, Ky.: Westminster/John Knox, 1986.

Augustine, St. *City of God*. Translated by Gerald Walsh et al. New York: Image Books, 1958.

_____. *Confessions*. Translated by Rex Warner. New York: New American Library, 1963.

_____. *On Free Choice of Will*. Translated by Anna S. Benjamin and L. H. Hackstoff. Indianapolis: Bobbs-Merrill, 1964.

Baxter, Richard. *The Reformed Pastor*. Edited by Hugh Martin. Richmond: John Knox Press, 1956.

Belenky, Mary Field, et al. *Women's Ways of Knowing*. New York: Basic Books, 1986.

Bergman, Stephen J. "Men's Psychological Development: A Relational Perspective." In *A New Psychology of Men*, ed. Ronald Levant and William Pollack. New York: Basic Books, 1995, 68–90.

Boisen, Anton. *Out of the Depths*. New York: Harper & Brothers, 1960.

Bowen, Murray. *Family Therapy in Clinical Practice*. New York: Jacob Aronson, 1985.

Browning, Don S. *The Moral Context of Pastoral Care*. Philadelphia: Westminster Press, 1976.

_____. *Religious Thought and the Modern Psychologies: A Critical Conversation in the Theology of Culture*. Minneapolis: Augsburg Fortress, 1988.

Brunner, Emil. *The Misunderstanding of the Church*. Philadelphia: Westminster Press, 1953.

Bruzina, Ronald, and Bruce Wilshire, eds. *Crosscurrents in Phenomenology*. Boston: Martinus Nijhoff, 1978.

Calvin, John. *Institutes of the Christian Religion*. 2 Vols. Translated by Ford Lewis Battles. Philadelphia: Westminster Press, 1960.

_____. *Letters of Jean Calvin*. Edited and compiled by Jules Bonnet. Philadelphia: Presbyterian Board of Education, 1858.

Capps, Donald. *The Depleted Self*. Minneapolis: Fortress Press, 1993.

Carroll, Jackson. *As One with Authority*. Louisville, Ky.: Westminster/ John Knox, 1991.

Cooper-White, Pamela. *The Cry of Tamar*. Minneapolis: Fortress Press, 1995.

Couture, Pam. "Ritual and Pastoral Care." In *Dictionary of Pastoral Care and Counseling*, ed. Rodney Hunter. Nashville: Abingdon Press, 1990.

Cass, Vivienne. "The Implications of Homosexual Identity Formation for the Kinsey Model and Scale of Sexual Preference." In *Homosexuality/ Heterosexuality*, ed. David McWhirter et al. New York: Oxford University Press, 1990.

The Constitution of the Presbyterian Church (U.S.A.). Part II: Book of Order. Louisville, Ky: Office of the General Assembly, 1991.

Draper, Edgar, et al. "On the Diagnostic Value of Religious Ideation." *Archives of General Psychiatry* 13 (September 1965): 202–7.

Driver, Tom. *The Magic of Ritual*. San Francisco: Harper, 1991.

Dunfee, Susan Nelson. *Beyond Servanthood: Christianity and the Liberation of Women*. Lanham, Md.: University Press of America, 1989.

Dykstra, Craig. "The Formative Power of Congregations." *Religious Education* 82/4 (Fall 1987): 530–46.

Edwards, Jonathan. *Religious Affections*. Edited by John E. Smith. New Haven: Yale University Press, 1959.

Eilts, Mitzi. "Saving the Family: When Is Covenant Broken?" In Marie Fortune, *Violence in the Family*. Cleveland, Oh.: Pilgrim Press, 1991.

Erikson, Erik. *Childhood and Society*. 2d ed. New York: W. W. Norton, 1963.

_____. *Identity and the Life Style*. New York: W. W. Norton, 1980.

Falco, Kristine. *Psychotherapy with Lesbian Clients: Theory in Practice*. New York: Brunner/Mazel, 1991.

Farley, Edward. *Good and Evil*. Minneapolis: Fortress Press, 1990.

_____. "Psychopathology and Human Evil: Toward a Theory of Differentiation." In *Crosscurrents in Phenomenology*, ed. Ronald Bruzina and Bruce Wilshire. Boston: Martinus Nijhoff, 1978.

Fenn, Richard, and John McDargh, eds. *Losing the Soul: Essays in the Social Psychology of Religion*. Buffalo: State University of New York Press, 1995.

Finkelhor, David. *Child Sexual Abuse*. New York: Free Press, 1984.

Fitchett, George. *Spiritual Assessment in Pastoral Care: A Guide to Selected Resources*. Decatur, Ga.: Journal of Pastoral Care Publications, 1993.

Fortune, Marie. *Violence in the Family*. Cleveland, Oh.: Pilgrim Press, 1991.

Fossum, Merle A., and Marilyn Mason. *Facing Shame*. New York: W. W. Norton, 1986.

Freud, Sigmund. *Civilization and Its Discontents*. Translated and edited by James Strachey. New York: W. W. Norton, 1962.

_____. *The Ego and the Id*. Translated by Joan Rivier. Revised and edited by James Strachey. New York: W. W. Norton, 1962.

_____. *The Future of an Illusion*. Edited by James Strachey. New York: W. W. Norton, 1989.

_____. *New Introductory Lectures on Psychoanalysis*. Translated and edited by James Strachey. New York: W. W. Norton, 1966.

Fulkerson, Mary McClintock. *Changing the Subject*. Minneapolis: Fortress Press, 1994.

Gerkin, Charles V. "Is Pastoral Counseling a Credible Alternative in the Ministry?" *Journal of Pastoral Care* 26 (December 1972): 257–60.

Gilligan, Carol. *In a Different Voice*. Cambridge, Mass.: Harvard University Press, 1982.

Glaz, Maxine, and Jeanne Stevenson-Moessner, eds. *Women in Travail and Transition*. Minneapolis: Fortress Press, 1991.

Grant, Jacquelyn. *White Women's Christ and Black Women's Jesus*. American Academy of Religion Academy Series 64. Atlanta: Scholars Press, 1989.

Gregory the Great. *Pastoral Care*. Translated and annotated by Henry Davis. Westminster, Md.: Newman Press, 1960.

Hahn, Celia A. *A Sexual Paradox: Creative Tensions in Our Lives and in our Congregations*. New York: Pilgrim Press, 1991.

Hare-Mustin, Rachel. "The Problem of Gender in Family Therapy Theory." In Monica McGoldrick et al., *Women in Families*. New York: W. W. Norton, 1989, 61–77.

Harrison, Beverly. "The Power of Anger in the Work of Love." In Carol S. Robb, ed., *Making the Connections*. Boston: Beacon Press, 1985, 3–21.

Hendrix, Harville. "Pastoral Counseling: In Search of a New Paradigm." *Pastoral Psychology* 25 (Spring 1977): 157–72.

Hester, David. "Fear of God and the Beginning of Knowledge: Wisdom and Church Education." Convocation Address, Louisville Presbyterian Theological Seminary, Louisville, Ky., September 3, 1991.

Heyward, Carter. "Notes on Historical Grounding: Beyond Sexual Essentialism." In *Sexuality and the Sacred*, ed. James B. Nelson and Sandra Longfellow. Louisville, Ky.: Westminster/John Knox, 1994, 9–18.

Hiltner, Seward. "Toward Autonomous Pastoral Diagnosis." *Bulletin of the Menninger Clinic* 40 (September 1975): 574–78.

Hodgson, Peter C. *Revisioning the Church*. Minneapolis: Fortress Press, 1988.

Hodgson, Peter C., and Robert H. King, eds. *Christian Theology*. Minneapolis: Fortress Press, 1982.

Ivy, Stephen. "Pastoral Assessment: Issue and Directions." *Religious Studies Review* 16/3 (July 1990): 212–18.

_____. "Pastoral Diagnosis as Pastoral Caring." *Journal of Pastoral Care* 42 (Spring 1988): 81–89.

James, William. *Varieties of Religious Experience*. New York: Modern Library, 1936.

Janssens, Louis. "Norms and Priorities in a Love Ethic." *Louvain Studies* 6 (Spring 1977), 20–28.

Johnson, Elizabeth. *She Who Is*. New York: Crossroad, 1993.

Jordan, Judith. "Women and Empathy." In Judith Jordan et al., eds., *Women's Growth in Connnection*. New York: Guilford, 1991.

_____, et al., eds. *Women's Growth in Connection*. New York: Guilford, 1991.

Kaschak, Ellyn. *Engendered Lives*. New York: Basic Books, 1992.

Kaufman, Gershen. *Shame: The Power of Caring*. 2d ed. revised. Cambridge, Mass.: Schenkman Books, 1985.

Kegan, Robert. *The Evolving Self*. Cambridge, Mass.: Harvard University Press, 1982.

Kohlberg, Lawrence. *The Philosophy of Moral Development*. San Francisco: Harper & Row, 1981.

Lebaqcz, Karen. *Professional Ethics*. Nashville: Abingdon, 1985.

Levant, Ronald, and William Pollack, eds. *A New Psychology of Men*. New York: Basic Books, 1995.

Levinas, Emmanuel. *Ethics and Infinity*. Translated by R. A. Cohen. Pittsburgh: Duquesne University Press, 1985.

Levinson, Daniel J. *The Seasons of a Man's Life*. New York: Knopf, 1978.

Loomer, Bernard. "Two Kinds of Power." *Criterion* 15/1 (Winter 1975): 15–18.

Lowe, Walter. "Christ and Salvation." In *Christian Theology*, ed. Peter C. Hodgson and Robert H. King. Minneapolis: Fortress Press, 1982, 196–222.

Luepnitz, Deborah. *The Family Interpreted*. New York: Basic Books, 1988.

Luther, Martin. *Christian Liberty*. Translated by W. A. Lambert. Edited by Harold J. Grimm. Philadelphia: Fortress Press, 1957.

_____. *Lectures on Romans*. Translated and edited by Wilhelm Pauck. Philadelphia: Westminster Press, 1961.

Marshall, Joretta. *Counseling Lesbian Partners*. Louisville, Ky.: Westminster/ John Knox, 1997.

_____. "Internal Pastoral Authority in an Ecclesial Tradition: Psychological and Theological Dynamics." Ph.D. diss., Vanderbilt University, 1992.

_____. "Toward the Development of a Pastoral Soul: Reflections on Identity and Theological Education." *Pastoral Psychology* 43/1 (September 1994): 13

McCarthy, Marie. "The Role of Mutuality in Family Structure and Relationships: A Critical Examination of Select Systems of Family Therapy from the Perspective of Selected Options in Contemporary Theological Ethics." Ph.D. diss., University of Chicago, 1985.

McGoldrick, Monica, Carol M. Anderson, and Froma Walsh. *Women in Families*. New York: W. W. Norton, 1989.

McGoldrick, Monica, John Pearce, and Joseph Giordano, eds. *Ethnicity and Family Therapy*. New York: Guilford, 1982.

McWhirter, David P., Stephanie A. Sanders, and June M. Reinish, eds. *Homosexuality/Heterosexuality*. New York: Oxford University Press, 1990.

Miller, Jean Baker. "The Development of Women's Sense of Self." In Judith Jordan et al., eds., *Women's Growth in Connection*. New York: Guilford, 1991, 11–26.

Mount, Eric. *Professional Ethics in Context*. Louisville, Ky.: Westminster/John Knox, 1990.

Nelson, James B. *Between Two Gardens*. New York: Pilgrim Press, 1983.

_____. *Embodiment*. Minneapolis: Augsburg, 1979.

_____. *The Intimate Connection*. Louisville, Ky.: Westminster/ John Knox, 1988.

_____, and Sandra Longfellow, eds. *Sexuality and the Sacred*. Louisville, Ky.: Westminster/John Knox, 1994.

Nelson, Susan L. "Soul-Loss and Sin." In *Losing the Soul*, ed. Richard Fenn and John McDargh. Buffalo: State University of New York Press, 1995.

Niebuhr, H. Richard. *Christ and Culture*. New York: Harper & Row, 1951.

Niebuhr, Reinhold. *The Nature and Destiny of Man*. 2 vols. New York: Scribner's, 1949.

Noddings, Nel. *Caring*. Berkeley: University of California Press, 1984.

Nygren, Anders. *Agape and Eros*. Translated by Philip Watson. Philadelphia: Westminster Press, 1953.

Oates, Wayne. "Do Pastoral Counselors Bring a New Consciousness to the Health Professions?" *Journal of Pastoral Care* 26 (December 1972): 255–57.

_____. *Pastoral Counseling*. Philadelphia: Westminster Press, 1974.

_____. *The Religious Care of the Psychiatric Patient*. Philadelphia: Westminster Press, 1978.

Orr, Judith. "Ministry with Working-Class Women." *Journal of Pastoral Care* 45/4 (Winter 1991): 343–53.

Ostdiek, Gilbert. "Ritual and Transformation." *Liturgical Ministry* 2 (Spring 1993): 38–48.

Outka, Gene. *Agape: An Ethical Analysis.* New Haven: Yale University Press, 1972.

_____. "Universal Love and Impartiality." In *The Love Commandments*, ed. Edmund Santurri and William Werpehowski. Washington, D.C.: Georgetown University Press, 1992.

Pasewark, Kyle. *A Theology of Power: Being Beyond Domination.* Minneapolis: Fortress Press, 1993.

Patterson, T. T. *Management Theory.* London: Business Publication, 1967.

Patton, John, and Brian Childs. *Christian Marriage and Family.* Nashville: Abingdon, 1988.

Pellauer, Mary, Barbara Chester, and Jane Boyajian, eds. *Sexual Assault and Abuse.* San Francisco: Harper & Row, 1987.

Pfister, Oskar, *Christianity and Fear.* Translated by W. H. Johnson. London: George Allen and Unwin, 1948.

Placher, William C., and David Willis-Watkins. *Belonging to God.* Louisville, Ky.: Westminster/John Knox, 1992.

_____. *Narratives of a Vulnerable God.* Louisville, Ky.: Westminster/John Knox, 1994.

Plaskow, Judith. *Sex, Sin and Grace.* Lanham, Md.: University Press of America, 1980.

Plaskow, Judith and Carol Christ, eds. *Womanspirit Rising.* San Francisco: Harper, 1979.

Polanyi, Michael. *Personal Knowledge.* Chicago: University of Chicago Press, 1962.

Poling, James Newton. *The Abuse of Power.* Nashville: Abingdon, 1991.

Presbyterian Church (U.S.A.). "A Brief Statement of Faith." In *The Book of Confessions.* Louisville, Ky.: Office of the General Assembly, 1991.

Pruyser, Paul. *The Minister as Diagnostician.* Philadelphia: Westminster Press, 1976.

_____. *The Psychological Examination: A Guide for Clinicians.* New York: International Universities Press, 1979.

Ramsay, Nancy J. "Sexual Abuse and Shame: The Travail of Recovery," 112–23. In *Women in Travail and Transition*, ed. Maxine Glaz and Jeanne Stevenson-Moessner, 112–23. Minneapolis: Fortress Press, 1991.

Ramshaw, Elaine. *Ritual and Pastoral Care.* Philadelphia: Fortress Press, 1987.

Robb, Carol S., ed. *Making the Connections.* Boston: Beacon Press, 1985.

Rogers, Carl R. *On Becoming a Person.* Boston: Houghton Mifflin, 1961.

_____. *Person to Person: The Problem of Being Human.* Lafayette, Calif.; Real People Press, 1967.

Russell, Letty. *The Future of Partnership.* Philadelphia: Westminster Press, 1979.

Saiving, Valerie. "The Human Situation: A Feminine View." In *Womanspirit Rising*, ed. Judith Plaskow and Carol Christ. San Francisco: Harper, 1979, 25–42.

Santurri, Edmund, and William Werphehowski, eds. *The Love Commandments*. Washington, D.C.: Georgetown University Press, 1992.

Schreiter, Robert J. *Constructing Local Theologies*. Maryknoll, N.Y.: Orbis, 1985.

Schüssler Fiorenza, Elizabeth. *In Memory of Her*. New York: Crossroad, 1983.

Sennett, Richard. *Authority*. New York: Random House, 1980.

Siegler, Miriam, and Humphrey Osmond. "Aesculapian Authority." *The Hastings Center Studies* 1 (1973): 41–52.

_____. *Models of Madness, Models of Medicine*. New York: Macmillan, 1974.

Smith, Harmon L. "Language, Belief, Authority: Crisis for Christian Ministry and Professional Identity," *Pastoral Psychology* 23 (April 1972): 15–21.

Stancil, David C. "The Spiritual Values Inventory." Ph.D. diss., Southern Baptist Theological Seminary, Louisville, Ky., 1989.

Suchocki, Marjorie. *The End of Evil*. Albany, N.Y.: State University of New York Press, 1988.

_____. *God, Christ, Church*. New rev. ed. New York: Crossroad, 1993.

Sue, Derald Wing, and David Sue. *Counseling the Culturally Different*. 2d ed. New York: John Wiley and Sons, 1990.

Surrey, Janet L. "Relationship and Empowerment." In Judith Jordan et al., eds., *Women's Growth in Connection*. New York: Guilford, 1991.

_____. "The Self-in-Relation: A Theory of Women's Development." In Judith Jordan, et al., eds., *Women's Growth in Connection*. New York: Guilford, 1991.

Tannen, Deborah. *You Just Don't Understand*. New York: Ballantine, 1990.

Theological Dictionary of the New Testament, vol. 1. Edited by Gerhard Kittel. Translated by Geoffrey Bromily. Grand Rapids: Eerdmans, 1964–1976.

Theology and Worship Ministry Unit, Presbyterian Church (U.S.A.). *Growing in the Life of Christian Faith*. Louisville, Ky.: Distribution Management Services, 1989.

Tracy, David. "The Catholic Model of Caritas: Self-Transcendence and Transformation." In *The Family in Crisis or in Transition*, Concilium, 121 (New York: Seabury, 1979), 100–110.

Trepper, Terry S., and Mary Jo Barrett. *Systemic Treatment of Incest*. New York: Brunner/Mazel, 1989.

Underwood, Ralph. "Personal and Professional Integrity in Relation to Pastoral Assessment." *Pastoral Psychology* 31 (Winter 1982): 109–17.

United Methodist Church. *Book of Discipline*. Nashville: United Methodist Publishing House, 1992.

Van den Blink, A. J. "The Helping Response." Ph.D. diss., Princeton University, 1972.

Walsh, Froma. "Reconsidering Gender in the Marital Quid Pro Quo." In *Women in Families*, ed. Monica McGoldrick, Carol M. Anderson, and Froma Walsh. New York: W. W. Norton, 1989.

Weber, Max. *On Charisma and Institution Building*. Edited and introduced by S. N. Eisenstadt. Chicago: University of Chicago Press, 1968.

Williams, Daniel Day. *The Minister and the Care of Souls*. San Francisco: Harper & Row, 1961.

———. *The Spirit and the Forms of Love*. New York: Harper & Row, 1968.

———. "What Psychiatry Means to Theological Education." *Journal of Pastoral Care* 18 (Fall 1964): 129–31.

Williams, Delores. *Sisters in the Wilderness*. Maryknoll, N.Y.: Orbis, 1993.

William, Robert R. "Sin and Evil." In *Christian Theology*, ed. Peter Hodgson and Robert King. Minneapolis: Fortress Press, 1982.

INDEX

AUTHOR

SUBJECT